Sriranga Veeraraghavan

SAMS
Teach Yourself
Shell Programming
in 24 Hours

SAMS

A Division of Macmillan Computer Publishing
201 West 103rd St., Indianapolis, Indiana, 46290 USA

EXECUTIVE EDITOR
Jeff Koch

ACQUISITIONS EDITOR
Gretchen Ganser

DEVELOPMENT EDITOR
Hugh Vandivier

TECHNICAL EDITOR
Aron Hsiao

MANAGING EDITOR
Brice Gosnell

PROJECT EDITOR
Gretchen Uphoff

COPY EDITORS
Michael Dietsch
Kelly Talbot

INDEXER
Bruce Clingaman

PROOFREADER
Andrew Beaster

INTERIOR DESIGN
Gary Adair

COVER DESIGN
Aren Howell

LAYOUT TECHNICIANS
Brandon Allen
Stacey DeRome
Tim Osborn
Staci Somers

Contents at a Glance

Table of Contents

Contents

About the Author

Sriranga Veeraraghavan works in the Enterprise Network Management group at Cisco Systems, Inc. He has several years of experience developing software in C, Java, Perl, and Bourne Shell and has contributed to several books, including UNIX Unleashed and Special Edition Using UNIX. Sriranga graduated from the University of California at Berkeley in 1997 with a degree in engineering and is currently pursuing further studies at Stanford University. Among other interests, Sriranga enjoys mountain biking, classical music, and playing Marathon with his brother Srivathsa.

Dedication

For my grandmother, who taught me to love the English language.

For my mother, who taught me to love programming languages.

Acknowledgments

Writing a book on shell programming is a daunting task, due to the myriad of UNIX versions and shell versions that are available. Thanks to the work of my development editor Hugh Vandivier and my technical editor Aron Hsiao, I was able to make sure the book covered all the material completely and correctly. Their suggestions and comments have helped me enormously.

In addition to the technical side of the book, many things about the publishing process were new to me. Thanks to my acquisitions editor Gretchen Ganser and my executive editor Jeff Koch for handling all of the editorial issues and patiently working with me to keep this book on schedule. I would also like to thank Jane Brownlow who got me started on this project.

Working on a book takes a lot of time from work, as I found out. Thanks to the cooperation and understanding of my managers Pat Shriver and Larry Coryell, I was able to balance work and authoring. I know there is a thing called regular work, Pat. I'll get to it soon. I promise.

I need to thank my parents; my brother, Srivathsa; and my aunt and uncle, Srinivasa and Suma; who put off family activities so that I could finish this book. I promise we'll go to Lake Tahoe next year. Also thanks to my cousin's wife, Katherine, who wanted to see her name in my book.

Thanks to everyone else on the excellent team at Sams who worked on this book. Without their support, this book would not exist.

Tell Us What You Think!

As the reader of this book, you are our most important critic and commentator. We value your opinion and want to know what we're doing right, what we could do better, what areas you'd like to see us publish in, and any other words of wisdom you're willing to pass our way.

As an executive editor for the Operating Systems team at Macmillan Computer Publishing, I welcome your comments. You can fax, email, or write me directly to let me know what you did or didn't like about this book—as well as what we can do to make our books stronger.

Please note that I cannot help you with technical problems related to the topic of this book, and that due to the high volume of mail I receive, I might not be able to reply to every message.

When you write, please be sure to include this book's title and author as well as your name and phone or fax number. I will carefully review your comments and share them with the author and editors who worked on the book.

Fax: 317.581.4663
Email: opsys@mcp.com
Mail: Executive Editor
         Operating Systems
         Macmillan Computer Publishing
         201 West 103rd Street
         Indianapolis, IN 46290 USA

Introduction

In recent years, the UNIX operating system has seen a huge boost in its popularity, especially with the emergence of Linux. For programmers and users of UNIX, this comes as no surprise: UNIX was designed to provide an environment that's powerful yet easy to use.

One of the main strengths of UNIX is that it comes with a large collection of standard programs. These programs perform a wide variety of tasks from listing your files to reading email. Unlike other operating systems, one of the key features of UNIX is that these programs can be combined to perform complicated tasks and solve your problems.

One of the most powerful standard programs available in UNIX is the shell. The *shell* is a program that provides you with a consistent and easy-to-use environment for executing programs in UNIX. If you have ever used a UNIX system, you have interacted with the shell.

The main responsibility of the shell is to read the commands you type and then ask the UNIX kernel to perform these commands. In addition to this, the shell provides sophisticated programming constructs that enable you to make decisions, repeatedly execute commands, create functions, and store values in variables.

This book concentrates on the standard UNIX shell called the Bourne shell. When Dennis Ritche and Ken Thompson were developing much of UNIX in the early 1970s, they used a very simple shell. The first real shell, written by Stephen Bourne, appeared in the mid 1970s. The original Bourne shell has changed slightly over the years; some features were added and others were removed, but its syntax and its resulting power have remained the same.

The most attractive feature of the shell is that it enables you to create scripts. *Scripts* are files that contain a list of commands you want to run. Because every script is contained in a file and every file has a name, scripts enable you to combine existing programs to create completely new programs that solve your problems. This book teaches you how to create, execute, modify, and debug shell scripts quickly and easily. After you get used to writing scripts, you will find yourself solving more and more problems with them.

How This Book Is Organized

I assume that you have some familiarity with UNIX and know how to log in, create and edit files, and work with files and directories to a limited extent. If you haven't used

UNIX in a while or you aren't familiar with one of these topics, don't worry. The first part of this book reviews this material thoroughly.

This book is divided into three parts:

- Part I is an introduction to UNIX, the shell, and some common tools.
- Part II covers programming using the shell.
- Part III covers advanced topics in shell programming.

Part I consists of Chapters 1 through 6. The following material covered in the individual chapters:

- Chapter 1, "Shell Basics," discusses several important concepts related to the shell and describes the different versions of the shell.
- Chapter 2, "Script Basics," describes the process of creating and running a shell script. It also covers the login process and the different modes in which the shell executes.
- Chapters 3, "Working with Files," and 4, "Working with Directories," provide an overview of the commands used when working with files and directories. These chapters show you how to list the contents of a directory, view the contents of a file, and manipulate files and directories.
- Chapter 5, "Manipulating File Attributes," introduces the concept of file attributes. It covers the different types of files along with modifying a file's permissions.
- In UNIX every program runs as a process. Chapter 6, "Processes," shows you how to start and stop a process. It also explains the term *process ID* and how you can view them.

By this point, you should have a good foundation in the UNIX basics. This will enable you to start writing shell scripts that solve real problems using the concepts covered in Part II. Part II is the heart of this book, consisting of Chapters 7 through 18. It teaches you about all the tools available when programming in the shell. The following material is covered in these chapters:

- Chapter 7, "Variables," explains the use of variables in shell programming, shows you how to create and delete variables, and explains the concept of environment variables.
- Chapters 8, "Substitution," and 9, "Quoting," cover the topics of substitution and quoting. Chapter 8 shows you the four main types of substitution: filename, variables, command, and arithmetic substitution. Chapter 9 shows you the behavior of the different types of quoting and its effect on substitution.

- Chapters 10, "Flow Control," and 11, "Loops," provide complete coverage of flow control and looping. The flow control constructs `if` and `case` are covered along with the loop constructs `for` and `while`.

- Chapter 12, "Parameters," shows you how to write scripts that use command line arguments. The special variables and the `getopts` command are covered in detail.

- Chapter 13, "Input/Output," covers the `echo`, `printf`, and `read` commands along with the < and > input redirection operators. This chapter also covers using file descriptors.

- Chapter 14, "Functions," discusses shell functions. Functions provide a mapping between a name and a set of commands. Learning to use functions in a shell script is a powerful technique that helps you solve complicated problems.

- Chapters 15, "Text Filters," 16, "Filtering Text Using Regular Expressions," and 17, "Filtering Text with awk," cover text filtering. These chapters show you how to use a variety of UNIX commands including `grep`, `tr`, `sed`, and `awk`.

- Chapter 18, "Miscellaneous Tools," provides an introduction to some tools that are used in shell programming. Some of the commands that are discussed include `type`, `find`, `bc`, and `remsh`.

At this point, you will know enough about the shell and the external tools available in UNIX that you can solve most problems. The last part of the book, Part III, is designed to help you solve the most difficult problems encountered in shell programming. Part III spans Chapters 19 through 24 and covers the following material:

- Chapter 19, "Dealing with Signals," explains the concept of signals and shows you how to deliver a signal and how to deal with a signal using the `trap` command.

- Chapter 20, "Debugging," discusses the shell's built-in debugging tools. It shows you how to use syntax checking and shell tracing to track down bugs and fix them.

- Chapters 21, "Problem Solving with Functions," and 22, "Problem Solving with Shell Scripts," cover problem solving. Chapter 21 covers problems that can be solved using functions. Chapter 22 introduces some real-world problems and shows you how to solve them using a shell script.

- Chapter 23, "Scripting for Portability," covers the topic of portability. In this chapter, you rewrite several scripts from previous chapters to be portable to different versions of UNIX.

- Chapter 24, "Shell Programming FAQs," is a question-and-answer chapter. Several common programming questions are presented along with detailed answers and examples.

Each chapter in this book includes complete syntax descriptions for the various commands along with several examples to illustrate the use of commands. The examples are designed to show you how to apply the commands to solve real problems. At the end of each chapter are a few questions that you can use to check your progress. Some of the questions are short answer while others require you to write scripts.

After Chapter 24, three appendixes are available for your reference:

- Appendix A, "Command Quick Reference," provides you with a complete command reference.
- Appendix B, "Glossary," contains the terms used in this book.
- Appendix C, "Quiz Answers," contains the answers to all the questions in the book.

About the Examples

As you work through the chapters, try typing in the examples to get a better feeling of how the computer responds and how each command works. After you get an example working, try experimenting with the example by changing commands. Don't be afraid to experiment. Experiments (both successes and failures) teach you important things about UNIX and the shell.

Many of the examples and the answers to the questions are available for downloading from the following URL:

```
http://www.csua.berkeley.edu/~ranga/downloads/tysp1.tar.Z
```

After you have downloaded this file, change to the directory where the file was saved and execute the following commands:

```
$ uncompress tysp1.tar.Z
$ tar -xvf tysp1.tar
```

This creates a directory named tysp1 that contains the examples from this book.

There is no warranty of any kind on the examples in this book. I have tried to make the examples as portable as possible, and to this end I have tested each example on the following versions of UNIX:

- Sun Solaris versions 2.5.1, 2.6, 2.7
- Hewlett-Packard HP-UX versions 10.10, 10.20, 11.0
- Red Hat Linux versions 4.2, 5.1, 5.2
- FreeBSD version 2.2.6

It is possible that some of the examples might not work on other versions of UNIX. If you encounter a problem or have a suggestion about improvements to the examples or the content of the book, please feel free to contact me at the following email address:

`ranga@soda.berkeley.edu`

I appreciate any suggestions and feedback you have regarding this book.

Conventions Used in This Book

Features in this book include the following:

Notes give you comments and asides about the topic at hand, as well as full explanations of certain concepts.

Tips provide great shortcuts and hints on how to program in shell more effectively.

Cautions warn you against making your life miserable and avoiding the pitfalls in programming.

NEW TERM   Paragraphs containing new terms feature the New Term icon. The new term appears in *italic*.

At the end of each chapter, you'll find a handy Summary and a Quiz section (with answers found in Appendix C). Many times, you'll also find a Terms section.

In addition, you'll find various typographic conventions throughout this book:

- Commands, variables, directories, and files appear in text in a special `monospaced font`.
- Commands and such that you type appear in **boldface type**.
- Placeholders in syntax descriptions appear in a `monospaced italic` typeface. This indicates that you will replace the placeholder with the actual filename, parameter, or other element that it represents.

PART I

Introduction to UNIX and Shell Tools

Hour

HOUR 1

Shell Basics

My father has a tool chest that holds all his woodworking tools, from screwdrivers and chisels to power sanders and power drills. He has used these tools to build several desks, a shed, a bridge, and many toys. By applying the same tools, he has been able to build all the different elements required for his projects.

NEW TERM Shell scripting is similar to a woodworking project. To build something out of wood, you need to use the right tools. In UNIX, the tools you use are called *utilities* or *commands*. There are simple commands like ls and cd, and there are power tools like awk, sed, and the shell.

One of the biggest problems in woodworking is using the wrong tool or technique while building a project. Knowing which tool to use comes from experience. In this book, you will learn how to use the UNIX tools via examples and exercises.

The simple tools are easy to learn. You probably already know how to use many of them. The power tools take longer to learn, but when you get the hang of them, you'll be able to tackle any problem. This book teaches you how to use both the simple tools and the power tools. The main focus is on the most powerful tool in UNIX, the shell.

Before you can build things using the shell, you need to learn some basics. This chapter looks at the following topics:

- Commands
- The shell

It's time to get started.

What Is a Command?

NEW TERM In UNIX, a *command* is a program that you can run. In other operating systems, such as Mac OS or Windows, you point to the program you want to run and click it. To run a command in UNIX, you type its name and press Enter.

For example:

```
$ date [ENTER]
Wed Dec  9 08:49:13 PST 1998
$
```

Here, the date command has been entered. This command displays the current day, date, time, and year. After the current date appears, notice that the $ character is displayed.

In this book, I use the $ character to indicate the *prompt*. Wherever you see a prompt, you can type the name of a command and press Enter. This executes the command that you type. While a command executes, the prompt is not displayed. When the command finishes executing, the prompt is displayed again.

> The $ character is a prompt for you to enter a command. It is not part of the command itself.
>
> For example, to execute the date command, you type the word date at the prompt, $. Don't type $ date. Depending on your version of UNIX, an error message might be displayed if you type $ date instead of date at the prompt.

Now look at another example of running a command:

```
$ who
vathsa     tty1     Dec  6 19:36
sveerara   ttyp2    Dec  6 19:38
ranga      ttyp0    Dec  9 09:23
$
```

Here, I entered the command who at the prompt. This command displays a list of all the people, or users, who are currently using the UNIX machine.

The first column of the output lists the usernames of the people who are logged in. On my system, you can see that there are three users, vathsa, sveerara, and ranga. The second column lists the terminals they are logged in to, and the final column lists the time they logged in.

The output varies from system to system. Try it on your system to see who is logged in.

For those readers who are not familiar with the process of logging in to a UNIX system, the details are discussed in Chapter 2, "Script Basics."

Simple Commands

NEW TERM The who and date commands are examples of *simple* commands. A simple command is one that you can execute by just giving its name at the prompt:

```
$ command
```

Here, *command* is the name of the command you want to execute. Simple commands in UNIX can be small commands like who and date, or they can be large commands like a Web browser or a spreadsheet program. You can execute most commands in UNIX as simple commands.

Complex Commands

You can use the who command to gather information about yourself when you execute it as follows:

```
$ who am i
ranga        pts/0         Dec  9 08:49
$
```

This tells me the following information:

- My username is ranga.
- I am logged in to the terminal pts/0.
- I logged in at 8:49 on Dec 9.

NEW TERM This command also introduces the concept of a *complex* command, which is a command that consists of a command name and a list of arguments.

NEW TERM *Arguments* are command modifiers that change the behavior of a command. In this case, the command name is who, and the arguments are am and i.

NEW TERM When the who command runs as a simple command, it displays information about everyone who is logged in to a UNIX system. The output that is generated when a command runs as a simple command is called the *default* behavior of that command.

The arguments am and i change the behavior of the who command to list information about you only. In UNIX, most commands accept arguments that modify their behavior.

The formal syntax for a complex command is:

```
$ command argument1 argument2 argument3 ... argumentN
```

Here, *command* is the name of the command you want to execute, and *argument1* through *argumentN* are the arguments you want to give *command*.

Compound Commands

One of the most powerful features of UNIX is the capability to combine simple and complex commands together to obtain *compound* commands.

NEW TERM A compound command consists of a list of simple and complex commands separated by the semicolon character (;). An example of a complex command is

```
$ date ; who am i ;
Wed Dec  9 10:10:10 PST 1998
ranga       pts/0         Dec  9 08:49
$
```

Here, the compound command consists of the simple command date and the complex command who am i. As you can see from the output, the date command executes first, followed by the who am i command. When you give a compound command, each of the individual commands that compose it execute in order.

In this example, the complex command behaves as if you typed the commands in the following order:

```
$ date
Wed Dec  9 10:25:34 PST 1998
$ who am i
ranga       pts/0         Dec  9 08:49
$
```

The main difference between executing commands in this fashion and using a complex command is that in a complex command you do not get the prompt back between the two commands.

The formal syntax for a complex command is:

```
$ command1 ; command2 ; command3 ; ... ; commandN ;
```

Here, *command1* through *commandN* are either simple or complex commands. The order of execution is *command1*, followed by *command2*, followed by *command3,* and so on. When *commandN* finishes executing, the prompt returns.

Command Separators

NEW TERM   The semicolon character (;) is treated as a command *separator*, which indicates where one command ends and another begins.

If you don't use it to separate each of the individual commands in a complex command, the computer will not be able to tell where one command ends and the next command starts. If you execute the previous example without the first semicolon

```
$ date who am i
```

an error message similar to the following will be produced:

```
date: bad conversion
```

Here, the `date` command thinks that it is being run as a complex command with the arguments `who`, `am`, and `i`. The `date` command is confused by these arguments and displays an error message. When using complex commands, remember to use the semicolon character.

You can also terminate individual simple and complex commands using the semicolon character. For example, the commands

```
$ date
```

```
and$ date ;
```

produce the same output due to the order in which commands execute.

In the first case, the simple command `date` executes, and the prompt returns.

In the second case, the computer thinks that a complex command is executing. It begins by executing the first command in the complex command. In this case, it is the date command. When this command finishes, the computer tries to execute the next command. Because no other commands are left to execute, the prompt returns.

You will frequently see the semicolon used to terminate simple and complex commands in scripts.Because the semicolon is required to terminate commands in other languages, such as C, Perl, and Java, many script programmers use it the same way in scripts. No extra overhead is incurred by using the semicolon in this manner.

What Is the Shell?

In the preceding section, I explained that when you type the command

```
$ date
```

the computer executes the `date` command and displays the result.

But how does the computer know that you wanted to run the command `date`?

NEW TERM   The computer uses a special program called the *shell* to figure this out. The shell
provides you with an interface to the UNIX system. It gathers input from you
and executes programs based on that input. When a program finishes executing, it displays that program's output.

For this reason, the shell is often referred to as the UNIX system's *command interpreter*.
For users familiar with Windows, the UNIX shell is similar to the DOS shell,
`COMMAND.COM`.

The real power of the UNIX shell lies in the fact that it is much more than a command
interpreter. It is also a powerful programming language, complete with conditional statements, loops, and functions.

If you are familiar with these types of statements from other programming languages,
great. You'll pick up shell programming quickly. If you haven't seen these before, don't
fret. By the time you finish this book, you'll know how to use each of these statements.

The Shell Prompt

The prompt, $, which was discussed in the beginning of this chapter, is issued by the
shell.

While the prompt is displayed, you can type a command. The shell reads your input after
you press Enter. It determines the command you want executed by looking at the first
word of your input. A word is an unbroken set of characters. Spaces and tabs separate
words.

To the shell, your input looks like the following:

```
$ word1 word2 word3 ... wordN
```

The shell always picks *word1* as the name of the command you want executed. If there is
only one word

```
$ date
```

the shell's job is easy. It executes the command. If there are more words

```
$ who am i
```

the shell passes the extra words as arguments to the command specified by *word1*.

Different Types of Shells

You might notice that your prompt looks slightly different than the $ prompt I am using. The actual prompt that is displayed depends on the type of shell you are using.

In UNIX there are two major types of shells:

- The Bourne shell (includes sh, ksh, and bash)
- The C shell (includes csh and tcsh)

If you are using a Bourne-type shell, the default prompt is the $ character. If you are using a C-type shell, the default prompt is the % character. This book covers only Bourne-type shells because the C-type shells are not powerful enough for shell programming.

> In UNIX there are two types of accounts, regular user accounts and the root account. Normal users are given regular user accounts. The root account is an account with special privileges the administrator of a UNIX system (called the *sysadmin*) uses to perform maintenance and upgrades.
>
> If you are using the root account, both the Bourne and C shells display the # character as a prompt. Be extremely careful when executing commands as the root user because your commands effect the whole system.
>
> None of the examples in this book require that you have access to the root account to execute them.

The different Bourne-type shells follow:

- Bourne shell (sh)
- Korn shell (ksh)
- Bourne Again shell (bash)
- POSIX shell (sh)

The different C-type shells follow:

- C shell (csh)
- TENEX/TOPS C shell (tcsh)

Unless explicitly noted, the examples and exercise answers in this book will work with any Bourne-type shell.

The Original Bourne Shell

The original UNIX shell was written in the mid-1970s by Stephen R. Bourne while he was at AT&T Bell Labs in New Jersey. The Bourne shell was the first shell to appear on UNIX systems, thus it is referred to as "the shell." In this book, when I refer to the shell, I am referring to the Bourne shell.

The Bourne shell is usually installed as /bin/sh on most versions of UNIX. For this reason, it is the shell of choice for writing scripts to use on several different versions of UNIX.

In addition to being a command interpreter, the Bourne shell is a powerful language with a programming syntax similar to that of the ALGOL language. It contains the following features:

- Process control (see Chapter 6, "Processes")
- Variables (see Chapter 7, "Variables")
- Regular expressions (see Chapter 8, "Substitution")
- Flow control (see Chapter 10, "Flow Control," and Chapter 11, "Loops")
- Powerful input and output controls (see Chapter 13, "Input/Output")
- Functions (see Chapter 14, "Functions")

All Bourne-type shells support these features.

One of the main drawbacks of the original Bourne shell is that it is hard to use interactively. The three major drawbacks are

- No file name completion
- No command history or command editing
- Difficulty in executing multiple background processes or jobs

The C Shell

Bill Joy developed the C shell while he was at the University of California at Berkeley in the early 1980s. It was designed to make interactive use of the shell easier for users. Another design goal was to change the syntax of the shell from the Bourne shell's older ALGOL style to the newer C style.

The C language style of the C shell was intended as an improvement because the C language was familiar to the programmers working on UNIX at Berkeley. The idea was that a shell that used C language style syntax would be easier to write scripts in than a shell that used the ALGOL style syntax.

As it turned out, the C shell could not be used for much more than the most trivial scripts. Some of the major drawbacks are

- Weak input and output controls
- Lack of functions
- Confusing syntax due to a "lazy" command interpreter

Although the C shell did not catch on for scripts, it has become extremely popular for interactive use. Some of the key improvements responsible for this popularity follow:

- Command History. You can recall commands you previously executed for re-execution. You can also edit the command before it is re-executed.
- Aliases. You can create short mnemonic names for commands. Aliases are a simplified form of the Bourne shell functions.
- File Name Completion. You can have the C shell automatically complete a filename by just typing a few characters of the file's name.
- Job Controls. The C shell enables you to execute multiple processes and control them using the `jobs` command.

The C shell is usually installed on most systems as `/bin/csh`.

The TENEX/TOPS C shell, `tcsh`, is a newer version of the C shell that enables you to scroll through the command history using the up and down arrow keys. It also enables you to edit commands using right and left arrow keys.

Although it is widely available in educational UNIX machines, `tcsh` is not always present on corporate UNIX machines. For more information on obtaining `tcsh`, take a look at the following URL:

`http://www.primate.wisc.edu/software/csh-tcsh-book/`

This page includes information on obtaining and installing `tcsh` in both source and binary form.

The Korn Shell

For a long time, the only two shells to choose from were the Bourne shell and the C shell. This meant that most users had to know two shells, the Bourne shell for programming and the C shell for interactive use.

To rectify this situation, David Korn of AT&T Bell Labs wrote the Korn shell, `ksh`, which incorporates all the C shell's interactive features into the Bourne shell's syntax. For this reason, the Korn shell has become a favorite with users.

In recent years, most vendors have started to ship the Korn shell with their versions of UNIX. Usually you will find it installed as `/bin/ksh` or `/usr/bin/ksh`.

In general, `ksh` can be treated as fully compatible with `sh`, but some differences will prevent scripts from functioning correctly. These exceptions are noted throughout the book.

Some of the additional features that the Korn shell brings to the Bourne shell include the following:

- Command history and history substitution
- Command aliases and functions
- File name completion
- Arrays (see Chapter 7)
- Built-in integer arithmetic (see Chapter 8)

There are three major versions of `ksh` available:

- The Official version (`ksh`)
- The Public Domain version (`pdksh`)
- The Desktop version (`dtksh`)

The Official version is available in binary format (no sources) from

`http://www.kornshell.com`

The Public Domain version is available in both binary and source format from

`ftp://ftp.cs.mun.ca:/pub/pdksh`

For the shell programmer, there is no difference between the Official and the Public Domain versions of `ksh`—all scripts that run in one version will run in the other.

For shell users, the Official version provides a few nice features like command line completion with the Tab key rather than the Esc key.

The Desktop version comes with all major implementations of CDE. This version provides the capability to create and display Graphical User Interfaces (GUIs) using `ksh` syntax. Scripts written for the other two versions of `ksh` will run correctly under this version.

The POSIX shell is another variant of the Korn shell. Currently, the only major vendor shipping the POSIX shell is Hewlett-Packard. In HP-UX 11.0, the POSIX shell is installed as `/bin/sh`. The Bourne shell is installed as `/usr/old/bin/sh`.

The Bourne Again Shell

The Bourne Again shell, `bash`, was developed as part of the GNU project and has replaced the Bourne shell, `sh`, for GNU-based systems like Linux. All major Linux distributions, including Red Hat, Slackware, and Caldera, ship with `bash` as their `sh` replacement.

Although it includes C shell (`csh` and `tcsh`) and Korn shell (`ksh`) features, `bash` retains syntax compatibility with the Bourne shell, enabling it to run almost all Bourne shell scripts.

`bash` was written by Brian Fox (`bfox@gnu.ai.mit.edu`) of the Free Software Foundation and is currently maintained by Chester Ramey (`chet@ins.cwru.edu`) of Case Western Reserve University.

`bash` is available for anonymous FTP from any of the GNU archive sites, including the main GNU archive site:

`ftp://prep.ai.mit.edu/pub/gnu/`

As of this writing, the most recent release version of `bash` is 2.02.1.

Because `bash` is an implementation of the IEEE POSIX 1003.2/ISO 9945.2 Shell and Tools specification, it is extremely portable and can be built on most UNIX systems. It has also been ported to QNX, Minix, OS/2, and Windows 95/NT.

Currently, only Linux ships with the Bourne Again shell. It is installed as `/bin/bash`. On most Linux systems, it is also installed as `/bin/sh`.

Some features that `bash` includes in addition to those of the Korn shell are

- Name completion for variable names, usernames, host names, commands, and filenames
- Spelling correction for pathnames in the `cd` command
- Arrays of unlimited size
- Integer arithmetic in any base between 2 and 64

Summary

In this chapter, you looked at the shell basics. You saw how to execute simple commands, complex commands, and compound commands. You also covered the concept of a shell along with descriptions of the different shells that you are likely to encounter.

In the next chapter, "Script Basics," you explore the function of the shell in greater detail, starting with its use, interactively. I then show you how to use the shell for shell scripts.

One chapter down, only 23 more to go until you are a shell programming expert.

Questions

1. Classify each of the following as simple, complex, or compound commands:

   ```
   $ ls
   $ date ; uptime          [Complex]
   $ ls -l
   $ echo "hello world"
   ```

   If you haven't seen some of these commands before, try them out on your system. As you progress through the book, each will be formally introduced.

2. What is the effect of putting a semicolon at the end of a single simple command or a complex command?

   For example, will the output of the following commands be different?

   ```
   $ who am i
   $ who am i ;     → tries to execute but nothing there
                       next command
   ```
   [Same results]

3. What are the two major types of shells? Give an example of a shell that falls into each type.

   [Bourne]
   [C]

Terms

Commands   A command is a program you can run. To run a command, type its name and press Enter.

Prompts   When you see a prompt, type the name of a command and press Enter. In this book, the $ character is used to indicate the prompt.

Simple Commands   A simple command is a command that you can execute by giving its name at the prompt.

Default Behavior   The output that is generated when a command runs as a simple command is called the default behavior of that command.

Complex Commands   A complex command is a command that consists of a command name and a list of arguments.

Arguments   Arguments are command modifiers that change the behavior of a command.

Compound Commands   A compound command consists of a list of simple and complex commands separated by the semicolon character (;).

Command Separators   A command separator indicates where one command ends and another begins. The most common command separator is the semicolon character (;).

Shell   The shell provides you with an interface to the UNIX system. It gathers input from you and executes programs based on that input. When a program has finished executing, it displays that program's output. The shell is sometimes called a command interpreter.

Words   A word is an unbroken set of characters. The shell uses spaces and tabs to separate words.

HOUR **2**

Script Basics

In Chapter 1, "Shell Basics," I introduced the concept of a shell and commands. I showed you how the shell reads your input and executes the command you requested.

In this chapter I will explain in detail what the shell is and how it works. You will learn how the shell is started during the login process and what happens when you log out.

After I explain this behavior, I will show you how to group commands that are normally executed interactively into a file to create a script. Scripts are the power behind the shell because they enable you to group commands together to create new commands.

The UNIX System

The UNIX system consists of two components:

- Utilities
- The kernel

NEW TERM *Utilities* are programs you can run or execute. The programs who and date that you saw in the previous chapter are examples of utilities. Almost every program that you know is considered a utility.

NEW TERM *Commands* are slightly different than utilities. The term *utility* refers to the name of a program, whereas the term *command* refers to the program and any arguments you specify to that program to change its behavior. You might see the term *command* used instead of the term *utility* for simple commands, where only the program name to execute is given.

The kernel is the heart of the UNIX system. It provides utilities with a means of accessing a machine's hardware. It also handles the scheduling and execution of commands.

When a machine is turned off, both the kernel and the utilities are stored on the machine's hard disks. But when the computer is booted, the kernel is loaded from disk into memory. The kernel remains in memory until the machine is turned off.

Utilities, on the other hand, are stored on disk and loaded into memory only when they are executed. For example, when you execute the command

```
$ who
```

the kernel loads the who command from the machine's hard disk, places it in memory, and executes it. When the program finishes executing, it remains in the machine's memory for a short period of time before it is removed. This enables frequently used commands to execute faster. Consider what happens when you execute the date command three times:

```
$ date
Sun Dec 27 09:42:37 PST 1998
$ date
Sun Dec 27 09:42:38 PST 1998
$ date
Sun Dec 27 09:42:39 PST 1998
```

The first time the date command can be loaded from the machine's hard disk, but the second and third time the date command usually remains in the machine's memory allowing it to execute faster.

The shell is a program similar to the who command. The main difference is that the shell is loaded into memory when you log in.

Logging In

When you first connect to a UNIX system, you usually see a prompt such as the following:

```
login:
```

You need to enter your username at this prompt. After you enter your username, another prompt is presented:

```
login: ranga
Password:
```

You need to enter your password at this prompt.

These two prompts are presented by a program called getty. These are its tasks:

1. Display the prompt login.
2. Wait for a user to type a username.
3. After a username has been entered, display the password prompt.
4. Wait for a user to enter a password.
5. Give the username and password entered by the user to the login command and exit.

After login receives your username and password, it looks through the file /etc/passwd for an entry matching the information you provided. If it finds a match, login executes a shell and exits.

As an example, on my system the matching entry for my username, ranga, in file /etc/passwd is:

```
ranga:x:500:100:Sriranga Veeraraghavan:/home/ranga:/bin/bash
```

As you progress through the book, I will explain the information stored here.

> For those readers who are not familiar with UNIX files or filenames such as /etc/passwd, this topic is covered extensively in Chapters 3, "Working with Files," and 4, "Working with Directories."
>
> I will discuss files briefly in this chapter. A general idea from other operating systems of what files are is enough to understand these examples.

If no match is found, the login program issues an error message and exits. At this point the getty program takes over and displays a new login prompt.

The shell that login executes is specified in the file /etc/passwd. Usually this is one of the shells that I covered in the previous chapter.

In this book I assume that the shell started by the login program is /bin/sh. Depending on the version of UNIX you are running, this might or might not be the Bourne shell:

- On Solaris and FreeBSD, it is the Bourne shell.
- On HP-UX, it is the POSIX shell.
- On Linux, it is the Bourne Again shell.

Shell Initialization

When the login program executes a shell, that shell is *uninitialized*. When a shell is uninitialized, important parameters required by the shell to function correctly are not defined.

The shell undergoes a phase called *initialization* to set up these parameters. This is usually a two step process that involves the shell reading the following files:

- /etc/profile
- profile

The process is as follows:

1. The shell checks to see whether the file /etc/profile exists.
2. If it exists, the shell reads it. Otherwise, this file is skipped. No error message is displayed.
3. The shell checks to see whether the file .profile exists in your home directory. Your *home directory* is the directory that you start out in after you log in.
4. If it exists, the shell reads it; otherwise, the shell skips it. No error message is displayed.

As soon as both of these files have been read, the shell displays a prompt:

$

This is the prompt where you can enter commands in order to have them execute.

> The shell initialization process detailed here applies to all Bourne type shells, but some additional files are used by bash and ksh.
>
> You can obtain more information about this process for a particular shell using the man command explained later in this chapter.

Interactive Versus Noninteractive Shells

When the shell displays a prompt for you, it is running in interactive mode.

NEW TERM *Interactive mode* means that the shell expects to read input from you and execute the commands that you specify. This mode is called *interactive* because the shell is interacting with a user. This is usually the mode of the shell that most users are familiar with: you log in, execute some commands, and log out. When you log out using the `exit` command, the shell exits.

NEW TERM The shell can be run in another mode, called *noninteractive mode*. In this mode, the shell does not interact with you; instead it reads commands stored in a file and executes them. When it reaches the end of the file, the shell exits.

How `login` Starts a Shell

When the `login` program starts a shell, it basically executes the following command:

```
/bin/sh
```

By issuing this command, it puts the shell into interactive mode. You can start a shell in interactive mode by issuing the same command at the prompt:

```
$ /bin/sh
$
```

The first prompt $ is displayed by the shell that `login` started; the second one is displayed by the shell you started. To exit from this shell, use the `exit` command:

```
$ exit
$
```

The prompt that is displayed now is from the original shell started by `login`. Typing **exit** at this prompt logs you out.

How to Start the Shell Noninteractively

You can start the shell noninteractively as follows:

```
$ /bin/sh filename
```

Here *filename* is the name of a file that contains commands to execute. As an example, consider the compound command:

```
$ date ; who
```

Put these commands into a file called `logins`. First open a file called `logins` in an editor and type the command shown previously. Assuming that the file is located in the current directory, after the file is saved, the command can run as

```
$ /bin/sh logins
```

This executes the compound command and displays its output.

NEW TERM   This is the first example of a *shell script*. Basically, a shell script is a list of commands stored in a file that the shell executes noninteractively.

Initialization File Contents

Usually the shell initialization files are quite short. They are designed to provide a complete working environment with as little overhead as possible for both interactive and noninteractive shells.

The file /etc/profile is maintained by the system administrator of your UNIX machine and contains shell initialization information required by all users on a system.

The file .profile is under your control. You can add as much shell customization information as you want to this file. The minimum set of information that you need to configure includes

- The type of terminal you are using
- A list of directories in which to locate commands
- A list of directories in which to locate manual pages for commands

Setting the Terminal Type

Usually the type of terminal you are using is automatically configured by either the login or getty programs. Sometimes, the autoconfiguration process guesses your terminal incorrectly. This can occur when you are using a dial-up or modem connection.

If your terminal is set incorrectly, the output of commands might look strange, or you might not be able to interact with the shell properly. To make sure that this is not the case, most users set their terminal to the lowest common denominator as follows:

```
TERM=vt100
```

When I introduce the case statement in Chapter 10, "Flow Control," you will see a more advanced method of setting the terminal type that enables access to advanced terminal features.

Setting the PATH

When you type the command

```
$ date
```

the shell has to locate the command date before it can be executed. The PATH specifies the locations in which the shell should look for commands. Usually it is set as follows:

```
PATH=/bin:/usr/bin
```

Each of the individual entries separated by the colon character, :, are directories. Directories are discussed in Chapter 4.

If you request the shell to execute a command and it cannot find it in any of the directories given in the PATH variable, a message similar to the following appears:

```
$ hello
hello: not found
```

Setting the MANPATH

In UNIX, online help has been available since the beginning. In the section "Getting Help" I will discuss how to access it using the man command.

In order for you to access all the available help, you have to tell the shell where to look for the online help pages. This information is specified using the MANPATH. A common setting is

```
MANPATH=/usr/man:/usr/share/man
```

Like the path, each of the individual entries separated by the colon character, :, are directories.

When you use the man command to request online help as follows, the man command searches every directory given in the MANPATH for an online help page corresponding to the topic you requested.

```
$ man who
```

In this case it looks for the online help page corresponding to the who command. If this page is found, it is displayed as discussed in the next section.

Making a Shell Script Executable

One of the most important tasks in writing shell scripts is making the shell script executable and making sure that the correct shell is invoked on the script.

In a previous example, you created the logins script that executes the following compound command:

```
date ; who ;
```

If you wanted to run the script by typing its name, you need to do two things:

- Make it executable.
- Make sure that the right shell is used when the script is run.

To make this script executable, do the following:

```
chmod a+x ./logins
```

Here you are using the `chmod` command. For a complete discussion of how to use this command, please see Chapter 5, "Manipulating File Attributes."

To ensure that the correct shell is used to run the script, you must add the following "magic" line to the beginning of the script:

```
#!/bin/sh
```

Your script then has two lines:

```
#/bin/sh
date ; who ;
```

The magic line causes a new shell (in this case, `/bin/sh`) to be called to execute the script. Without the magic line, the current shell is always used to evaluate the script, regardless of which shell the script was written for. For example, without a magic line, `csh` and `tcsh` users might not be able to get a Bourne shell (`sh`) script to run correctly.

THE MAGIC OF `#!/bin/sh`

The `#!/bin/sh` must be the first line of a shell script in order for `sh` to be used to run the script. If this appears on any other line, it is treated as a comment and ignored by all shells.

Comments

NEW TERM   The magic first line `#!/bin/sh` introduces the topic of comments. A *comment* is a statement that is embedded in a shell script but should not be executed by the shell.

In shell scripts, comments start with the # character. Everything between the # and end of the line are considered part of the comment and are ignored by the shell.

Adding comments to a script is quite simple: Open the script using an editor and add lines that start with the # character. For example, to add the following line to the `logins` shell script:

```
# print out the date and who's logged on
```

I opened the file `logins` with my editor and inserted this line as the second line in the file. The shell script is now as follows:

```
#!/bin/sh
# print out the date and who's logged on
date ; who ;
```

There is no change in the output of the script because comments are ignored. Also comments do not slow down a script because the shell can easily skip them.

You can also add comments to lines that contain commands by adding the # character after the commands. For example, you can add a comment to the line `date ; who ;` as follows:

```
date ; who ; # execute the date and who commands
```

When you are writing a shell script, make sure to use comments to explain what you are doing in case someone else has to look at your shell script. You might find that this helps you figure out what your own scripts are doing, months after you write them.

Getting Help

As you read through this book, you will want to get more information about the commands and features I discuss. This information is available by using the online help feature of UNIX.

Every version of UNIX comes with an extensive collection of online help pages called manual pages. These are often referred to as *man pages*. The man pages are the authoritative source about your UNIX system. They contain complete information about both the kernel and all the utilities.

Using the man Command

To access a man page you need to use the man (*man* as in *manual*) command as follows:

```
man command
```

Here, `command` is the name of a command that you want more information about. As an example,

```
$ man uptime
```

displays the following on a Solaris machine:

```
User Commands                                          uptime(1)

NAME
     uptime - show how long the system has been up

SYNOPSIS
     uptime
```

```
DESCRIPTION
      The uptime command prints the current time,  the  length  of
      time  the system has been up, and the average number of jobs
      in the run queue over the last 1, 5 and 15 minutes.  It  is,
      essentially,  the first line of a w(1) command.

EXAMPLE
      Below is an example of the output uptime provides:
           example% uptime
           10:47am  up 27 day(s), 50 mins,  1 user,
          ➥load average: 0.18, 0.26, 0.20

SEE ALSO
      w(1), who(1), whodo(1M), attributes(5)

NOTES
      who -b gives the time the system was last booted.
```

As you can see this man page is divided into several sections. These sections are described in Table 2.1.

TABLE 2.1 SECTIONS IN A MAN PAGE

Section	Description
NAME	This section gives the name of the command along with a short description of the command.
SYNOPSIS	This section describes all the different modes in which the command can be run. If a command accepts arguments they are shown in this section.
DESCRIPTION	This section includes a verbose description of the command. If a command accepts arguments, each argument will be fully explained in this section
EXAMPLE	This section usually shows you how to execute a command, along with some sample output.
SEE ALSO	This section lists other commands that are related to this command.
NOTES	This section usually lists some additional information about the command. Sometimes it lists known bugs with a particular command.

Most man pages include all the sections given in Table 2.1 and might include one or two optional sections described in Table 2.2.

TABLE 2.2 OPTIONAL SECTIONS FOUND IN MAN PAGES

Section	Description
AVAILABILITY	This section describes the versions of UNIX that include support for a given command. Sometimes it lists the optional software packages you need to purchase from the vendor to gain extra functionality from a command.
KNOWN BUGS	This section usually lists one or more known problems with a command. If you encounter a problem that is not included in this section, you should report it to your UNIX vendor.
FILES	This section lists the files that are required for a command to function correctly. It might also list the files that can be used to configure a command.
AUTHORS or CONTACTS	These sections list the command's authors or provide some contact information regarding a command.
STANDARDS COMPLIANCE	Some commands have behavior that is specified by a standards organization such as ISO (International Standards Organization), IEEE (Institute of Electrical and Electronic Engineers), or ANSI (American National Standards Institute). This section lists the standards with which a particular command complies.

Try using the man command to get more information on some of the commands I have discussed in this chapter.

If the man command cannot find a man page corresponding to the command you requested, it issues an error message. For example, the command

```
$ man apple
```

produces an error message similar to the following on my system:

```
No manual entry for apple
```

The exact error message depends on your version of UNIX.

Manual Sections

The term *manual page* comes from the original versions of UNIX, when the online pages were available as large bound manuals. In all, there were eight different manuals covering the main topics of the UNIX system. These manuals are described in Table 2.3.

TABLE 2.3   THE UNIX SYSTEM MANUALS

Manual Section	Description
1	Covers commands.
2	Covers UNIX system calls. *System calls* are used inside a program, such as date, to ask the kernel for a service.
3	Covers libraries. Libraries are used to store non–kernel-related functions used by C programmers.
4	Covers file formats. This manual specifies the format of files such as /etc/passwd.
5	Also covers file formats.
6	Includes the instructions for playing the games that came with UNIX.
7	Covers device drivers.
8	Covers system maintenance.

Unlike the printed version, where you had to know the section where you needed to look for a particular manual page, the man command looks in all the sections for the information you requested. This makes it much easier to get help using the man pages.

Summary

In this chapter, I explained in greater detail what the shell is and how it works. You saw how the login process works and what the login command does to start a shell. From this you were able to look at the two modes in which the shell can be run:

- Interactively   *PROmpt like £*
- Noninteractively   *Ocript NAme*

In shell programming, the noninteractive use of the shell should interest you the most. This mode enables you to specify commands inside a file and then have the shell execute the commands within that file. You also saw how to make a file containing commands executable. This enables you to treat shell scripts as new commands.

You also looked at some details of shell initialization and getting help using the man command.

The next chapter formally introduces the concept of files by showing you how to list files, view the contents of files, and manipulate files.

Questions

1. What are the two files used by the shell to initialize itself?   *[handwritten: /etc/profile .Profile]*

2. Why do you need to set PATH and MANPATH?   *[handwritten: where shell will look for commands   online manuals for help]*

3. What purpose does the following line

   ```
   #!/bin/sh
   ```

   serve in a script?   *[handwritten: Causes a new shell to be called to execute the script   sh = Bourne shell   ksh - Korn Shell]*

4. What command should you use to access the online help?   *[handwritten: MAN]*

Terms

Utilities   Utilities are programs, such as who and date, that you can run or execute.

Commands   A command is the name of a program and any arguments you specify to that program to cause its behavior to change. You might see the term *command* used instead of the term *utility* for simple commands, where only the program name to execute is given.

Kernel   The kernel is the heart of the UNIX system. It provides utilities with a means of accessing a machine's hardware. It also handles the scheduling and execution of commands.

Uninitialized Shell   When a shell is started it is uninitialized. This means that important parameters required by the shell to function correctly are not defined.

Shell Initialization   After a shell is started it undergoes a phase called initialization to set up some important parameters. This is usually a two step process that involves the shell reading the files /etc/profile and .profile.

Interactive Mode   In interactive mode the shell reads input from you and executes the commands that you specify. This mode is called interactive because the shell is interacting with a user.

Noninteractive Mode   In noninteractive mode, the shell does not interact with you; instead it reads commands stored in a file and executes them. When it reaches the end of the file, the shell exits.

Shell Script   A shell script is a list of commands stored in a file that the shell executes noninteractively.

Home Directory   Your home directory is the directory in which you start out after you log in.

Comments A comment is a statement that is embedded in a shell script but should not be executed by the shell.

Man Pages Every version of UNIX comes with an extensive collection of online help pages called *man pages* (short for *manual pages*). The man pages are the authoritative source about your UNIX system. They contain complete information about both the kernel and all the utilities.

Hour **3**

Working with Files

In UNIX there are three basic types of files:

- Ordinary Files
- Directories
- Special Files

An *ordinary file* is a file on the system that contains data, text, or program instructions. In this chapter, you look at working with ordinary files.

NEW TERM *Directories*, covered in Chapter 4, "Working with Directories," store both special and ordinary files. For users familiar with Windows or Mac OS, UNIX directories are equivalent to folders.

Special files are covered in Chapter 5, "Manipulating File Attributes." Some special files provide access to hardware such as hard drives, CD-ROM drives, modems, and Ethernet adapters. Other special files are similar to aliases or shortcuts and enable you to access a single file using different names.

Listing Files

First, list the files and directories stored in the current directory. Use the following command:

```
$ ls
```

Here's a sample directory listing:

```
bin          hosts      lib        res.03
ch07         hw1        pub        test_results
ch07.bak     hw2        res.01     users
docs         hw3        res.02     work
```

This output indicates that several items are in the current directory, but this output does not tell us whether these items are files or directories. To find out which of the items are files and which are directories, specify the -F option to ls:

```
$ ls -F
```

Now the output for the directory is slightly different:

```
bin/         hosts      lib/       res.03
ch07         hw1        pub/       test_results
ch07.bak     hw2        res.01     users
docs/        hw3        res.02     work/
```

As you can see, some of the items now have a / at the end: each of these items is a directory. The other items, such as hw1, have no character appended to them. This indicates that they are ordinary files.

When the -F option is specified to ls, it appends a character indicating the file type of each of the items it lists. The exact character depends on your version of ls. For ordinary files, no character is appended. For special files, a character such as !, @, or # is appended to the filename.

For more information on the exact characters your version of ls appends to the end of a filename when the -F option is specified, please check the UNIX manual page for the ls command. You can do this as follows:

```
$ man ls
```

So far, you have seen ls list more than one file on a line. Although this is fine for humans reading the output, it is hard to manipulate in a shell script. Shell scripts are geared toward dealing with lines of text, not the individual words on a line. Without using external tools, such as the awk language covered in Chapter 17, "Filtering Text Using awk," it is hard to deal with the words on a line.

In a shell script it is much easier to manipulate the output when each file is listed on a separate line. Fortunately `ls` supports the `-1` option to do this. For example,

```
$ ls -1
```

produces the following listing:

```
bin
ch07
ch07.bak
docs
hosts
hw1
hw2
hw3
lib
pub
res.01
res.02
res.03
test_results
users
work
```

Hidden Files

NEW TERM   So far you have used `ls` to list *visible* files and directories, but `ls` can also list *invisible* or *hidden* files and directories. An invisible file is one whose first character is the dot or period character (`.`). UNIX programs (including the shell) use most of these files to store configuration information. Some common examples of hidden files include the files

- `.profile`, the Bourne shell (`sh`) initialization script
- `.kshrc`, the Korn shell (`ksh`) initialization script
- `.cshrc`, the C shell (`csh`) initialization script
- `.rhosts`, the remote shell configuration file

All files that do not start with the `.` character are considered visible.

To list invisible files, specify the `-a` option to `ls`:

```
$ ls -a
```

The directory listing now looks like this:

```
.             .profile      docs          lib           test_results
..            .rhosts       hosts         pub           users
.emacs        bin           hw1           res.01        work
.exrc         ch07          hw2           res.02
.kshrc        ch07.bak      hw3           res.03
```

As you can see, this directory contains many invisible files.

Notice that in this output, the file type information is missing. To get the file type information, specify the -F and the -a options as follows:

```
$ ls -a -F
```

The output changes to the following:

```
./              .profile      docs/      lib/       test_results
../             .rhosts       hosts      pub/       users
.emacs          bin/          hw1        res.01     work/
.exrc           ch07          hw2        res.02
.kshrc          ch07.bak      hw3        res.03
```

With the file type information you see that there are two hidden directories (. and ..). These two directories are special entries that are present in all directories. The first one, ., represents the current directory. The second one, .., represents the parent directory. We discuss these concepts in greater detail in section "The Directory Tree" of Chapter 4.

Option Grouping

In the previous example, the command that you used specified the options to ls separately. These options can also be grouped together. For example, the commands

```
$ ls -aF
$ ls -Fa
```

are the same as the command

```
$ ls -a -F
```

As you can see, the order of the options does not matter to ls. As an example of option grouping, consider the equivalent following commands:

```
ls -1 -a -F
ls -1aF
ls -a1F
ls -Fa1
```

Any combination of the options -1, -a, and -F produces identical output:

```
./
../
.emacs
.exrc
.kshrc
.profile
.rhosts
bin/
ch07
```

```
ch07.bak
docs/
hosts
hw1
hw2
hw3
lib/
pub/
res.01
res.02
res.03
test_results
users
work/
```

Viewing the Content of a File

3

The ability to list files is very important, but shell scripts also need to be able to view the contents of a file.

cat

NEW TERM   To view the content of a file, use the cat (short for *concatenate*) command. Its syntax is as follows:

```
cat files
```

Here *files* are the names of the files that you want to view. For example,

```
$ cat hosts
```

prints out the contents of a file called hosts:

```
127.0.0.1       localhost         loopback
10.8.11.2       kanchi.bosland.us kanchi
10.8.11.9       kashi.bosland.us  kashi
128.32.43.52    soda.berkeley.edu soda
```

You can specify more than one file as follows:

```
$ cat hosts users
```

If the users file contains a list of users, this produces the following output:

```
127.0.0.1       localhost         loopback
10.8.11.2       kanchi.bosland.us kanchi
10.8.11.9       kashi.bosland.us  kashi
128.32.43.52    soda.berkeley.edu soda
```

```
ranga
sveerara
vathsa
amma
```

Numbering Lines

NEW TERM The cat command also understands several options. One of these is the -n option, which numbers the output lines. You can use it as follows:

```
$ cat -n hosts
```

This produces the output

```
1   127.0.0.1       localhost           loopback
2   10.8.11.2       kanchi.bosland.us   kanchi
3   10.8.11.9       kashi.bosland.us    kashi
4   128.32.43.52    soda.berkeley.edu   soda
5
```

NEW TERM The numbered output shows us that the last line in this file is blank. You can ask cat to skip numbering blank lines using the -b option:

```
$ cat -b hosts
```

In this case the output looks like the following:

```
1   127.0.0.1       localhost           loopback
2   10.8.11.2       kanchi.bosland.us   kanchi
3   10.8.11.9       kashi.bosland.us    kashi
4   128.32.43.52    soda.berkeley.edu   soda
```

Although the blank line is still there, it is no longer numbered.

Counting Words (wc)

Now that you know how to view the contents of a file, look at how to get some information about the contents.

NEW TERM You can use the wc command to get a count of the total number of lines, words, and characters contained in a file. The basic syntax of this command is

```
wc [options] files
```

Here *options* are one or more of the options given in Table 3.1 and *files* are the files you want examined.

If no options are specified, the output contains a summary of the number of lines, words, and characters. For example, the command

```
$ wc .rhosts
```

produces the following output for my `.rhosts` file:

```
7 14 179 .rhosts
```

The first number, in this case 7, is the number of lines in the file. The second number, in this case 14, is the number of words in the file. The third number, in this case 179, is the number of characters in the file. Finally, the filename is listed. The filename is important if more than one file is specified.

If you specify more than one file, wc gives the individual counts along with a total. For example, the command

```
$ wc .rhosts .profile
```

produces the following output:

```
7 14 179 .rhosts
133 405 2908 .profile
140 419 3087 total
```

You can also use wc to get the individual counts as shown in the next sections. The options covered in these sections are given in Table 3.1.

TABLE 3.1   wc OPTIONS

Option	Description
-l	Counts the number of lines
-w	Counts the number of words
-m or -c	Counts the number of characters

The -m option is available on Solaris and HP-UX. It is not available on Linux. On Linux systems, you need to use the -c option instead.

Number of Lines

NEW TERM To count the number of lines, use the -l (*l* as in *lines*) option. For example, the command

```
$ wc -l .profile
```

produces the output

```
133 .profile
```

Number of Words

 To count the number of words in a file, use the -w (*w* as in *words*) option. For example, the command

```
$ wc -w .rhosts
```

produces the output

```
14 .rhosts
```

which is what you expected.

Number of Characters

 To count the number of characters, use either the -m option or the -c option. As mentioned, the -m option should be used on Solaris and HP-UX. The -c option should be used on Linux systems.

For example, the command

```
$ wc -m .profile
```

produces the output

```
2908 .profile
```

In Linux or GNU, the equivalent command is

```
$ wc -c .profile
```

Combining Options

Like the ls command, the options to wc can be grouped together and given in any order.

For example, if you wanted a count of the number of words and characters in the file test_results you can use any of the following commands:

```
$ wc -w -m test_results
$ wc -wm test_results
$ wc -mw test_results
```

The output from each of these commands is identical:

```
606 3768 test_results
```

The output lists the words in the files first, the number of characters in the file, and the name of the file.

In this case, there are 606 words and 3,768 characters in the file test_results.

Manipulating Files

In the preceding sections, you looked at listing files and viewing their content. In this section you look at the following methods of manipulating files:

- Copying files
- Renaming files
- Removing files

Copying Files (cp)

To make a copy of a file use the cp command. The basic syntax of the command is

```
cp source destination
```

Here source is the name of the file that is copied and destination is the name of the copy. For example, the following command makes a copy of the file test_results and places the copy in a file named test_results.orig:

```
$ cp test_results test_results.orig
```

Common Errors

There is no output from the cp command, unless it encounters an error. Two common errors occur when

- The source is a directory
- The source does not exists

An example of the first case is the command

```
$ cp work docs
```

This causes an error message similar to the following:

```
cp: work: is a directory
```

An example of the second case is the command

```
$ cp test_relsuts test_results.orig
```

Here I have mistyped the filename test_results as test_relsuts and cp gives the following error:

```
cp: cannot access test_relsuts: No such file or directory
```

Interactive Mode

NEW TERM   No error message is generated if the destination already exists. In this case, the destination file is automatically overwritten. This can lead to serious problems.

To avoid this behavior you can specify the -i (*i* as in *interactive*) options to cp.

If the file test_results.orig exists, the command

```
$ cp -i test_results test_results.orig
```

results in a prompt something like the following:

```
overwrite test_results.orig? (y/n)
```

If you choose y (yes), the file will is overwritten. If you choose n (no), the file test_results.orig isn't changed.

Copying Files to a Different Directory

If the *destination* is a directory, the copy has the same name as the *source* but is located in the *destination* directory. For example, the command

```
$ cp test_results work/        ──→ means directory
```

places a copy of the file test_results in the directory work.

Multiple Inputs

If more than two inputs are given, cp treats the last argument as the *destination* and the other files as *sources*. This works only if the *sources* are files and the *destination* is a directory, as in the following example:

```
$ cp res.01 res.02 res.03 work/
```

If one or more of the *sources* are directories the following error message is produced. For example, the command

```
$ cp res.01 work/ docs/ pub/        ──→ WILL copy to last directory
```

produces the following error:

```
cp: work: is a directory
cp: docs: is a directory
```

Although cp reports errors, the *source* file, in this case res.01, is correctly copied to the directory pub.

If the destination is a file, but multiple inputs are given, as in the following example,

```
$ cp hw1 hw2 hw3
```

an error message similar to the following

```
cp: hw3: No such file or directory
```

is generated. In this case no files are copied.

Renaming Files (mv)

NEW TERM   To change the name of a file use the mv command. Its basic syntax is

```
mv source destination
```

Here *source* is the original name of the file and *destination* is the new name of the file. As an example,

```
$ mv test_result test_result.orig
```

changes the name of the file test_result to test_result.orig. A new file called test_result.orig is not produced like in cp; only the name of the file is changed. There is no output from mv if the name change is successful.

If the source does not exist, as in the following example,

```
$ mv test_reslut test_result.orig
```

an error similar to the following is reported:

```
mv: test_reslut: cannot access: No such file or directory
```

Interactive Mode

Like cp, mv does not report an error if the *destination* already exists: it simply overwrites the file. to avoid this problem you can specify the -i option.

For example, if the file ch07.bak already exists, the following command

```
$ mv -i ch07 ch07.bak
```

results in a confirmation prompt:

```
remove ch07.bak? (n/y)
```

If you choose n (no), the *destination* file is not touched. If you choose y (yes), the *destination* file is removed and the *source* file is renamed.

The actual prompt varies between the different versions of UNIX.

Removing Files (rm)

NEW TERM   To remove files use the `rm` command. The syntax is

```
rm files
```

Here `files` is a list of one or more files to remove. For example, the command

```
$ rm res.01 res.02
```

removes the files `res.01` and `res.02`.

Common Errors

The two most common errors using `rm` are

- One of the specified files does not exist
- One of the specified files is a directory

As an example of the first case, the command

```
$ rm res.01 res.02 res.03
```

produces an error message if the file `res.02` does not exist:

```
rm: res.02 non-existent
```

The other two files are removed.

An example of the second case is the command

```
$ rm res.01 res.03 work/
```

This command produces another error message:

```
rm: work directory
```

The two files are removed.

Interactive Mode

Because there is no way to recover a file that has been deleted using `rm`, you can specify the `-i` option. In interactive mode, `rm` prompts you for every file that is requested for deletion.

For example, the command

```
$ rm -i hw1 hw2 hw3
```

produces confirmation prompts similar to the following:

```
hw1: ? (n/y) y
hw2: ? (n/y) n
hw3: ? (n/y) y
```

In this case I answer y to deleting hw1 and hw3, but I answer n to deleting hw2.

Summary

In this chapter, you covered the following topics:

- Listing files using ls
- Viewing the content of a file using cat
- Counting the words, lines, and characters in a file using wc
- Copying files using cp
- Renaming files using mv
- Removing files using rm

Knowing how to perform each of these tasks is essential to becoming a good shell programmer. In the chapters ahead you use these basics to create scripts for solving real world problems.

Questions

1. What are invisible files? How do you use ls to list them?

2. Will there be any difference in the output of the following commands?

   a. $ ls -a1

   b. $ ls -1 -a

   c. $ ls -1a

3. Which options should be specified to wc in order to count the number of lines and characters in a file?

4. Given that hw1, hw2, ch1, and ch2 are files and book and homework are directories, which of the following commands generates an error message?

   a. $ cp hw1 ch2 homework

   b. $ cp hw1 homework hw2 book

   c. $ rm hw1 homework ch1

   d. $ rm hw2 ch2

Terms

ls   The command that lists the files in a directory.

cat   The command that views the contents of a file.

wc   The command that counts the words, lines, and characters in a file.

cp   The command that copies files.

mv   The command that renames files.

rm   The command that removes files.

Ordinary File   A file on the system that contains data, text, or program instructions.

Directories   A type of file that stores other files. For users familiar with Windows or Mac OS, UNIX directories are equivalent to folders.

Invisible Files or **Hidden Files**   Files whose names start with the . character. By default the ls command does not list these files. You can list them by specifying the -a option to ls.

HOUR 4

Working With Directories

/ root

NEW TERM UNIX uses a hierarchical structure for organizing files and directories. This structure is often referred to as a *directory tree*. The tree has a single root node, the slash character (/), and all other directories are contained below it.

You can use every directory, including /, to store both files and other directories. Every file is stored in a directory, and every directory except / is stored in another directory.

This is slightly different from the multiroot hierarchical structure used by Windows and Mac OS. In those operating systems, all devices (floppy disk drives, CD-ROMs, hard drives, and so on) are mounted at the highest directory level. The UNIX model is slightly different, but after a short time most users find it extremely convenient.

This chapter introduces the directory tree and shows you how to manipulate its building blocks: directories.

The Directory Tree

To explain the origin and advantages of the directory tree, consider a project that requires organization, such as writing a book.

When you start out, it is easiest to put all the documents related to the book in one location. As you work on the book, you might find it hard to locate the material related to a particular chapter.

If you are writing the book with pen and paper, the easiest solution to this problem is to take all the pages related to the first chapter and put them into a folder labeled "Chapter 1." As you write more chapters, you can put the material related to these chapters into separate folders.

In this method, when you finish the book, you will have many separate folders. You might put all the folders into a box and label that box with the name of the book. (Then you can stack the boxes in your closet.)

By grouping the material for the different chapters into folders and grouping the folders into boxes, the multitude of pages required to write a book becomes organized and easily accessible. When you want to see Chapter 5 from a particular book, you can grab that box from your closet and look only at the folder pertaining to Chapter 5.

You can carry this same method over to a project on your computer. When you start out, all the files for the book might be in your home directory, but as you write more chapters, you can create directories to store the material relating to a particular chapter. Finally, you can group all the directories for the book into a directory named after the book.

NEW TERM   As you can probably see, this arrangement creates an upside-down *tree* with the *root* at the top and the directories *branching* off from the root. The files stored in the directories can be though of as *leaves*.

NEW TERM   This brings up the notion of *parent* directories and *child* or *subdirectories*. For example, consider two directories A and B, where directory A contains directory B. In this case, A is called the parent of B, and B is called a child of A.

The depth of the directory tree is limited only by the fact that the *absolute* path to a file cannot have more than 1,024 characters. I cover absolute paths later in the chapter.

Filenames

In UNIX, every file and directory has a name associated with it. This name is referred to as the file or directory's *filename*.

In addition to their filenames, every file and directory is associated with the name of its parent directory. When a filename is combined with the parent directory's name, the result is called a *pathname*. Two examples of pathnames are

```
/home/ranga/docs/book/ch5.doc
/usr/local/bin/
```

As you can see, each of these pathnames consists of several "words" separated by the slash (/) character. In UNIX, the slash separates directories, whereas the individual words are the names of files or directories. The sum of all the words and the / characters makes up the pathname.

The last set of characters in a pathname is the actual name of the file or directory being referred to: The rest of the characters represent its parent directories. In the first example, the filename is ch5.doc.

The name of a file can be up to 255 characters long and can contain any ASCII character except /. Generally, the characters used in pathnames are the alphanumeric characters (a to z, A to Z, and 0 to 9) along with periods (.), hyphens (-), and underscores (_).

Other characters, especially the space, are usually avoided because many programs cannot deal with them properly. For example, consider a file with the following name:

```
A Farewell To Arms
```

Most programs treat this a four separate files named A, Farewell, To, and Arms, instead of one file. You look at a workaround to this problem in Chapter 9, "Quoting."

One thing to keep in mind about filenames is that two files in the same directory cannot have the same name. Thus both of the following filenames

```
/home/ranga/docs/ch5.doc
/home/ranga/docs/ch5.doc
```

refer to the same file, but the following filenames

```
/home/ranga/docs/ch5.doc
/home/ranga/docs/books/ch5.doc
```

refer to different files because they are located in different directories. In addition, because UNIX is case-sensitive, you can have two files in the same directory whose names differ only by case. UNIX considers the following

```
/home/ranga/docs/ch5.doc
/home/ranga/docs/CH5.doc
```

to be different files. This often confuses users coming from the Windows or DOS environments.

4

Pathnames

In order to access a file or directory, its pathname must be specified. As you have seen, a pathname consists of two parts: the name of the directory and the names of its parents. UNIX offers two ways to specify the names of the parent directory. This leads to two types of pathnames:

- Absolute
- Relative

AN ANALOGY FOR PATHNAMES

The following statements illustrate a good analogy for the difference between absolute and relative pathnames:

"I live in San Jose."

"I live in San Jose, California, USA."

The first statement gives only the city in which I live. It does not give any more information, thus the location of my house is relative. It could be located in any state or country containing a city called San Jose. The second statement fully qualifies the location of my house, thus it is an absolute location.

Absolute Pathnames

NEW TERM   An *absolute* pathname represents the location of a file or directory starting from the root directory and listing all the directories between the root and the file or directory of interest.

Because absolute pathnames list the path from the root directory, they always start with the slash (/) character. Regardless of what the current directory is, an absolute path points to an exact location of a file or directory. The following is an example of an absolute pathname:

```
/home/ranga/work/bugs.txt
```

This absolute path tells you that the file bugs.txt is located in the directory work, which is located in the directory ranga, which in turn is located in the directory home. The slash at the beginning of the path tells you that the directory home is located in the root directory.

Relative Pathnames

NEW TERM A *relative* pathname enables you to access files and directories by specifying a path to that file or directory within your current directory. When your current directory changes, the relative pathname to a file can also change.

NEW TERM To find out what the current directory is, use the pwd (*print working directory*) command, which prints the name of the directory in which you are currently located. For example

```
$ pwd
/home/ranga/pub
```

tells me that I am located in the directory /home/ranga/pub.

When you're specifying a relative pathname, the slash character is not present at the beginning of the pathname. This indicates that a relative pathname is being used instead of an absolute pathname. The relative pathname is a list of the directories located between your current directory and the file or directory you are representing.

If you are pointing to a directory in your pathname that is below your current one, you can access it by specifying its name. For example, the directory name:

```
docs/
```

refers to the directory docs located in the current directory.

In order to access the current directory's parent directory or other directories at a higher level in the tree than the current level, use the special name of two dots (. .).

The UNIX file system uses two dots (. .) to represent the directory above you in the tree, and a single dot (.) to represent your current directory.

Look at an example that illustrates how relative pathnames are used. Assume that the current directory is

```
/home/ranga/work
```

Then the relative pathname

```
../docs/ch5.doc
```

represents the file

```
/home/ranga/docs/ch5.doc
```

whereas

```
./docs/ch5.doc
```

4

represents the file

```
/home/ranga/work/docs/ch5.doc
```

You can also refer to this file using the following relative path:

```
docs/ch5.doc
```

As mentioned previously, you do not have to append the ./ to the beginning of path-names that refer to files or directories located within the current directory or one of its subdirectories.

Switching Directories

NEW TERM
Now that you have covered the basics of the directory tree, look at moving around the tree using the cd (change directory) command.

Home Directories

First print the working directory:

```
$ pwd
/home/ranga
```

This indicates that I am in my home directory. Your home directory is the initial directory where you start when you log in to a UNIX machine. Most systems use either /home or /users as directories under which home directories are stored. On my system I use /home.

The easiest way to determine the location of your home directory is to do the following:

```
$ cd
$ pwd
/home/ranga
```

When you issue the cd command without arguments, it changes the current directory to your home directory. Therefore, after the cd command completes, the pwd command prints the working directory that is your home directory.

Changing Directories

You can use the cd command to do more than change to a home directory: You can use it to change to any directory by specifying a valid absolute or relative path. The syntax is as follows:

```
cd directory
```

Here, *directory* is the name of the directory that you want to change to. For example, the command

```
$ cd /usr/local/bin
```

changes to the directory /usr/local/bin. Here, you used an absolute path.

Say that the current directory is

```
$ pwd
/home/ranga
```

From this directory, you can cd to the directory /usr/local/bin using the following relative path:

```
$ cd ../../usr/local/bin
```

Changing the current directory means that all your relative path specifications must be relative to the new directory rather than the previous directory. For example, consider the following sequence of commands:

```
$ pwd
/home/ranga/docs
$ cat names
ranga
vathsa
amma
$ cd /usr/local
$ cat names
cat: cannot open names
```

When the first cat command was issued, the working directory was /home/ranga/docs. The file, names, was located in this directory, thus the cat command found it and displayed its contents.

After the cd command, the working directory became /usr/local. Because no file was called names in that directory, cat produces an error message stating that it could not open the file. To access the file names from the new directory, you need to specify either the absolute path to the file or a relative path from the current directory.

Common Errors

The most common errors are

- Specifying more than one argument
- Trying to cd to a file
- Trying to cd to a directory that does not exist

An example of the first case is

```
$ cd /home /tmp /var
$ pwd
/home
```

As you can see, cd uses only its first argument. The other arguments are ignored. Sometimes in shell programming, this becomes an issue. When you issue a cd command in a shell script, make sure that you end up in the directory you intended to reach.

An example of the second case is

```
$ pwd
/home/ranga
$ cd docs/ch5.doc
cd: docs/ch5.doc: Not a directory
$ pwd
/home/ranga
```

Here, you tried to change to a location that was not a directory, and cd reported an error. If this error occurs, the working directory does not change. The final pwd command in this example illustrates this.

An example of the third case is

```
$ pwd
/home/ranga
$ cd final_exam_answers
cd: final_exam_answers: No such file or directory
$ pwd
/home/ranga
```

Here, I tried to change into the directory final_exam_answers, but because this directory did not exist, cd reported an error. The final pwd command shows that the working directory did not change.

The problem in this last example occurs because none of my professors were kind enough to make a copy of the directory final_exam_answers for me.

Listing Files and Directories

In Chapter 3, "Working with Files," you looked at using the ls command to list the files in the current directory. Now look at using the ls command to list the files in any directory.

Listing Directories

To list the files in a directory you can use the following syntax:

```
ls directory
```

Here, *directory* is the absolute or relative pathname of the directory whose contents you want listed.

For example, both of the following commands list the contents of the directory /usr/local (assuming the working directory is /home/ranga):

```
$ ls /usr/local
$ ls ../../usr/local
```

On my system the listing looks like

```
X11             bin             gimp            jikes           sbin
ace             doc             include         lib             share
atalk           etc             info            man             turboj-1.1.0
```

The listing on your system might look quite different.

You can use any of the options you covered in Chapter 3 to change the output. For example, the command

```
$ ls -aF /usr/local
```

produces the following output

```
./              atalk/          gimp/           lib/            turboj-1.1.0/
../             bin/            include/        man/
X11/            doc/            info/           sbin/
ace/            etc/            jikes/          share/
```

You can specify more than one directory as an argument. For example

```
$ ls /home /usr/local
```

produces the following output on my system:

```
/home:
amma    ftp     httpd   ranga   vathsa

/usr/local:
X11             bin             gimp            jikes           sbin
ace             doc             include         lib             share
atalk           etc             info            man             turboj-1.1.0
```

A blank line separates the contents of each directory.

4

Listing Files

If you specify the name of a file instead of a directory, ls lists only that one file. For example

```
$ ls .profile
.profile
```

You can intermix files and directories as arguments to ls:

```
$ ls .profile docs/ /usr/local /bin/sh
```

This produces a listing of the specified files and the contents of the directories.

If you don't want the contents of the directory listed, specify the -d option to ls. This forces ls to display only the name of the directory, not its contents:

```
$ ls -d /home/ranga
/home/ranga
```

You can combine the -d option with any of the other ls options you have covered. An example of this is

```
$ ls -aFd /usr/local /home/ranga /bin/sh
/bin/sh*        /home/ranga/   /usr/local/
```

Common Errors

If the file or directory you specify does not exist, ls reports an error. For example

```
$ ls tomorrows_stock_prices.txt
tomorrows_stock_prices.txt: No such file or directory
```

If you specify several arguments instead of one, ls reports errors only for those files or directories that do not exist. It correctly lists the others. For example

```
$ ls tomorrows_stock_prices.txt /usr/local .profile
```

produces an error message

```
tomorrows_stock_prices.txt: No such file or directory
/usr/local:
X11          bin        gimp        jikes       sbin
ace          doc        include     lib         share
atalk        etc        info        man         turboj-1.1.0

.profile
```

Manipulating Directories

Now that you have covered using directories, look at manipulating them. The most common manipulations are

- Creating directories
- Copying directories
- Moving directories
- Removing directories

Creating Directories

You can create directories with the mkdir command. Its syntax is

```
mkdir directory
```

Here, *directory* is the absolute or relative pathname of the directory you want to create. For example, the command

```
$ mkdir hw1
```

creates the directory hw1 in the current directory. Here is another example:

```
$ mkdir /tmp/test-dir
```

This command creates the directory test-dir in the /tmp directory. The mkdir command produces no output if it successfully creates the requested directory.

If you give more than one directory on the command line, mkdir creates each of the directories. For example

```
$ mkdir docs pub
```

creates the directories docs and pub under the current directory.

Creating Parent Directories

Sometimes when you want to create a directory, its parent directory or directories might not exist. In this case, mkdir issues an error message. Here is an illustration of this:

```
$ mkdir /tmp/ch04/test1
mkdir: Failed to make directory "/tmp/ch04/test1"; No such file or
➥directory
```

In such cases, you can specify the -p (p as in parent) option to the mkdir command. It creates all the necessary directories for you. For example

```
$ mkdir -p /tmp/ch04/test1
```

creates all the required parent directories.

4

The `mkdir` command uses the following procedure to create the requested directory:

1. The `mkdir` command checks whether the directory `/tmp` exists. If it does not exist, it is created.

2. The `mkdir` command checks whether the directory `/tmp/ch04` exists. If it does not exist, it is created.

3. The `mkdir` command checks whether the directory `/tmp/ch04/test1` exists. If it does not, it is created.

Common Errors

The most common error in using `mkdir` is trying to make a directory that already exists. If the directory `/tmp/ch04` already exists, the command

```
$ mkdir /tmp/ch04
```

generates an error message similar to the following:

```
mkdir: cannot make directory '/tmp/ch04': File exists
```

An error also occurs if you try to create a directory with the same name as a file. For example, the following commands

```
$ ls -F docs/names.txt
names
$ mkdir docs/names
```

result in the error message

```
mkdir: cannot make directory 'docs/names': File exists
```

If you specify more than one argument to `mkdir`, it creates as many of these directories as it can. Any directory that could not be created generates an error message.

Copying Files and Directories

In Chapter 3, you looked at using the `cp` command to copy files. Now look at using it to copy directories.

To copy a directory, you specify the `-r` option to `cp`. The syntax is as follows:

```
cp -r source destination
```

Here, *source* is the pathname of the directory you want to copy, and *destination* is where you want to place the copy. For example

```
$ cp -r docs/book /mnt/zip
```

copies the directory `book` located in the `docs` directory to the directory `/mnt/zip`. It creates a new directory called `book` under `/mnt/zip`.

Copying Multiple Directories

In the same way that you can copy multiple files with cp, you can also copy multiple directories. If cp encounters more than one source, all the source directories are copied to the destination. The destination is assumed to be the last argument.

For example, the command

```
$ cp -r docs/book docs/school work/src /mnt/zip
```

copies the directories school and book, located in the directory docs, to /mnt/zip. It also copies the directory src, located in the directory work, to /mnt/zip. After the copies finish, /mnt/zip looks like the following:

```
$ ls -aF /mnt/zip
./    ../    book/    school/    src/
```

You can also mix files and directories in the argument list. For example

```
$ cp -r .profile docs/book .kshrc doc/names work/src /mnt/jaz
```

copies all the requested files and directories to the directory /mnt/jaz.

If your argument list consists only of files, the -r option has no effect.

Common Errors

The most common error in copying files and directories is in the requested destination. The most common problems in copying directories involve using a destination that is not a directory.

An example of this is

```
$ cp -r docs /mnt/zip/backup
cp: cannot create directory '/mnt/zip/backup': File exists
$ ls -F /mnt/zip/backup
/mnt/zip/backup
```

As you can see, the cp operation fails because a file called /mnt/zip/backup already exists.

Moving Files and Directories

You have looked at the mv command to rename files, but its real purpose is to move files and directories between different locations in the directory tree. The basic syntax is this:

```
mv source destination
```

Here *source* is the name of the file or directory you want to move, and *destination* is the directory where you want the file or directory to end up. For example

```
$ mv /home/ranga/names /tmp
```

moves the file `names` located in the directory `/home/ranga` to the directory `/tmp`.

Moving a directory is exactly the same:

```
$ mv docs/ work/
```

moves the directory `docs` into the directory `work`. To move the directory `docs` back to the current directory you can use the command:

```
$ mv work/docs .
```

One nice feature of `mv` is that you can move and rename a file or directory all in one command. For example

```
$ mv docs/names /tmp/names.txt
```

moves the file `names` in the directory `docs` to the directory `/tmp` and renames it `names.txt`.

Moving Multiple Items

As you can with `cp`, you can specify more than one file or directory as the source. For example

```
$ mv work/ docs/ .profile pub/
```

moves the directories `work` and `docs` along with the file `.profile` into the directory `pub`.

When you are moving multiple items, you cannot rename them. If you want to rename an item and move it, you must use a separate `mv` command for each item.

Common Errors

You can encounter three common errors with `mv`:

- Moving multiple files and directories to a directory that does not exist
- Moving files and directories to a file
- Trying to move directories across file systems

The first and second cases produce the same error message, so look at one example that illustrates what happens:

```
$ mv .profile docs pub /mnt/jaz/backup
mv: when moving multiple files, last argument must be a directory
$ ls -aF /mnt/jaz
./              ../              archive/     lost+found/  old/
```

As you can see, no directory named backup exists in the /mnt/jaz directory, so mv reports an error. The same error is reported if backup was a file in the /mnt/jaz directory.

The third case occurs when you try to move a directory from one file system to another. For the purposes of this book, you can think of a file system as either a hard drive or a hard drive partition.

assume that /home and /tmp are on separate partitions. In this case, the command

```
$ mv /tmp/ch01 /home/ranga/docs
```

returns error output

```
mv: cannot move '/tmp/ch01' across filesystems: Not a regular file
```

The most common workaround to this is to use the cp -r to copy the directory and then remove the original with rm:

```
$ cp -r /tmp/ch01 /home/ranga
$ rm -r /tmp/ch01
```

I cover the -r option of rm later in this chapter.

Sometimes, you might use the tar (as in tape archive) command instead of cp:

```
$ ( cd /tmp ; tar -cvpf - ch01 ¦ ( cd /home/ranga ; tar -xvpf -) )
$ rm -r /tmp/ch01
```

I explain the tar version of moving directories in Chapter 22, "Problem Solving with Shell Scripts."

Removing Directories

You can use two commands to remove directories:

- rmdir   *removes empty directories*
- rm -r   *removes directories & their contents*

Use the first command to remove empty directories. It is considered "safe" because in the worst case, you can accidentally lose an empty directory, which you can quickly re-create with mkdir.

The second command removes directories along with their contents. It is considered "unsafe" because in the worst case of rm -r, you could lose your entire system.

When using rm to remove either files or directories, make sure that you remove only those files that you don't want.

There is no way to restore files deleted with rm, so mistakes can be very hard to recover from.

rmdir

To remove an empty directory, you can use the rmdir command. Its syntax is

```
rmdir directories
```

Here, directories includes the names of the directories you want removed. For example, the command

```
$ rmdir ch01 ch02 ch03
```

removes the directories ch01, ch02, and ch03 if they are empty. The rmdir command produces no output if it is successful.

Common Errors

You might encounter two common error messages from rmdir. These occur when you

- Try to remove a directory that is not empty
- Try to remove files with rmdir

For the first case, you need to know how to determine whether a directory is empty. You can do this by using the -A option of the ls command. An empty directory produces no output. If there is some output, the directory you specified is not empty.

For example, if the directory bar is empty, the following command

```
$ ls -A bar
```

returns nothing.

Now say that the directory docs is not empty. The following command

```
$ rmdir docs
```

produces an error message

```
rmdir: docs: Directory not empty
```

To illustrate the second error, assume that names is a file. The following command

```
$ rmdir names
```

produces an error message

```
rmdir: names: Not a directory
```

rm -r

You can specify the -r option to rm to remove a directory and its contents. The syntax is as follows:

```
rm -r directories
```

Here *directories* includes the names of the directories you want removed.

For example, the command

```
$ rm -r ch01/
```

removes the directory ch01 and its contents. This command produces no output.

You can specify a combination of files and directories as follows:

```
$ rm -r ch01/ test1.txt ch01-old.txt ch02/
```

In order to make rm safer, you can combine the -r and -i options.

Common Errors

Usually the only error reported by rm is that a requested file or directory cannot be removed. If the file or directory midterm_answers does not exist, rm reports an error:

```
$ rm -r midterm_answers
rm: midterm_answers: No such file or directory
```

Summary

In this chapter, you have looked at working with directories. Specifically, you covered the following topics:

- Working with filenames and pathnames
- Switching directories
- Listing files and directories
- Creating directories
- Copying and moving directories
- Removing directories

You reviewed each of these topics because it is important to know how to perform these functions when writing shell scripts. As you progress further into this book, you see how common directory manipulations occur in shell scripts.

Questions

1. Which of the following are absolute pathnames? Which are relative?

   a. `/usr/local/bin`

   b. `../../home/ranga`

   c. `docs/book/ch01`

   d. `/`

2. What is the output of the `pwd` command after the following sequence of `cd` commands have been issued?

   ```
   $ cd /usr/local
   $ cd bin
   $ cd ../../tmp
   $ cd
   ```

3. What command should be used to copy the directory `/usr/local` to `/opt/pgms`?

4. What command(s) should be used to move the directory `/usr/local` to `/opt/pgms`?

5. Given the following listing for the directory `backup`, can you use the `rmdir` command to remove this directory? If not, please give a command that can be used.

   ```
   $ ls -a backup
   ./    ../   sysbak-980322 sysbak-980112
   ```

HOUR 5

Manipulating File Attributes

In addition to working with files and directories, shell scripts are often called on to manipulate the attributes of a file. In this chapter, you learn how to manipulate the following file attributes:

- Permissions
- Owners
- Groups

You will examine the different types of files available on UNIX systems and how to identify them.

File Types

UNIX supports several different types of files. Files can contain your important data, such as files from a word processor or graphics package, or they can represent devices, directories, or symbolic links. In this section, you will look at the different types of files available under UNIX.

Determining a File's Type

To determine a file's type, specify the `-l` option to the `ls`. When this option is specified, `ls` lists the file type for the specified files. For example, the command

```
$ ls -l /home/ranga/.profile
```

produces the following output:

```
-rwxr-xr-x   1 ranga    users        2368 Jul 11 15:57 .profile*
```

Here, you see that the very first character is a hyphen (-). This indicates that the file is a regular file. For special files, the first character will be one of the letters given in Table 5.1.

To obtain file type information about a directory, you must specify the `-d` option along with the `-l` option:

```
$ ls -ld /home/ranga
```

This produces the following output:

```
drwxr-xr-x  27 ranga    users        2048 Jul 23 23:49 /home/ranga/
```

TABLE 5.1 SPECIAL CHARACTERS FOR DIFFERENT FILE TYPES

Character	File Type
-	Regular file
l	Symbolic link
c	Character special
b	Block special
p	Named pipe
s	Socket
d	Directory file

I'll provide the actual descriptions of each of these file types in the following sections.

Regular Files

NEW TERM   *Regular files* are the most common type of files you will encounter. These files store any kind of data. This data can be stored as plain text, an application-specific format, or a special binary format that the system can execute.

UNIX does not have to understand the data contained in a regular file. A regular file can store any form of raw data because UNIX does not interpret the data that is in the file.

[handwritten margin note: file shows what kind of file it is]

Often simply determining that a file is a regular file tells you very little about the file itself. Usually you need to know whether a particular file is a binary program, a shell script, or a library. In these instances, the `file` program is very useful.

It is invoked as follows:

```
file filename
```

Here, *filename* is the name of the file you want to examine. As an example, on my system, the command

```
$ file /sbin/sh
```

produces the following output:

```
/sbin/sh: ELF 32-bit MSB executable SPARC Version 1,
➥statically linked, stripped
```

Here you see that the file, /sbin/sh, is an executable program. Try it out on a few files to get an idea of the kind of information that it can give you.

Symbolic Links

NEW TERM   A *symbolic link* is a special file that points to another file on the system. When you access one of these files, it has a pathname stored inside it. Use this pathname to advance to the file or directory on the system represented by the pathname stored in the symbolic link.

For readers who are familiar with Windows or Mac OS, a symbolic link is similar to a shortcut or an alias.

You can use symbolic links to make a file appear as though it is located in many different places or has many different names in the file system. Symbolic links can point to any type of file or directory.

The `ls -1` output for a symbolic link looks like this:

```
lrwxrwxrwx   1 root      root          9 Oct 23 13:58 /bin/ -> ./usr/bin/
```

The output indicates that the directory /bin is really a link to the directory ./usr/bin.

The relative path in the output is not relative to your current working directory: it is relative to the directory where the link resides. In this case, the link /bin resides in the / directory, thus ./usr/bin indicates that /bin is a link to the directory /usr/bin.

5

Creating Symbolic Links

Create symbolic links using the `ln` command with the `-s` option. The syntax is as follows:

```
ln -s source destination
```

Here, *source* is either the absolute or relative path to the original version of the file, and *destination* is the name you want the link to have.

For example, the following command

```
$ ln -s /home/httpd/html/users/ranga /home/ranga/public_html
```

creates a link in my home directory to my Web files. If you encounter an error while creating a link, `ln` will display an error message. Otherwise, it displays no output.

In this example, you used absolute paths. In practice, relative paths are preferred for the source and the destination. For example, the actual commands I used to create a link to my Web files are the following:

```
$ cd
$ ln -s ../httpd/html/users/ranga ./public_html
```

You can see the relative path by using `ls -l`:

```
$ ls -l ./public_html

lrwxrwxrwx   1 ranga    users    26 Nov  9  1997 public_html -> ../httpd/
➥html/users/ranga
```

This output indicates that the file is a link and also shows the file or directory that the link points to.

Common Errors

The two most common errors encountered when creating symbolic links happen when

- The destination already exists.
- The destination is a directory.

If the specified destination is a file, it does not create the requested link. For example, if the file `.exrc` exists in my home directory, the command

```
$ ln -s /etc/exrc .exrc
```

produces the following error message:

```
ln: cannot create .exrc: File exists
```

If the specified destination is a directory, ln creates a link in that directory with the same name as the source. For example, if the directory pub exists in the current directory, the following command

```
$ ln -s /home/ftp/pub/ranga pub
```

creates the link pub/ranga rather than complaining that the destination is a directory. I mention this behavior of ln as a common error because forgetting about that fact is a common shell script bug.

Device Files

You can access UNIX devices through reading and writing to device files. These device files are access points to the device within the file systems.

Usually, device files are located under the /dev directory. The two main types of device files are

- Character special files
- Block special files

Character Special Files

NEW TERM   *Character special* files provide a mechanism for communicating with a device one character at a time. Usually character devices represent a "raw" device. The output of ls on a character special file looks like the following:

```
crw-------   1 ranga     users     4,   0 Feb  7 13:47 /dev/tty0
                                   MAJOR   MINOR
```

NEW TERM   The first letter in the output is c, therefore you know that this particular file is a character special file, but you also see two extra numbers before the date. The first number is called the *major* number and the second number is called the *minor* number. UNIX uses these two numbers to identify the device driver that this file communicates with.

Block Special Files

NEW TERM   *Block special* files also provide a mechanism for communicating with device drivers via the file system. These files are called *block devices* because they transfer large blocks of data at a time. This type of file typically represents hard drives and removable media.

Look at the ls -l output for a typical block device. For example, /dev/sda:

```
brw-rw----   1 root      disk      8,   0 Feb  7 13:47 /dev/sda
```

Here the first character is b, indicating that this file is a block special file. Just like the character special files, these files also have a major and a minor number.

Named Pipes

NEW TERM One of the greatest features of UNIX is that you can redirect the output of one program to the input of another program with very little work. For example, the command who ¦ grep ranga takes the output of the who command and makes it the input to the grep command. This is called *piping* the output of one command into another. You will examine input and output redirection in great detail in Chapter 13, "Input/Output."

On the command line, temporary anonymous pipes are used, but sometimes more control is needed than the command line provides. For such instances, UNIX provides a way to create a *named pipe*, so that two or more process can communicate with each other via a file that acts like a pipe. Because these files allow process to communicate with one another, they are one of the most popular forms of *interprocess communication* (IPC for short) available under UNIX.

Sockets

NEW TERM *Socket files* are another form of interprocess communication, but sockets can pass data and information between two processes that are not running on the same machine. Socket files are created when communication to a process on another machine located on a network is required. Internet tools in use today, such as Web browsers, use sockets to make a connection to the Web server.

Owners, Groups, and Permissions

File ownership is an important component of UNIX that provides a secure method for storing files. Every file in UNIX has the following attributes:

- Owner permissions
- Group permissions
- Other (world) permissions

The owner's permissions determine what actions the owner of the file can perform on the file. The group's permissions determine what actions a user, who is a member of the group that a file belongs to, can perform on the file. The permissions for others indicate what action all other users can perform on the file.

You can perform the following actions on a file:

- Read
- Write
- Execute

NEW TERM If a user has *read* permissions, that person can view the contents of a file. A user with *write* permissions can change the contents of a file, whereas a user with *execute* permissions can run a file as a program.

Viewing Permissions

You can display the permissions of a file using the `ls -l` command. For example, the following command

```
$ ls -l /home/ranga/.profile
```

produces the following output:

```
-rwxr-xr-x  1 ranga     users       2368 Jul 11 15:57 .profile*
```
Owner Group other

Because the first character is a hyphen (-), you know that this is a regular file. Several characters appear after this hyphen. The first three characters indicate the permissions for the *owner* of the file, the next three characters indicate the permissions for the *group* the file is associated with, and the last three characters indicate the permissions for all *other* users.

The permission block for this file indicates that the user has read, write, and execute permissions, whereas members of the group `users` and all other users have only read and execute permissions.

Three basic permissions that can be granted or denied on a file are read, write, and execute. These permissions are defined in Table 5.2.

After the permissions block, the *owner* and the *group* are listed. For this file, the *owner* is ranga and the *group* is *users*.

TABLE 5.2 BASIC PERMISSIONS

Letter	Permission	Definition
r	Read	The user can view the contents of the file.
w	Write	The user can alter the contents of the file.
x	Execute	The user can run the file, which is likely a program. For directories, the execute permission must be set in order for users to access the directory.

5

Directory Permissions

The x bit on a directory grants access to the directory. The read and write permissions have no effect if the access bit is not set.

The read permission on a directory enables users to use the ls command to view files and their attributes that are located in the directory.

The write permission on a directory is the permission to watch out for because it lets a user add and also remove files from the directory.

A directory that grants a user only execute permission will not enable the user to view the contents of the directory or add or delete any files from the directory, but it will let the user run executable files located in the directory.

> To ensure that your files are secure, check both the file permissions and the permissions of the directory where the file is located.
>
> If a file has write permission for owner, group, and other, the file is insecure. Inversely, if a file is in a directory that has write and execute permissions for owner, group, and other, all files located in the directory are insecure, no matter what the permissions on the files themselves are.

SUID and SGID File Permission

Often when a command is executed, it will have to be executed with special privileges in order to accomplish its task.

As an example, when you change your password with the passwd command, your new password is stored in the file /etc/shadow. As a regular user, you do not have read or write access to this file for security reasons, but when you change your password, you need to have write permission to this file. This means that the passwd program has to give you additional permissions so that you can write to the file /etc/shadow.

Additional permissions are given to programs via a mechanism known as the *Set User ID* (*SUID*) and *Set Group ID* (*SGID*) bits. When you execute a program that has the SUID bit enabled, you inherit the permissions of that program's owner. Programs that do not have the SUID bit set are run with the permissions of the user who started the program.

This is true for SGID as well. Normally programs execute with your group permissions, but instead your group will be changed just for this program to the group owner of the program.

As an example, the `passwd` command, used to change your password, is owned by the root and has the set SUID bit enabled. When you execute it, you effectively become root while the command runs.

NEW TERM The SUID and SGID bits will appear as the letter "s" if the permission is available. The SUID "s" bit will be located in the permission bits where the owners execute permission would normally reside. For example, the command

```
$ ls -l /usr/bin/passwd
```

produces the following output:

```
-r-sr-xr-x   1 root     bin          19031 Feb  7 13:47 /usr/bin/passwd*
```

which shows that the SUID bit is set and that the command is owned by the root. A capital letter *S* in the execute position instead of a lowercase *s* indicates that the execute bit is not set.

The *SUID bit* or `stick bit` imposes extra file removal permissions on a directory. A directory with write permissions enabled for a user enables that user to add and delete any files from this directory. If the sticky bit is enabled on the directory, files can only be removed if you are one of the following users:

- The owner of the sticky directory
- The owner the file being removed
- The super user, root

You should consider enabling the sticky bit for any directories that nonprivileged users can write. Examples of such directories would include temporary directories and public file upload sites.

Directories can also take advantage of the SGID bit. If a directory has the SGID bit set, any new files added to the directory automatically inherit that directories group, instead of the group of the user writing the file.

Changing File and Directory Permissions

You can change file and directory permissions with the `chmod` command. The basic syntax is as follows:

```
chmod expression  files
```

5

NEW TERM   Here, *expression* is a statement of how to change the permissions. This expression can be of the following types:

- Symbolic
- Octal

The symbolic expression method uses letters to alter the permissions, and the octal expression method uses numbers. The numbers in the octal method are base-8 (octal) numbers ranging from 0 to 7.

Symbolic Method

The symbolic expression has the syntax of

`(who)(action)(permissions)`

Table 5.3 shows the possible values for *who*, Table 5.4 shows the possible *actions*, and Table 5.5 shows the possible *permissions* settings. Using these three reference tables, you can build an expression.

TABLE 5.3   *who*

Letter	Represents
u	Owner
g	Group
o	Other
a	All

TABLE 5.4   *actions*

Symbol	Represents
+	Adding permissions to the file
-	Removing permission from the file
=	Explicitly set the file permissions

TABLE 5.5   *permissions*

Letter	Represents
r	Read
w	Write
x	Execute
s	SUID or SGID

Now look at a few examples of using chmod.

To give the "world" read access to all files in a directory, you can use one of the following commands:

```
$ chmod a=r *
```

or

```
$ chmod guo=r *
```

If the command is successful, it produces no output.

To stop anyone except the owner of the file .profile from writing to it, try this:

```
$ chmod go-w .profile
```

To deny access to the files in your home directory, you can try the following:

```
$ cd ; chmod go= *
```

or

```
$ cd ; chmod go-rwx *
```

> If you do this, be warned because some users will call you a *file miser*.

When specifying the users part or the permissions part, the order in which you give the letters is irrelevant. Thus these commands are equivalent:

```
$ chmod guo+rx *
$ chmod uog+xr *
```

If you need to apply more than one set of permissions changes to a file or files, use a comma separated list: For example

```
$ chmod go-w,a+x a.out
```

removes the groups and "world" write permission on a.out and adds the execute permission for everyone.

To set the SUID and SGID bits for your home directory, try the following:

```
$ cd ; chmod ug+s .
```

5

So far, the examples you have examined involve changing the permissions for files in a directory, but `chmod` also enables you to change the permissions for every file in a directory including the files in subdirectories. You can accomplish this by specifying the `-R` option.

For example, if the directory `pub` contains the following directories:

```
$ ls pub
./         ../        README    faqs/    src/
```

you can change the permission read permissions of the file `README` along with the files contained in the directories `faqs` and `src` with the following command:

```
$ chmod -R o+r pub
```

Be careful when doing this to large subtrees because you *can* change the permissions of a file in a way that you did not intend.

Octal Method

By changing permissions with an octal expression, you can only explicitly set file permissions. This method uses a single number to assign the desired permission to each of the three categories of users (owner, group, and other).

The values of the individual permissions are the following:

- Read permission has a value of 4
- Write permission has a value of 2
- Execute permission has a value of 1

Adding the value of the permissions that you want to grant will give you a number between 0 and 7. This number will be used to specify the permissions for the owner, group, and finally the other category.

Setting SUID and SGID using the octal method places these bits out in front of the standard permissions. The permissions SUID and SGID take on the values 4 and 2, respectively.

Go through some of the examples covered in the previous section to get an idea of how to use the octal method of changing permissions.

In order to set the "world" read access to all files in a directory, do this:

```
chmod 0444 *
```

To stop anyone except the owner of the file `.profile` from writing to it, do this:

```
chmod 0600 .profile
```

Common Errors

Many new users find the octal specification of file permissions confusing. The most important thing to keep in mind is that the octal method sets or assigns permissions to a file, but it does not add or delete them.

This means that the octal mode does not have an equivalent to

```
chmod u+rw .profile
```

The closest possible octal version would be

```
chmod 0600 .profile
```

But this removes permissions for everyone except the user. It can also reduce the user's permissions by removing that person's execute permission.

Just keep in mind that the octal mode sets the permissions of files not to modify them, and you will not run into any problems.

Changing Owners and Groups

Two commands are available to change the owner and the group of files:

- chown
- chgrp

NEW TERM   The chown command stands for "change owner" and is used to change the owner of a file.

The chgrp command stands for "change group" and is used to change the group of a file.

On some older systems, the chgrp command might not be available, and the chown command must be used instead. You will learn how to use both chown and chgrp to change the group of a file. For maximum portability, you should stick to using chown to change both the owner and the group of a file.

Changing Ownership

The chown command changes the ownership of a file. The basic syntax is as follows:

```
chown options user:group files
```

Here, *options* can be one or more of the options listed in the man page for chown. Because considerable variation exists in the available options, please consult the man page on your system for a complete list.

5

The value of *user* can be either the name of a user on the system or the user id (uid) of a user on the system. The value of *group* can be the name of a group on the system or the group ID (GID) of a group on the system. To just change the owner, you can omit the group value.

As an example

```
chown ranga: /home/httpd/html/users/ranga
```

changes the owner of the given directory to the user `ranga`.

Restrictions

The super user, root, has the unrestricted capability to change the ownership of a file, but some restrictions occur for normal users.

Normal users can change only the owner of files they own. This means that if you give another user ownership of a file, you will not be able to regain ownership of that file. Only the new owner of the file or the super user can return the ownership to you.

On some systems, the `chown` command will be disabled for normal user use. This generally happens if the system is running disk quotas. Under a disk quota system, users might be allowed to store only 100MB of files, but if they change the ownership of some files, their free available disk space increases, and they still have access to their files.

The `chown` command will recursively change the ownership of all files when the `-R` option is included. For example, the command

```
chown -R ranga: /home/httpd/html/users/ranga
```

changes the owner of all the files and subdirectories located under the given directory to be the user `ranga`.

Changing Group Ownership

You can change group ownership of a file with the `chgrp` command. Its basic syntax is as follows:

```
chgrp options group files
```

Here, *options* is one or more of the options listed in the man page for `chgrp`. The value of *group* can be either the name of a group or the GID of a group on the system. As an example

```
chgrp authors /home/ranga/docs/ch5.doc
```

changes the group of the given file to be the group authors. Just like `chown`, all versions of `chgrp` understand the `-R` option also.

On systems without this command, you can use chown to change the group of a file. For example, the command

```
chown :authors /home/ranga/docs/ch5.doc
```

changes the group of the given file to the group authors.

Summary

In this chapter, I covered several important topics relating to files and file permissions. Specifically, I covered the following tasks:

- Determining a file's type
- Changing file and directory permissions using symbolic and octal notation
- Enabling SUID and SGID permissions for files and directories
- Changing the owner of a file or directory
- Changing the group of a file or directory

As you will see in subsequent chapters, each of these tasks is important in shell scripts.

Questions

For the three questions, refer to the following ls -l output:

```
crw-r-----  1 bin      sys         188 0x001000 Oct 13 00:31 /dev/
➥rdsk/c0t1d0
-r--r--r--  1 root     sys         418 Oct 13 16:25 /etc/passwd
drwxrwxrwx 10 bin      bin        1024 Oct 15 20:27 /usr/local/
-r-sr-xr-x  1 root     bin       28672 Nov  6  1997 /usr/sbin/ping
```

1. Identify the file type of each of the files given above.
2. Identify the owner and group of each of the files given above.
3. Describe the permissions for the owner, group, and all "other" users for each of the files given above.

5

Hour 6

Processes

By David B. Horvath, CCP

In this chapter you learn the concepts of processes and jobs. In UNIX every program runs as a process. I explain background and foreground processes and how to start a process. You are introduced to the commands that list and kill processes. Finally, the concept of parent and child processes are explained.

In this chapter you look at the four major topics involving processes provided with the shell:

- Starting processes
- Listing running processes
- Killing processes
- Parent and child processes

Starting a Process

Whenever you issue a command in UNIX, it creates, or *starts*, a new process. When you tried out the ls command to list directory contents in Chapter 4, "Working with Directories," you started a process (the ls command).

The operating system tracks processes through a five digit ID number known as the *pid* or *process ID*. Each process in the system has a unique pid. Pids eventually repeat because all the possible numbers are used up and the next pid rolls or starts over. At any one time, no two processes with the same pid exist in the system because it is the pid that UNIX uses to track each process. You might be interested in the fact that the pid usually rolls over at the 16-bit signed boundary. The highest it gets before rolling over is 32,767.

You can use the ps command to see what processes you are running and all processes on the system. The ps command is described in the "Listing Running Processes" section of this chapter.

When you start a process (run a command), there are two ways you can run it—in the *foreground* or *background*. The difference is how the process interacts with you at the terminal.

Foreground Processes

By default, every process that you start runs in the foreground. It gets its input from the keyboard and sends its output to the screen. You can redirect process input and output (see Chapter 13, "Input/Output"), but by default, input and output are connected to your terminal.

You can see this happen with the ls command. If I want to list all the files in my current directory (various chapters that start with a zero), I can use the following command:

```
$ ls ch0*.doc
```

On my screen, I see the following output:

```
ch01-1.doc   ch010.doc    ch02.doc     ch03-2.doc   ch04-1.doc
➥ch040.doc    ch05.doc     ch06-2.doc
ch01-2.doc   ch02-1.doc   ch020.doc    ch03.doc     ch04-2.doc
➥ch05-1.doc   ch050.doc    ch06.doc
ch01.doc     ch02-2.doc   ch03-1.doc   ch030.doc    ch04.doc
➥ch05-2.doc   ch06-1.doc   ch060.doc
```

The process runs in the foreground, the output is directed to my screen, and if the ls command wants any input (which it does not), it waits for it from the keyboard.

While this command is running, I cannot run any other commands (start any other processes). I can enter commands, but no prompt appears and nothing happens until this one completes because UNIX buffers keystrokes. For the `ls` command, which usually runs very quickly, this is not a problem. But if I have something that runs for a long time—such as a large compile, database query, program that calculated pi, or a server—my terminal will be tied up.

Fortunately, I do not have to wait for one process to complete before I can start another. UNIX provides facilities for starting processes in the background, suspending foreground processes, and moving processes between the foreground and background.

> When you log off or are disconnected from the system by a communication problem, your processes are terminated. If you have a long running process that you do not want terminated, you need to use the nohup command. nohup stands for no HUP (Hang UP). The nohup command is described later, in the section "Keeping Background Processes Around (nohup Command)."

long Running process

Background Processes

A background process runs without being connected to your keyboard. If the background process requires any keyboard input, it waits.

The advantage of running a process in the background is that you can run other commands; you do not have to wait until it completes to start another!

The simplest way to start a background process is to add an ampersand (&) at the end of the command.

Running the same `ls` command as in the foreground example, I use the following:

```
$ ls ch0*.doc &
```
BAckground

On the screen, I see the following:

```
[1]      20757
$ ch01-1.doc  ch010.doc   ch02.doc    ch03-2.doc  ch04-1.doc
 ➥ch040.doc   ch05.doc    ch06-2.doc
ch01-2.doc  ch02-1.doc  ch020.doc   ch03.doc    ch04-2.doc
 ➥ch05-1.doc  ch050.doc   ch06.doc
ch01.doc    ch02-2.doc  ch03-1.doc  ch030.doc   ch04.doc
 ➥ch05-2.doc  ch06-1.doc  ch060.doc
```
Process ID

Job No

6

I can see from the first line of output that the process runs in the background. The output is directed to my screen. If the `ls` command wants any input (which it does not), it goes into a stop state until I move it into the foreground and give it the data from the keyboard.

Background

That first line contains information about the background process—the job number and process ID. You need to know the job number to manipulate it between background and foreground.

If you run this command yourself, you might notice that you do not get a prompt back after the last line of the directory listing. That's because the prompt actually appears immediately after the job/pid line, next to `ch01-1.doc`. You are able to enter a command immediately instead of waiting for `ls` to finish.

If you press the Enter key now, you see the following:

```
[1]  +  Done                    ls ch0*.doc &
$
```

The first line tells you that the `ls` command background process finishes successfully. The second is a prompt for another command.

> If you try this command and do not see the completion messages, it might be because your shell has been told not to show it to you. When enabled, those messages are part of process or job monitoring. You can enable monitoring with the following:
>
> `set -o monitor`   *Enable messages*
>
> To disable the monitoring messages, you use +o:
>
> `set +o monitor`   *Disable message*
>
> You can also check all the shell options with the following:
>
> `set -o`   *Check option*

You see a different completion message if an error occurs. There is no file with the name `no_such_file` in my directory, so if I try to list it with `ls`, I get an error. The command is

```
$ ls no_such_file &
```

resulting in output that looks like

```
[1]      25389
$ no_such_file: No such file or directory
```

The first line is the background process information, and the second shows the prompt for the next command and the output from `ls`—the error message. I get the same error message if I run `ls` as a foreground process.

If you have process and job monitoring enabled, pressing Enter again results in the following appearing on your screen:

```
[1]  +  Done(2)                 ls no_such_file &
$
```

[handwritten: Command prompt]

[handwritten: → Did not RUN successfully]

The `ls` command returns a nonzero status. That value (2) is shown after the `Done` message to inform you that it did not run successfully. Of course, the dollar sign ($) on the next line is the command prompt.

BACKGROUND PROCESSES THAT REQUIRE INPUT

If you run a background process that requires input and do not redirect it to read a file instead of the keyboard, the process stops. If you have process and job monitoring enabled, pressing Enter at an empty command prompt or starting a command returns a message. The following is an example of running a command in the background that needs input (using a simple program I created that is not part of UNIX):

```
$ i_need_input &
```

Because this command does not produce any output until you give it input, all you see is the command prompt. Pressing Enter results in a message as follows:

```
[1] + Stopped (SIGTTIN)        i_need_input &
```

[handwritten: waiting for terminal input]

On some systems the message looks like the following:

```
[1] + Stopped (tty input)       i_need_input &
```

SIGTTIN (seen in the first example) is a signal (SIG) that tells me the program is waiting for terminal (TT) input (IN). See Chapter 19, "Dealing with Signals," for more information on signals.

If you get a message like this, you have two choices. You can kill the process and rerun it with input redirected, or you can bring the process to the foreground, give it the input it needs, and then let it continue as a foreground or background process. This chapter explains how to handle either of these choices.

6

Background Processes That Write Output

Some processes force their output to the screen and go into a stop state if they run in the background and want to write output. These processes display a message like:

```
[1] + Stopped (SIGTTOU)        i_write &
```

On some systems the message might display as follows:

```
[1] + Stopped (tty output)     i_write &
```

SIGTTOU (seen in the first example) is a signal (SIG) that tells me that the program wants to write output (OU) to the terminal (TT) but is in the background. See Chapter 19 for more information on signals.

If you get a message like this, you have two choices. You can kill the process and rerun it with output redirected, or you can bring the process to the foreground where it writes its output and let it continue as a foreground or background process. This chapter explains how to handle either of those choices.

(handwritten: Wants to write output to the terminal)

Moving a Foreground Process to the Background

In addition to running a process in the background using &, you can move a foreground process into the background. While a foreground process runs, the shell does not process any new commands. Before you can enter any commands, you have to suspend the foreground process to get a command prompt. The suspend key on most UNIX systems is Ctrl+Z.

(handwritten: Suspend process)

You can determine which key performs which function by using the stty command. By entering

```
$ stty -a
```

you are shown the following, along with a lot of other information:

```
intr = ^C; quit = ^\; erase = ^H; kill = ^U;
➥ eof = ^D; eol = ^@
eol2 = ^@; start = ^Q; stop = ^S; susp = ^Z;
➥ dsusp = ^Y; reprint = ^R
discard = ^O; werase = ^W; lnext = ^V
```

The entry after susp (^Z in this example) is the key that suspends a foreground process. The character ^ stands for Ctrl. If Ctrl+Z does not work for you, use the stty command as shown previously to determine the key for your system.

(handwritten: shows key functions)

When a foreground process is suspended, a command prompt enables you to enter more commands; the original process is still in memory but is not getting any CPU time. To resume the foreground process, you have two choices—background and foreground. The bg command enables you to resume the suspended process in the background; the fg command returns it to the foreground. fg is covered in the next section.

For example, you start a long running process. I'm using long_running_process for the following example:

```
$ long_running_process
```

While it is running, you decide that it should run in the background so your terminal is not tied up. To do that, you press the Ctrl+Z key and see the following (the ^Z is your Ctrl+Z key being echoed):

```
^Z[1] + Stopped (SIGTSTP)          long_running_process
$
```

You are told the job number (1) and that the process is Stopped. You then get a prompt. To resume the job in the background, you enter the bg command as follows:

```
$ bg
[1]     long_running_process &
$
```

As a result, the process runs in the background. Look at the last character on the second line, the ampersand (&). As a reminder, the shell displays the ampersand there to remind you that the job is running in the background. It behaves just like a command where you type the ampersand at the end of the line.

By default, the bg command moves the most recently suspended process to the background. You can have multiple processes suspended at one time. To differentiate them, put the job number prefixed with a percent sign (%) on the command line.

In the following example, I start two long running processes, suspend both of them, and put the first one into the background. The next few lines show starting and suspending two foreground processes:

```
$ long_running_process
^Z[1] + Stopped (SIGTSTP)          long_running_process
$ long_running_process2
^Z[2] + Stopped (SIGTSTP)          long_running_process2
$
```

To move the first one to the background, I use the following:

```
$ bg %1
[1]     long_running_process &
$
```

The second process is still suspended and can be moved to the background as follows:

```
$ bg %2
[2]     long_running_process2 &
$
```

6

The capability to specify which job to perform an action on (move to foreground or background for instance) shows the importance of having job numbers assigned to background processes.

Moving a Background Process to the Foreground (fg Command)

When you have a process that is in the background or suspended, you can move it to the foreground with the fg command. By default, the process most recently suspended or moved to the background moves to the foreground. You can also specify which job, using its job number, you want to make foreground.

> If you're ever in doubt about which job will be moved to the background or foreground, don't guess. Put the job number on the bg or fg command, prefixed with a percent sign.

Using the long running process in the previous section, a foreground process is suspended and moved into the background in the following example:

```
$ long_running_process
^Z[1] + Stopped (SIGTSTP)          long_running_process
$ bg
[1]       long_running_process &
$
```

You can move it back to the foreground as follows:

```
$ fg %1
long_running_process
```

The second line shows you which command you moved back to the foreground. The same thing would have happened if it was moved back to the foreground after being suspended.

Keeping Background Processes Around (nohup Command)

You can prevent a background process from terminating, which is the default action, when you sign off or are disconnected. The nohup command prevents your process from getting the HUP (Hang UP) signal and enables it to continue processing.

The nohup command is simple to use—just add it before the command you actually want to run. Because nohup is designed to run when there is no terminal attached, it wants you to redirect output to a file. If you do not, nohup redirects it automatically to a file known as nohup.out.

Running a process in the background with nohup looks like the following:

```
$ nohup ls &  - Background
[1]     6695
$ Sending output to nohup.out
```

Because I do not redirect the output from nohup, it does it for me. If I redirect the output (nohup ls > results &), I do not see the second message.

After waiting a few moments and pressing Enter, I see the following:

```
[1] + Done                        nohup ls &
$
```

You can look at the file nohup.out using cat, more, pg, vi, view, or your preferred tool to see the results.

Waiting for Background Processes to Finish (wait Command)

There are two ways to wait for a background process to finish before doing something else. You can press the Enter key every few minutes until you get the completion message, or you can use the wait command.

There are three ways to use the wait command—with no options (the default), with a process ID, or with a job number prefixed with a percent sign. The command will wait for the completion of the job or process you specify.

If you do not specify a job or process (the default setting), the wait command waits for all background jobs to finish. Using wait without any options is useful in a shell script that starts a series of background jobs. When they are all done, it can continue processing.

With the ls command from the previous example running, I can force a wait with the following:

```
$ wait %1
```

I can not enter another command until job number 1 finishes. If I use wait, I do not get the completion message (Done).

Listing Running Processes

You can start processes in the foreground and background, suspend them, and move them between the foreground and background, but how do you know what is running? There are two commands to help you find out—jobs and ps.

6

jobs Command

The jobs command shows you the processes you have suspended and the ones running in the background. Because the jobs command is a foreground process, it cannot show you your active foreground processes.

In the following example, I have three jobs. The first one (job 3) is running, the second (job 2) is suspended (a foreground process after I used Ctrl+Z), and the third one (job 1) is stopped in the background to wait for keyboard input:

[handwritten note in left margin: indicates most recent job]

```
$ jobs
[3]  ±  Running                  first_one &   Background
[2]  -  Stopped (SIGTSTP)  suspend second_one
[1]     Stopped (SIGTTIN)  waiting third_one &  Background
                           input
```

I can manipulate these jobs with the fg and bg commands. The most recent job is job number 3 (shown with a plus sign); this is the one that bg or fg act on if no job number is supplied. The most recent job before that is job number two (shown with a minus sign).

> The reason for the plus and minus symbols on the jobs listing is that job numbers are reassigned when one completes and another starts. In the previous example, if job number 2 finishes and you start another job, it is assigned job number 2 and a plus sign because it is the most recent job.

ps Command

Another command that shows all processes running is the ps (Process Status) command. By default, it shows those processes that you are running. It also accepts many different options, a few of which are shown here.

There are different flavors, or versions, of UNIX. ps is one command where the differences are very obvious. The examples in this chapter are based on System V, a UNIX standard developed by UNIX Systems Labs (USL) when it was part of AT&T. If you are using a version of UNIX based on Berkeley Systems Division (BSD), like Linux, your output will be different.

The simplest example (with the same three jobs running as the previous example) is the ps command alone:

```
$ ps
   PID TTY       TIME CMD
  6738 pts/6     0:00 first_one
```

Process ID *Terminal* *Time* *Command* (handwritten annotations)

```
 6739 pts/6    0:00 second_one
 3662 pts/6    0:00 ksh
 8062 pts/6    0:00 ps
 6770 pts/6    0:01 third_one
```

For each running process, this provides me with four pieces of information: the pid, the TTY (terminal running this process), the Time or amount of CPU consumed by this process, and the command name running.

I am running three jobs but have five processes. Of course, one of the extra processes is the ps command itself. The remaining process, ksh, is the command shell that interprets what I type at the keyboard and manages the processes and jobs. It is my interface to the operating system and nothing would happen without it. ksh is the Korn shell.

> If you are using a version of UNIX based on BSD, like Linux, your output is different and looks like the following:
>
> ```
> $ ps
>   PID  TT  STAT      TIME COMMAND
> 13049  q0  Ss     0:00.06 -ksh (ksh)
> 13108  q0  R+     0:00.01 ps
> ```
> *State of the job* (handwritten annotation)
>
> For each running process, this provides you with five pieces of information: the pid, the TT (terminal running this process), STAT (the state of the job), the TIME or amount of CPU consumed by this process, and finally the command name running.
>
> Use the man ps command for an explanation of the states and options available.

> In some versions of UNIX, the ps command does not show itself in the listing. That's just the way it works. I used a version that does show it. If you don't see it on your system, don't worry.

6

One of the most commonly used flags for ps is the -f (*f* for *full*) option, which provides more information as shown in the following example:

```
$ ps -f
    UID   PID  PPID  C    STIME TTY         TIME CMD
dhorvath 6738  3662  0 10:23:03 pts/6       0:00 first_one
dhorvath 6739  3662  0 10:22:54 pts/6       0:00 second_one
dhorvath 3662  3657  0 08:10:53 pts/6       0:00 -ksh
dhorvath 6892  3662  4 10:51:50 pts/6       0:00 ps -f
dhorvath 6770  3662  2 10:35:45 pts/6       0:03 third_one
```

Table 6.1 shows the meaning of each of these columns.

TABLE 6.1 PS -F COLUMNS

Column Heading	Description
UID	User ID that this process belongs to (the person running it).
PID	Process ID.
PPID	Parent process ID (the ID of the process that started it).
C	CPU utilization of process.
unlabeled	Nice value—used in calculating process priority.
STIME	Process start time (when it began).
CMD	The command that started this process. CMD with -f is different from CMD without it; it shows any command line options and arguments.

Note that the PPID of all my commands is 3662, which is the pid of ksh. Everything I do runs under ksh.

> You might be wondering why TIME changed for third_one. Between the time I entered the ps and the ps -f commands, third_one used some CPU time—two seconds. On larger UNIX servers, a lot of work can be done with very little CPU time. That's why the ps command itself is showing with zero CPU time; it used time, but not enough to round up to one second.

Two more common options are -e (*e* for *every*) and -u (*u* for *user*). The -e option is handy if you want to see whether the database is running or who is playing Zork (an old text-based computer game). Because so many processes run on a busy system, it is common to pipe the output of ps -e to a text filter like grep (see Chapter 15, "Text Filters"). The -u option is handy if you want to see what a specific user is doing—are they busy or do they have time to chat; is your boss busy or checking to make sure you're not playing Zork?. With -u, you specify the user you want to list after the -u.

You can combine the -f option with -e or -u, but you cannot combine -e with -u.

Table 6.2 shows more BSD ps command options.

TABLE 6.2   MORE BSD PS COMMAND OPTIONS.

Column Heading	Description
ps -a	Shows information about all users
ps -x	Shows information about processes without terminals (daemons and jobs running nohup)
ps -u	Shows additional information (like the System V ps -f)

Use the man ps command for an explanation of all the available options. If you are ever in doubt about a command or option, use the man command to obtain information about that command. For the ps command, man ps gets you the manual page.

Killing a Process (`kill` Command)

Another handy command to use with jobs and processes is the kill command. As the name implies, the kill command *kills*, or ends, a process.

Just like the fg and bg commands, the job number is prefixed with a percent sign. To kill job number 1 in the earlier example regarding waiting for keyboard input, I use the following:

```
$ kill %1
[1] - Terminated              third_one &
$
```

You can also kill a specific process by specifying the process ID on the command line without the percent sign used with job numbers. To kill job number 2 (process 6738) in the earlier example using process ID, I use the following:

```
$ kill 6739
$
```

In reality, kill does not physically kill a process; it sends the process a signal. By default, it sends the TERM (value 15) signal. A process can choose to ignore the TERM signal or use it to begin an orderly shut down (flushing buffers, closing files, and so on). If a process ignores a regular kill command, you can use kill -9 or kill -KILL followed by the process ID or job number (prefixed with a percent sign). This forces the process to end.

6

Be very careful when specifying which process to kill, especially if you are using kill -9, because you can end a job by accident or even log yourself off. My command interpreter has the process ID of 3662, and I can try to kill it as follows:

```
$ ps -f
        UID   PID  PPID  C    STIME TTY      TIME CMD
 billing  3662  3657  0 08:10:53 pts/6      0:01 -ksh
$ kill 3662
$ ps -f
        UID   PID  PPID  C    STIME TTY      TIME CMD
 billing  3662  3657  0 08:10:53 pts/6      0:01 -ksh
```

ksh ignores a regular kill but not a kill -9, as follows:

```
$ kill -9 3662.
```

There is no command prompt after this command. I was disconnected from the system.

If your UNIX version does not support ps -f, you can use ps -ux.

Parent and Child Processes

In the ps -f example in the ps command section, each process has two ID numbers assigned to it: process ID (pid) and parent process ID (ppid). Each user process in the system has a parent process. Most commands that you run have the shell as their parent. The parent of your shell is usually the operating system or the terminal communications process (in.telnetd for telnet connections).

I have recreated this earlier example to demonstrate the ppid of all my commands is 3662, the pid of ksh, as follows:

```
$ ps -f
        UID   PID  PPID  C    STIME TTY      TIME CMD
 dhorvath 6738  3662  0 10:23:03 pts/6      0:00 first_one
 dhorvath 6739  3662  0 10:22:54 pts/6      0:00 second_one
 dhorvath 3662  3657  0 08:10:53 pts/6      0:00 -ksh
 dhorvath 6892  3662  4 10:51:50 pts/6      0:00 ps -f
 dhorvath 6770  3662  2 10:35:45 pts/6      0:03 third_one
```

The ppid of ksh is 3657. Using ps -ef (or ps -aux on some systems) and grep to find that number, I see the following:

```
$ ps -ef | grep 3657    Shell
 dhorvath 9778  3662  4 10:52:50 pts/6      0:00 ps -f
 dhorvath 9779  3662  0 10:52:51 pts/6      0:00 grep 3657
     root 3657   711  0 08:10:53 ?         0:00 in.telnetd
 dhorvath 3657  3662  0 08:10:53 pts/6      0:00 -ksh
```

This tells me that my terminal session is being handled by in.telnetd (the telnet daemon) that owns, or is the parent of, my Korn shell command interpreter.

There is a parent-child relationship between processes. in.telnetd is the parent of ksh, which is the child of in.telnetd but the parent of ps and grep.

When a child is *forked*, or created, from its parent, it receives a copy of the parent's environment, including environment variables. The child can change its own environment, but those changes do not reflect in the parent and go away when the child exits.

Job ID Versus Process ID

Background and suspended processes are usually manipulated via job number (job ID). This number is different from the process ID and is used because it is shorter. In addition, a job can consist of multiple processes running in series or at the same time, in parallel, so using the job ID is easier than tracking the individual processes.

Subshells

Whenever you run a shell script, in addition to any commands in the script, another copy of the shell interpreter is created. This new shell is known as a *subshell,* just as a directory contained in or under another is known as a subdirectory.

The best way to show this is with an example. I created a script known as psit and gave it execute permissions. This script runs ps and exits in the following example:

```
#! /bin/ksh
ps -ef | grep dhorvath
exit 0
```

When run, psit produces the following:

```
$ psit
 dhorvath 9830  3662  0 13:58:42 pts/6    0:00 ksh psit
 dhorvath 9831  9830 19 14:05:24 pts/6    0:00 ps -ef
 dhorvath 3662  3657  0 08:10:53 pts/6    0:00 -ksh
 dhorvath 9832  9830  0 13:58:42 pts/6    0:00 grep dhorvath
$
```

The subshell running as process 9830 is a child of process 3662, the original ksh shell. ps and grep are the children of process 9830 (ksh psit). When the psit script is done and exits, the subshell exits, and control is returned to the original shell.

You can also start a subshell by entering the shell name (ksh for Korn, sh for Bourne, and csh for C Shell). This feature is handy if you have one login (default) shell and want to use another. Starting out in Korn shell and starting C Shell would look like the following:

```
$ csh
% ps -f
     UID   PID  PPID  C    STIME TTY       TIME CMD
```

6

```
dhorvath 3662  3657  0 08:10:53 pts/6     0:00 -ksh
dhorvath 3266  8848 11 10:50:40 pts/6     0:00 ps -f
dhorvath 8848  3662  1 10:50:38 pts/6     0:00 csh
%
```

The C shell uses the percent sign as a prompt. After the csh command starts the shell, the prompt becomes the percent sign. The ps command shows csh as a child process and subshell of ksh. To exit csh and return to the parent shell, you enter exit.

Process Permissions

By default, a process runs with the permissions of the user running it. In most cases, this makes sense, enabling you to run a command or utility only on your files. There are times, however, when users need to access files that they do not own. A good example of this is the passwd command, which is usually stored as /usr/bin/passwd. It is used to change passwords and modify /etc/passwd and the shadow password file, if the system is so equipped.

It does not make sense for general users to have write access to the password files; they could create users on the fly. The program itself has these permissions. If you look at the file using ls, you see the letter s where x normally appears in the owner and group permissions. The owner of /usr/bin/passwd is root, and it belongs to the sys group. No matter who runs it, it has the permissions of the root user.

Overlaying the Current Process (exec Command)

In addition to creating (forking) child processes, you can overlay the current process with another. The exec command replaces the current process with the new one. Use this command only with great caution. If you use exec in your primary (login) shell interpreter, that shell interpreter (ksh with pid 3662 in the previous examples) is replaced with the new process.

Using the command exec ls at your login shell prompt gives you a directory listing and then disconnects you from the system, logging you out. Because exec overlays your shell (ksh, for example), there are no programs to handle commands for you when ls finishes and exits.

You can use exec to change your shell interpreter completely without creating a subshell. To convert from ksh to csh, you can use the following:

```
$ exec csh
% ps -f
      UID   PID  PPID  C    STIME TTY       TIME CMD
  dhorvath 3662  3657  0 08:10:53 pts/6     0:00 csh
  dhorvath 3266  3662 11 14:50:40 pts/6     0:00 ps -f
%
```

The prompt changes and `ps` shows `csh` instead of `ksh` but with the original pid and start time.

Summary

In this chapter, you looked at the four major topics involving processes provided with the shell:

- Starting a process
- Listing running processes
- Killing a process (`kill` command)
- Parent and child processes

As you write scripts and use the shell, knowing how to work with processes improves your productivity.

Questions

1. How do you run a command in the background?
2. How do you determine what processes you are running?
3. How do you change a foreground process into a background process?

Terms

Background—Background describes processes usually running at a lower priority and with their input disconnected from the interactive session. Input and output are usually directed to a file or other process.

Background Processes—Background processes are autonomous processes that run under UNIX without requiring user interaction.

bash—bash stands for the GNU Bourne Again Shell and is based on the Bourne shell, sh, the original command interpreter.

Bourne Shell—This shell is the original standard user interface to UNIX that supported limited programming capability.

BSD—BSD is an acronym for Berkeley Software Distribution.

BSD UNIX—This version of UNIX was developed by Berkeley Software Distribution and written at University of California, Berkeley.

6

C Shell—This user interface for UNIX, written by Bill Joy at Berkeley, features C programming-like syntax.

Child Processes—See *subprocesses*.

Child Shells—See *subshells*.

Daemons—Daemons are system-related background processes that often run with the permissions of root and services requests from other processes.

Korn Shell—This shell is a user interface for UNIX with extensive scripting (programming) support. It was written by David G. Korn. The shell features command-line editing and also accepts scripts written for the Bourne shell.

Parent Process Identifier—The parent process identifier is shown in the heading of the ps command as PPID. This is the process identifier of the parent process. See also *parent processes*.

Parent Processes—These processes control other processes that are often referred to as child processes or subprocesses. See *processes*.

Parent Shell—This shell controls other shells, which are often referred to as child shells or subshells. The login shell is typically the parent shell. See *shells*.

Process Identifier—The process identifier is shown in the heading of the ps command as pid. It is the unique number assigned to every process running in the system.

Processes—Processes are discrete, running programs under UNIX. The user's interactive session is a process. A process can invoke (run) and control another program that is then referred to as a subprocess. Ultimately, everything a user does is a subprocess of the operating system.

Shell—The shell is the part of UNIX that handles user input and invokes other programs to run commands. It includes a programming language. See also *Bourne shell*, *C shell*, *Korn shell*, tcsh, and bash.

Shell or Command Prompt—The prompt is a single character or set of characters that the UNIX shell displays at which a user can enter a command or set of commands.

Shell Scripts—Shell scripts are programs written using a shell programming language like those supported by Bourne, Korn, or C shells.

Subprocesses—Subprocesses run under the control of other processes, which are often referred to as parent processes. See *processes*.

Subshells—Subshells run under the control of another shell, which is often referred to as the parent shell. Typically, the login shell is the parent shell. See *shells*.

tcsh—This is a C shell-like user interface featuring command-line editing.

PART II
Shell Programming

Hour

Hour 7

Variables

NEW TERM   *Variables* are "words" that hold a *value*. The shell enables you to create, assign, and delete variables. Although the shell manages some variables, it is mostly up to the programmer to manage variables in shell scripts.

This chapter shows you how to

- Create variables
- Delete variables

This chapter also explains what environment variables are and how to use them properly. By using variables, you are able to make your scripts flexible and maintainable.

Defining Variables

Variables are defined as follows:

```
name=value
```

In this example, *name* is the name of the variable, and *value* is the value it should hold. For example,

```
FRUIT=peach
```

defines the variable `FRUIT` and assigns it the value `peach`.

Variables of this type are called *scalar* variables. A scalar variable can hold only one value at a time. Later in this chapter, you look at a different type of variable called an *array* variable that can hold multiple values.

Scalar variables are also referred to as *name value pairs*, because a variable's name and its value can be thought of as a pair.

Variable Names

The name of a variable can contain only letters (a to z or A to Z), numbers (0 to 9) or the underscore character (_). In addition, a variable's name can start only with a letter or an underscore.

The following examples are valid variable names:

```
_FRUIT
FRUIT_BASKET
TRUST_NO_1
TWO_TIMES_2
```

but

```
2_TIMES_2_EQUALS_4
```

is not a valid variable name. To make this a valid name, add an underscore at the beginning of its name:

```
_2_TIMES_2
```

Variable names, such as 1, 2 or 11, that start with numbers are reserved for use by the shell. You can use the value stored in these variables, but you cannot set the value yourself.

The reason you cannot use other characters such as !,*, or - is that these characters have a special meaning for the shell. If you try to make a variable name with one of these special characters it confuses the shell. For example, the variable names

```
FRUIT-BASKET
_2*2
TRUST_NO_1!
```

are invalid names. The error message generated by one of these variable name looks something like the following:

```
$ FRUIT-BASKET=apple
/bin/sh: FRUIT-BASKET=apple:  not found.
```

Variable Values

The shell enables you to store any value you want in a variable. For example,

```
FRUIT=peach
FRUIT=2apples
FRUIT=apple+pear+kiwi
```

The one thing to be careful about is using values that have spaces. For example,

```
$ FRUIT=apple orange plum
```

results in the following error message:

```
sh: orange:  not found.
```

In order to use spaces you need to *quote* the value. For example, both of the following are valid assignments:

```
$ FRUIT="apple orange plum"
$ FRUIT='apple orange plum'
```

The difference between these two quoting schemes is covered in Chapter 9, "Quoting."

Accessing Values

To access the value stored in a variable, prefix its name with the dollar sign ($). For example, the command

```
$ echo $FRUIT
peach
```

prints out the value stored in the variable FRUIT, in this case peach.

If you do not use the dollar sign ($) to access the value of a variable, the name of the variable is printed instead of its value. For example,

```
$ echo FRUIT
FRUIT
```

simply prints out FRUIT, not the value of the variable FRUIT.

The dollar sign ($) is used only to access a variable's value, not to define it. For example, the assignment

```
$ $FRUIT=apple
```

generates the following warning message

```
sh: peach=apple: not found
```

if FRUIT is defined as given previously.

7

If the variable FRUIT is undefined the error would be

```
sh: =apple: not found
```

Remember that when the dollar sign ($) character precedes a variable name, the value of the variable is substituted. For more information on the types of variable substitution available in sh, please consult the section, "Variable Substitution," in Chapter 8, "Substitution."

Array Variables

The Bourne shell, sh, supports only *scalar* variables, which are the type of variables you have seen so far. The Korn shell, ksh, extends this to include array variables. Version 2.0 and later of the Bourne Again shell, bash, also support array variables. The examples in the following section assume that you are using either ksh or bash 2.*x* or later.

Arrays provide a method of grouping a set of variables. Instead of creating a new name for each variable that is required, you can use a single array variable that stores all the other variables.

The difference between an array variable and a scalar variable can be explained as follows. Say that you are trying to represent the chapters in this book as a set of variables. Each of the individual variables is a scalar variable.

Some of these variables might be

```
CH01
CH02
CH15
CH07
```

Here is a format for each of the variable names: the letters *CH* followed by the chapter number. This format serves as a way of grouping these variables together. An array variable formalizes this grouping by using an array name in conjunction with a number that is called an *index*.

The simplest method of creating an array variable is to assign a value to one of its indices. This is expressed as follows:

```
name[index]=value
```

Here *name* is the name of the array, *index* is the index of the item in the array that you want to set, and *value* is the value you want to set for that item.

As an example, the following commands

```
$ FRUIT[0]=apple
$ FRUIT[1]=banana
```

```
$ FRUIT[2]=orange
```

set the values of the first three items in the array named FRUIT. You could do the same thing with scalar variables as follows:

```
$ FRUIT_0=apple
$ FRUIT_1=banana
$ FRUIT_2=orange
```

Although this works fine for small numbers of items, the array notation is much more efficient for large numbers of items. If you have to write a script using only sh, you can use this method for simulating arrays.

In the previous example, you set the array indices in sequence, but this is not necessary. For example, if you issue the command

```
$ FRUIT[10]=plum
```

the value of the item at index 10 in the array FRUIT is set to plum. One thing to note here is that the shell does not create a bunch of blank array items to fill the space between index 2 and index 10. Instead, it keeps track of only those array indices that contain values.

> In ksh, numerical indices for arrays must be between 0 and 1,023. In bash there is no such requirement.
>
> In addition, both ksh and bash support only integer array indices. This means that you cannot use floating point or decimal numbers such as 10.3.

If an array variable with the same name as a scalar variable is defined, the value of the scalar variable becomes the value of the element of the array at index 0. For example, if the following commands are executed

```
$ FRUIT=apple
$ FRUIT[1]=peach
```

the element FRUIT has the value apple. At this point any accesses to the scalar variable FRUIT are treated like an access to the array item FRUIT[0].

The second form of array initialization is used to set multiple elements at once. In ksh, this is done as follows:

```
set -A name value1 value2 ... valuen
```

In bash, the multiple elements are set as follows:

```
name=(value1 ... valuen)
```

7

Here, *name* is the name of the array and the values, *1* to *n*, are the values of the items to be set. When setting multiple elements at once, both ksh and bash use consecutive array indices beginning at 0. For example the ksh command

```
$ set -A band derri terry mike gene
```

or the bash command

```
$ band=(derri terry mike gene)
```

is equivalent to the following commands:

```
$ band[0]=derri
$ band[1]=terry
$ band[2]=mike
$ band[3]=gene
```

When setting multiple array elements in bash, you can place an array index before the value:

```
myarray=([0]=derri [3]=gene [2]=mike [1]=terry)
```

The array indices don't have to be in order, as shown previously, and the indices don't have to be integers.

This feature is not present in ksh.

Accessing Array Values

After you have set any array variable, you access it as follows:

```
${name[index]}
```

Here *name* is the name of the array, and *index* is the index that interests us. For example, if the array FRUIT was initialized as given previously, the command

```
$ echo ${FRUIT[2]}
```

produces the following output:

```
orange
```

You can access all the items in an array in one of the following ways:

```
${name[*]}
${name[@]}
```

Here *name* is the name of the array you are interested in. If the FRUIT array is initialized as given previously, the command

```
$ echo ${FRUIT[*]}
```

produces the following output:

```
apple banana orange
```

If any of the array items hold values with spaces, this form of array access will not work and will need to use the second form. The second form quotes all the array entries so that embedded spaces are preserved.

For example, define the following array item:

```
FRUIT[3]="passion fruit"
```

Assuming that FRUIT is defined as given previously, accessing the entire array using the following command

```
$ echo ${FRUIT[*]}
```

results in five items, not four:

```
apple banana orange passion fruit
```

Commands accessing FRUIT using this form of array access get five values, with passion and fruit treated as separate items.

To get only four items, you have to use the following form:

```
$ echo ${FRUIT[@]}
```

The output from this command looks similar to the previous commands:

```
apple banana orange passion fruit
```

but the commands see only four items because the shell quotes the last item as passion fruit.

Read-only Variables

The shell provides a way to mark variables as read-only by using the readonly command. After a variable is marked read-only, its value cannot be changed.

Consider the following commands:

```
$ FRUIT=kiwi
$ readonly FRUIT
$ echo $FRUIT
kiwi
$ FRUIT=cantaloupe
```
→ Cannot execute the command

7

The last command results in an error message:

```
/bin/sh: FRUIT: This variable is read only.
```

As you can see, the echo command can read the value of the variable FRUIT, but the shell did not enable us to overwrite the value stored in the variable FRUIT.

This feature is often used in scripts to make sure that critical variables are not overwritten accidentally.

In ksh and bash, the readonly command can be used to mark array and scalar variables as read-only.

Unsetting Variables

NEW TERM *Unsetting* a variable tells the shell to remove the variable from the list of variables that it tracks. This is like asking the shell to forget a piece of information because it is no longer required.

Both scalar and array variables are unset using the unset command:

```
unset name
```

Here *name* is the name of the variable to unset. For example,

```
unset FRUIT
```

unsets the variable FRUIT.

You cannot use the unset command to unset variables that are marked readonly.

Environment Variables

When a shell is running, three main types of variables are present:

- Local Variables
- Environment Variables
- Shell Variables

NEW TERM A *local variable* is a variable that is present within the current instance of the shell. It is not available to programs that are started by the shell. The variables that you looked at previously have all been local variables.

NEW TERM An *environment variable* is a variable that is available to any child process of the shell. Some programs need environment variables in order to function correctly. Usually a shell script defines only those environment variables that are needed by the programs that it runs.

NEW TERM A *shell variable* is a special variable that is set by the shell and is required by the shell in order to function correctly. Some of these variables are environment variables whereas others are local variables.

Table 7.1 gives a summary of the different types of variables discussed in this section. This table compares local variables set by the user, environment variables set by the user, and shell variables set by the shell.

TABLE 7.1 A COMPARISON OF LOCAL, ENVIRONMENT, AND SHELL VARIABLES

Attribute	Local	Environment	Shell
Accessible by child processes	No	Yes	Yes
Set by users	Yes	Yes	No
Set by the shell	No	No	Yes
User modifiable	Yes	Yes	No
Required by the shell	No	No	Yes

Exporting Environment Variables

NEW TERM You place variables in the environment by *exporting* them. Exporting can be done as follows:

```
export name
```

This command marks the variable with the specified *name* for export. This is the only form supported by sh, thus it is the most commonly encountered form. The standard shell idiom for exporting environment variables is

```
name=value ; export name
```

An example of this is

```
PATH=/sbin:/bin ; export PATH
```

Here you set the value of the variable PATH and then export it. Usually the assignment statement of an environment variable and the corresponding export statement are written on one line to clarify that the variable is an environment variable. This helps the next programmer who has to maintain the script quickly grasp the use of certain variables.

You can also use the export command to export more than one variable to the environment. For example,

7

```
export PATH HOME UID
```

exports the variables PATH, HOME, and UID to the environment.

Exporting Variables in ksh and bash

A second form for exporting variables is supported by ksh and bash:

```
export name=value
```

In this form, the variable specified by *name* is assigned the given *value*. Then that variable is marked for export. In this form, you can write the previous example as

```
export PATH=/sbin:/bin
```

In bash and ksh, any combination of *name* or *name=value* pairs can be given to the export command. For example, the command

```
export FMHOME=/usr/frame CLEARHOME=/usr/atria PATH
```

assigns the given values to the variables FMHOME and CLEARHOME and then exports the variables FMHOME, CLEARHOME, and PATH.

Shell Variables

NEW TERM   The variables that you have examined so far have all been *user variables*. A user variable is one that the user can manually set and reset.

In this section, you look at *shell variables*, which are variables that the shell sets during initialization and uses internally. Users can modify the value of these variables.

Table 7.2 gives a partial list of these shell variables. In addition to these variables, I cover several special variables in the section "Variable Substitution" in Chapter 8. Unless noted, all the variables given in Table 7.2 are available in sh, ksh, and bash.

TABLE 7.2   SHELL VARIABLES

Variable	Description
PWD	Indicates the current working directory as set by the cd command.
UID	Expands to the numeric user ID of the current user, initialized at shell startup.
SHLVL	Increments by one each time an instance of bash is started. This variable is useful for determining whether the built-in exit command ends the current session.
REPLY	Expands to the last input line read by the read built-in command when it is given no arguments. This variable is not available in sh.
RANDOM	Generates a random integer between 0 and 32,767 each time it is referenced. You can initialize the sequence of random numbers by assigning a value to $RANDOM. If $RANDOM is unset, it loses its special properties, even if it is subsequently reset. This variable is not available in sh.

Schell Variables

Variable	Description
SECONDS	Each time this parameter is referenced, it returns the number of seconds since shell invocation. If a value is assigned to $SECONDS, the value returned on subsequent references is the number of seconds since the assignment plus the value assigned. If $SECONDS is unset, it loses its special properties, even if it is subsequently reset. This variable is not available in sh.
IFS	Indicates the Internal Field Separator that is used by the parser for word splitting after expansion. $IFS is also used to split lines into words with the read built-in command. The default value is the string, " \t\n", where " " is the space character, \t is the tab character, and \n is the newline character.
PATH	Indicates search path for commands. It is a colon-separated list of directories in which the shell looks for commands. A common value is PATH=/bin:/sbin:/usr/bin:/usr/sbin:/usr/local/bin:/usr/ucb
HOME	Indicates the home directory of the current user: the default argument for the cd built-in command.

Summary

In this chapter, you looked at using variables for shell script programming. You learned how to define, access, and unset scalar and array variables. You also looked at special classes of variables known as environment variables and shell variables.

In the following chapters, you look at how variables are used to achieve a greater degree of flexibility and clarity in shell scripts. As you read, continue learning about shell programming until using variables becomes second nature to you.

Questions

1. Which of the following are valid variable names?

    a. _FRUIT_BASKET

    b. 1_APPLE_A_DAY

    c. FOUR-SCORE&7YEARS_AGO

    d. Variable

2. Is the following sequence of array assignments valid in sh, ksh, and bash?

```
$ adams[0]=hitchhikers_guide
$ adams[1]=restaurant
$ adams[3]=thanks_for_all_the_fish
$ adams[42]=life_universe_everything
$ adams[5]=mostly_harmless
```

7

3. Given the preceding array assignments, how would you access the array item at index 5 in the array adams? How about every item in the array?

4. What is the difference between an environment variable and a local variable?

Terms

Scalar Variable   A *scalar variable* can hold only one value at a time.

Array Variable   An *array variable* is a mechanism available in bash and ksh for grouping scalar variables together. The scalar variables stored in an array are accessed using a single name in conjunction with a number. This number is referred to as an index.

Local Variable   A *local variable* is a variable that is present within the current instance of the shell. It is not available to programs that are started by the shell.

Environment Variable   An *environment variable* is a variable that is available to any program that is started by the shell.

Shell Variable   A *shell variable* is a special variable that is set by the shell and is required by the shell in order to function correctly.

Exporting   A variable is placed in the environment by *exporting* it using the export command.

Hour **8**

Substitution

The shell performs substitution when it encounters an expression that contains one or more special characters.

NEW TERM In the last chapter, you learned how to access a variable's value using the special $ character. The process of retrieving the value of a variable is called *variable substitution*. In addition to this type of substitution, the shell can perform several other types of substitutions:

- Filename substitution (called *globbing*)
- Value-based variable substitution
- Command substitution
- Arithmetic substitution

In this chapter, you look at each of these types of substitution in detail.

Filename Substitution (Globbing)

NEW TERM The most common type of substitution is filename substitution. It is sometimes referred to as *globbing*.

Filename substitution is the process by which the shell expands a string containing wild-cards into a list of filenames. Table 8.1 provides the wildcards that the shell understands.

> Any command or script that operates on files can take advantage of file-name substitution. The examples in this section use the ls command so that the results of the filename substitution are clear. You can use any command in place of the ls command.

TABLE 8.1 WILDCARDS USED IN FILENAME SUBSTITUTION

Wildcard	Description
*	Matches zero or more occurrences of any character
?	Matches one occurrence of any character
[characters]	Matches one occurrence of any of the given characters

Using the * Wildcard

The simplest form of filename substitution is the * character. The * tells the shell to match zero or more occurrences of any character. If given by itself, it matches all file-names. For example, the command

```
$ ls *
```

lists every file and the contents of every directory in the current directory. If there are any invisible files or directories, they are not listed. You need to specify the -a option to ls, as described in Chapter 3, "Working with Files."

Using the * character by itself is required in many cases, but its strength lies in the fact that you can use it to match file suffixes, prefixes, or both.

Matching a File Prefix

To match a file prefix, use the * character as follows:

```
command prefix*
```

Here, command is the name of a command, such as ls, and prefix is the filename prefix you want to match. For example, the command

```
$ ls ch1*
```

8

matches all the files and directories in the current directory that start with the letters ch1. The output is similar to the following:

```
ch10-01   ch10-02   ch10-03   ch11-01   ch11-02   ch11-03
```

By varying the prefix slightly, you can change lists of files that are matched. For example, the command

```
$ ls ch10*
```

generates the following list of files on your system:

```
ch10-01   ch10-02   ch10-03
```

You can vary the suffix until it matches the list of files that you want to manipulate.

Matching a File Suffix

To match a file suffix, you use the * character as follows:

```
command *suffix
```

Here, *command* is the name of a command, such as ls, and *suffix* is the filename suffix you want to match. For example, the command

```
$ ls *doc
```

matches all the files and directories in the current directory that end with the letters doc:

```
Backup of ch10-01.doc   Backup of ch10-06.doc   ch10-05.doc
Backup of ch10-02.doc   ch10-01.doc             ch10-06.doc
Backup of ch10-03.doc   ch10-02.doc             ch10-07.doc
Backup of ch10-04.doc   ch10-03.doc
Backup of ch10-05.doc   ch10-04.doc
```

The command

```
$ ls *.doc
```

matches the same set of files because all the files that were matched end with the filename suffix .doc.

By varying the suffix, you can obtain the list of files you want to manipulate.

Matching Suffixes and Prefixes

You can match both the suffix and the prefix of files using the * character as follows:

```
command prefix*suffix
```

Here, *command* is the name of a command, such as ls, *prefix* is the filename prefix, and *suffix* is the filename suffix you want to match. For example, the command

```
$ ls Backup*doc
```

matches all the files in the current directory that start with the letters *Backup* and end with the letters *doc*:

```
Backup of ch10-01.doc  Backup of ch10-03.doc  Backup of ch10-05.doc
Backup of ch10-02.doc  Backup of ch10-04.doc  Backup of ch10-06.doc
```

You can also use more than one occurrence of the * character to narrow down the matches. For example, if the command

```
$ ls CGI*java
```

matches the following files

```
CGI.java      CGIGet.java   CGIPost.java  CGITester.java
```

and you want to list only the files that start with the characters *CGI*, end with *java*, and contain the characters *st*, you can use the following command:

```
$ ls CGI*st*java
```

The output is

```
CGIPost.java CGITester.java
```

GLOBBING IS CASE SENSITIVE

While using the * wildcard, it is important to specify the correct case for the prefix and suffix. For example, the command $ ls ch1* produces the following list of files:

```
ch10-01  ch10-02  ch10-03  ch11-01  ch11-02  ch11-03
```

whereas the command $ ls CH1* does not produce the same list of files.

Later in this chapter, I show you how to generate matches that are not case sensitive.

Using the ? Wildcard

One limitation of the * wildcard is that it matches one or more characters each time.

As an example, consider a situation where you need to list all files that have names of the form ch0*X*.doc, where *X* is a single number or letter. It seems like the command

```
$ ls ch0*.doc
```

would produce the appropriate match, but the actual output might look like:

```
ch01-1.doc  ch010.doc    ch02.doc     ch03-2.doc  ch04-1.doc  ch040.doc
➡ch05.doc    ch06-2.doc
ch01-2.doc  ch02-1.doc   ch020.doc    ch03.doc    ch04-2.doc  ch05-1.doc
➡ch050.doc   ch06.doc
ch01.doc    ch02-2.doc   ch03-1.doc   ch030.doc   ch04.doc    ch05-2.doc
➡ch06-1.doc  ch060.doc
```

In order to match only one character, the shell provides you with the ? wildcard. You can rewrite the command using this wildcard:

```
$ ls ch0?.doc
```

? 1 character

Now you see that the output matches only those files you are interested in:

```
ch01.doc  ch02.doc  ch03.doc  ch04.doc  ch05.doc  ch06.doc
```

Say that you now want to look for all files that have names of the form ch*XY*, where *X* and *Y* are any number or character. You can use the command

```
$ ls ch??.doc
```

?? two characters

to accomplish this.

Matching Sets of Characters

Two potential problems with the ? and * wildcards are

- They match any character, including special characters such as hyphens (-) or underlines (_).
- You have no way to indicate that you want to match only letters or only numbers to these operators.

Sometimes you need more control over the exact characters that you match. Consider the situation where you want to match filenames of the form ch0*X*, where *X* is a number between 0 and 9. Neither the * or the ? operator is cut out for this job.

Fortunately, the shell provides you with the capability to match sets of characters using the [wildcard. The syntax for using this wildcard is

command [*characters*]

Here *command* is the name of a command, such as ls, and *characters* represents the characters you want to match. For example, the following command fulfills the previous requirements:

```
$ ls ch0[0123456789].doc
ch01.doc  ch02.doc  ch03.doc  ch04.doc  ch05.doc  ch06.doc
```

One thing that you might have noticed is that you had to list all the characters that you wanted matched. The shell provides a mechanism to shorten the list. For example, the command

```
$ ls ch0[0-9].doc
```

produces the same list of files. As you can probably guess, this is most useful when you're trying to match sets of letters. For example,

```
$ ls [a-z]*
```

lists all the files starting with a lowercase letter. To match all the files starting with uppercase letters use the following:

```
$ ls [A-Z]*
```

The [wildcard also enables you to combine sets by putting the sets together. For example,

```
$ ls [a-zA-Z]*
```

matches all files that start with a letter, whereas the command

```
$ ls *[a-zA-Z0-9]
```

matches all files ending with a letter or a number.

As you can see from the previous examples, the maximum amount of flexibility in file-name substitution occurs when you couple the [wildcard with the other wildcards.

Negating a Set

Consider a situation where you need a list of all files except those that contain the letter *a*. You have two approaches to solving this problem:

1. Specify all the characters you want a filename to contain.
2. Specify that the filename should not include the letter *a*.

If you choose the first approach, you need to construct a set of all the characters that your filename can contain. You can start with:

```
[b-zA-Z0-9]
```

This set does not include the special characters that are allowed in filenames. Attempting to include all these characters creates a huge set that requires complicated quoting. An approximation of this set is

```
[b-zA-Z0-9\-_\+\=\\\'\"\{\[\}\]
```

Compared to this, the second approach is much better because you only need to specify the list of characters that you don't want.

The [wildcard provides you the capability to match all characters except those that are specified as the set. This is called *negating* the set, which you can accomplish by specify-ing the ! operator as the first character in a set. The syntax is

```
command [!characters]
```

8

Here, *command* is the name of a command, such as ls, and *characters* is the set of characters that you do not want to be matched. For example, to list all files except those that start with the letter *a*, you can use the command

```
$ ls [!a]*
```

Variable Substitution

Variable substitution enables the shell programmer to manipulate the value of a variable based on its state. Variable substitution falls into two categories:

- Actions taken when a variable has a value
- Actions taken when a variable does not have a value

The actions range from one time value substitution to aborting the script.

These categories are broken down into four forms of variable substitution. You can use variable substitutions as shorthand forms of expressions that would have to be written as explicit if-then-else statements, covered in Chapter 10, "Flow Control." Table 8.2 provides a summary of all variable substitution methods.

TABLE 8.2 VARIABLE SUBSTITUTION

Form	Description
${parameter:-word}	If *parameter* is null or unset, *word* is substituted for *parameter*. The value of *parameter* does not change.
${parameter:=word}	If *parameter* is null or unset, *parameter* is set to the value of *word*.
${parameter:?message}	If *parameter* is null or unset, *message* is printed to standard error. This checks that variables are set correctly.
${parameter:+word}	If *parameter* is set, *word* is substituted for *parameter*. The value of *parameter* does not change.

Substituting a Default Value

The first form enables a default value to be substituted when a variable is unset or null. This is formally described as

${parameter:-word}

Here *parameter* is the name of the variable, and *word* is the default value. A simple example of its use is

```
PS1=${HOST:-localhost}"$ " ; export PS1 ;
```

Default
value

You could use this in a user's `.profile` to make sure that the prompt is always set correctly. This form of variable substitution does not affect the value of the variable. It performs substitution only when the variable is unset.

Assigning a Default Value

To set the value of a variable, the second form of variable substitution must be used. This form is formally described as:

```
${parameter:=word}
```

Here, *parameter* is the name of the variable, and *word* is the default value to set the variable to if it is unset. Appending the previous example, you have

```
PS1=${HOST:=`uname -n`}"$ " ; export PS1 HOST ;
```

After the execution of this statement, both HOST and PS1 are set. This example also demonstrates the fact that the default string to use does not have to be a fixed string but can be the output of a command. If this substitution did not exist in the shell, the same line would have to be written as

```
if [ -z "$HOST" ] ; then HOST=`uname -n` ; fi ; PS1="$HOST$ ";
➥export PS1 HOST ;
```

As you can see, the variable substitution form is shorter and clearer than the explicit form.

Aborting Due to Variable Errors

Sometimes substituting default values can hide problems, thus sh supports a third form of variable substitution that enables a message to be written to standard error when a variable is unset. This form is formally described as

```
${parameter:?message}
```

A common use of this is in shell scripts and shell functions requiring certain variables to be set for proper execution. For example, the following command exits if the variable $HOME is unset:

```
: ${HOME:?"Your home directory is undefined."}
```

In addition to using the variable substitution form described previously, you are also making use of the no-op (*no-op* as in *no operation*) command, :, which simply evaluates the arguments passed to it. Here you are checking to see whether the variable HOME is defined. If it is not defined, an error message prints.

The final form of variable substitution is used to substitute when a variable is set. Formally this is described as

```
${parameter:+word}
```

Here *parameter* is the name of the variable, and *word* is the value to substitute if the variable is set. This form does not alter the value of the variable; it alters only what is substituted. A frequent use is to indicate when a script is running in debug mode:

```
echo ${DEBUG:+"Debug is active."}
```

Command and Arithmetic Substitution

Two additional forms of substitution provided by the shell are

- Command substitution
- Arithmetic substitution

NEW TERM   *Command substitution* enables you to capture the output of a command and substitute it in another command, whereas arithmetic substitution enables you to perform simple integer mathematics using the shell.

Command Substitution

Command substitution is the mechanism by which the shell performs a given set of commands and then substitutes their output in the place of the commands. Command substitution is performed when a command is given as

```
`command`
```

Here *command*, can be a simple command, a pipeline, or a list.

> Make sure that you are using the backquote, not the single quote character, when performing command substitution. Command substitution is performed by the shell only when the backquote, or backtick, character, `, is given. Using the single quote instead of the back quote is a common error in shell scripts leading to many hard to find bugs.

Command substitution is generally used to assign the output of a command to a variable. Each of the following examples demonstrate command substitution:

```
DATE=`date`
USERS=`who ¦ wc -l`
UP=`date ; uptime`
```

In the first example, the output of the date command becomes the value for the variable DATE. In the second example, the output of the pipeline becomes the value of the variable USERS. In the last example, the output of the list becomes the value of the variable UP.

You can also use command substitution to provide arguments for other commands. For example,

```
grep `id -un` /etc/passwd
```

looks through the file /etc/passwd for the output of the command:

```
id -un
```

In my case, the command substitution results in the string ranga, and thus grep returns the entry in the passwd file for my user name.

Arithmetic Substitution

In ksh and bash, the shell enables integer arithmetic to be performed. This avoids having to run an extra program such as expr or bc to do math in a shell script. This feature is not available in sh.

Arithmetic substitution is performed when the following form of command is given:

```
$((expression))
```

Expressions are evaluated according to standard mathematical conventions. Table 8.3 provides the available operators. The operators are listed in order of precedence.

TABLE 8.3 ARITHMETIC SUBSTITUTION OPERATORS

Operator	Description
/	The division operator. Divides two numbers and returns the result.
*	The multiplication operator. Multiples two numbers and returns the result.
-	The subtraction operator. Subtracts two numbers and returns the result.
+	The addition operator. Adds two numbers and returns the result.
()	The parentheses clarify which expressions should be evaluated before others.

You use the following command as an illustration of the operators and their precedence:

```
foo=$(( ((5 + 3*2) - 4) / 2 ))
```

After this command executes the value of foo to 3. Because this is integer arithmetic, the value is not 3.5, and because of operator precedence the value is not 6.

8

Summary

In this chapter, you have looked at the four main forms of substitution available in the shell:

- Filename substitution
- Variable substitution
- Command substitution
- Arithmetic substitution

As you write scripts and use the shell to solve problems, you find that these types of substitution help you extensively.

Questions

1. What combination of wildcards should you use to list all the files in the current directory that end in the form hw*XYZ*.*ABC*?

   Here *X* and *Y* can be any number; *Z* is a number between 2 and 6; and *A*, *B*, and *C* are any character.

2. What action is performed by the following line, if the variable MYPATH is unset:

   ```
   : ${MYPATH:=/usr/bin:/usr/sbin:/usr/ucb}
   ```

3. What is the difference between the actions performed by the command given in the previous problem and the action performed by the following command:

   ```
   : ${MYPATH:-/usr/bin:/usr/sbin:/usr/ucb}
   ```

4. What is the result of the following arithmetic substitution:

   ```
   $(( 3 * 2 + ( 4 - 3 / 4) ))
   ```

HOUR 9

Quoting

By Frank Watson

In the preceding chapter, you looked at shell substitution, which occurs automatically whenever you enter a command containing a wildcard character or a $ parameter. The way the shell interprets these and other special characters is generally useful, but sometimes it is necessary to turn off shell substitution and let each character stand for itself. Turning off the special meaning of a character is called *quoting*, and it can be done three ways:

- Using the backslash (\)
- Using the single quote (')
- Using the double quote (")

Quoting can be a very complex issue, even for experienced UNIX programmers. In this chapter you look at each of these forms of quoting and how to use them. You learn a series of simple rules to help you understand when quoting is needed and how to do it correctly.

Quoting with Backslashes

First, use the `echo` command to see what a special character is. The `echo` command is covered in more detail in Chapter 13, "Input/Output," but it is a simple command that just displays the arguments it has been given on the command line. For example,

```
echo Hello world
```

displays the following message on your screen:

```
Hello world
```

Here is a list of most of the shell special characters (also called *metacharacters*):

```
* ? [ ] ' " \ $  ; & ( ) ¦ ^ < > new-line space tab
```

Watch what happens if you add one of them to the `echo` command:

```
echo Hello; world
```

It now gives this error result:

```
Hello
sh: world: Command not found
```

The semicolon (;) character tells the shell that it has reached the end of one command and what follows is a new command. This character enables multiple commands on one line. Because `world` is not a valid command, you get the error shown.

You can resolve the problem by putting a backslash (\)in front of the ; character to take away its special meaning, enabling you to display it as a literal character:

```
echo Hello\; world
```

The backslash causes the ; character to be handled as any other normal character. The resulting output is

```
Hello; world
```

To display any shell special character reliably from `echo`, you must *escape* it, that is, precede it by a backslash. Using the backslash quotes the character that follows it, using it as a literal character. Each of the special shell characters previously listed causes a different problem symptom if you try to `echo` it without quoting it. This need to quote special characters occurs in many other UNIX commands as you see later.

Notice in the previous example that the quoting character, the backslash, is not displayed in the output. The shell preprocesses the command line, performing variable substitution, command substitution, and filename substitution, unless the special character that would normally invoke substitution is quoted. The quoting character is then removed from the command arguments, so the command being run never sees the quoting character. Here is a different example where quoting is needed:

```
echo You owe $1250
```

This seems like a simple echo statement, but notice that the output is not what you wanted because $1 is a special shell variable:

```
You owe 250
```

The $ sign is one of the metacharacters, so it must be quoted to avoid special handling by the shell:

```
echo You owe \$1250
```

Now you get the desired output:

```
You owe $1250
```

Notice the \ quoting character is not present in the output.

Using Single Quotes

Here is an echo command that must be modified because it contains many special shell characters:

```
echo <-$1250.**>; (update?) [y¦n]
```

Putting a backslash in front of each special character is tedious and makes the line difficult to read:

```
echo \<-\$1250.\*\*\>\; \(update\?\) \[y\¦n\]
```

There is an easy way to quote a large group of characters. Put a single quote (') at the beginning and at the end of the string:

```
echo '<-$1250.**>; (update?) [y¦n]'
```

Any characters within single quotes are quoted just as if a backslash is in front of each character. So now this echo command displays properly.

> Quoting regular characters is harmless. In the previous example, you put single quotes around a whole string, quoting both the special characters and the regular letters and digits that need no quoting. It does not hurt to quote regular characters because quoting takes away any special meaning from a character and does not mind if that character had no special meaning to begin with. This is true for the backslash, single quotes, and double quotes.

If a single quote appears within a string to be output, you should not put the whole string within single quotes:

```
echo 'It's Friday'
```
— WILL NOT work because of imbedded '

This fails and only outputs the following character, while the cursor waits for more input:

```
> _
```

The >sign is the secondary shell prompt (as stored in the PS2 shell variable), and it indicates that you have entered a multiple-line command—what you have typed so far is incomplete. Single quotes must be entered in pairs, and their effect is to quote all characters that occur between them. In case you are wondering, you cannot get around this by putting a backslash before an embedded single quote.

You can correct the previous example by not using single quotes as the method of quoting. Use one of the other quoting characters, such as the backslash:

```
echo It\'s Friday
```

Using Double Quotes

Single quotes can sometimes take away too much of the shell's special conveniences. The following echo statement contains many special characters that must be quoted in order to use them literally:

```
echo '$USER owes <-$1250.**>; [ as of (`date +%m/%d`) ]'
```

The output using single quotes is easy to predict—what you see is what you get:

```
$USER owes <-$1250.**>; [ as of (`date +%m/%d`) ]
```

However, this is not exactly what you want in this case. Single quotes prevent variable substitution (covered in Chapter 8, "Substitution"), so $USER is not replaced by the specific user name stored in that variable. Single quotes also prevent command substitution (covered in Chapter 8), so the attempt to insert the current month and day using the date command within backquotes fails.

Double quotes are the answer to this situation.

Double quotes take away the special meaning of all characters except the following:

- $ for parameter substitution.
- Backquotes for command substitution.
- \$ to enable literal dollar signs.
- \` to enable literal backquotes.

- \" to enable embedded double quotes.
- \\ to enable embedded backslashes.
- All other \ characters are literal (not special).

Watch what happens if you use double quotes like this:

```
echo "$USER owes <-$1250.**>; [ as of (`date +%m/%d`) ]"
```

Notice in the following output that the double quotes enable variable substitution to replace $USER and command substitution to replace `date +%m/%d`:

```
Fred owes <-250.**>; [ as of (12/21) ]
```

As you can see in this example, double quotes permit you to display many special characters literally while still enabling $ and backquote substitutions. However, notice the amount of money owed is incorrect because $1 is substituted. To correct this, always use a leading backslash to escape any $ within double quotes where substitution is not intended:

```
echo "$USER owes <-\$1250.**>; [ as of (`date +%m/%d`) ]""
```

The escaped dollar sign is no longer a special character, so the dollar amount appears correctly in the output now:

```
Fred owes <-$1250.**>;  [ as of (12/21) ]
```

Now that you have seen all three forms of quoting, here is a summary of their usage:

TABLE 9.1 THREE FORMS OF QUOTING

Quoting character	Effect
Single quote	*All* special characters between these quotes lose their special meaning.
Double quote	*Most* special characters between these quotes lose their special meaning with these exceptions: • $ • ` • \$ • \` • \" • \\
Backslash	*Any* character immediately following the backslash loses its special meaning.

9

This table also shows that double quotes or backslashes can be embedded in a double quoted string if they are escaped:

```
echo "The DOS directory is \"\\windows\\temp\""
```

The output looks like this:

```
The DOS directory is "\windows\temp"
```

Quoting Rules and Situations

Now that you know the basics, you can learn some additional rules to help you use quoting. You can also look at various UNIX commands and apply quoting to other situations.

Quoting Ignores Word Boundaries

In English, you are used to quoting whole words or sentences. In shell programming, the special characters must be quoted, but it does not matter whether the regular characters are quoted in the same word, as follows:

```
echo "Hello; world"
```

You can move the quotes off word boundaries as long as any special characters remain quoted. This command produces the same output as the preceding one:

```
echo Hel"lo; w"orld
```

Of course, it is easier to read the line if the quotes are on word boundaries. I present this point here to help you understand quoting and because you need this knowledge for more complex quoting situations.

Combining Quoting in Commands

You can freely switch from one type of quoting to another within the same command. This example contains single quotes, a backslash, and then double quotes:

```
echo The '$USER' variable contains this value \> "¦$USER¦"
```

Here is the output of this command if fred is the current content of $USER:

```
The $USER variable contains this value > ¦fred¦
```

Embedding Spaces in a Single Argument

To the shell, one or more spaces or tabs form a single command line argument separator. For example,

```
echo Name        Address
```

displays as

```
Name Address
```

Even though you put multiple spaces between Name and Address, the shell regards them as special characters forming one separator. The echo command simply displays the arguments it has received separated by a single space.

You can quote the spaces to achieve the desired result:

```
echo "Name            Address"
```

Now the multiple spaces are preserved in the output:

```
Name            Address
```

Spaces must also be quoted to embed them in a single command line argument:

```
mail -s Meeting tomorrow fred jane < meeting.notice
```

The mail command enables you to send mail to a list of users. The -s option enables the following argument to be used as the subject of the mail. The word tomorrow is supposed to be part of the subject, but it is taken as one of the users to receive the message and causes an error. You can solve this by quoting the embedded space within the subject using any of the three types of quoting:

```
mail -s Meeting\ tomorrow fred jane < meeting.notice
mail -s 'Meeting tomorrow' fred jane < meeting.notice
mail -s "Meeting tomorrow" fred jane < meeting.notice
```

Quoting Newlines to Continue on the Next Line

The newline character is found at the end of each line of a UNIX shell script; it is a special character that tells the shell that it has encountered the end of the command line. You insert the newline character by pressing Enter to go to the next line when inserting text in your shell script. Normally you can't see the newline character, but if you are in the vi editor, :set list will mark each newline character with a dollar sign. You can quote the newline character to enable a long command to extend to the next line:

```
$ cp file1 file2 file3 file4 file5 file6 file7 \
> file8 file9 /tmp
```

Notice the last character in the first line is a backslash, which is quoting the newline character implied at the end of the line. The shell recognizes this and displays > (the PS2 prompt) as confirmation that you are entering a continuation line or multiple-line command.

You must not enable any spaces after the final backslash for this to work. A quoted new-line is an argument separator just like a space or tab. Here is another example:

```
$ echo 'Line 1
> Line 2'
```

The newline is quoted because it is between a pair of single quotes found on two consecutive lines. Again, > is displayed by the shell and is not something you enter. Here is the output:

```
Line 1
Line 2
```

Quoting to Access Filenames Containing Special Characters

In the previous chapter, you learned that any word that contains the characters

```
* ? [ ]
```

is expanded to a list of files that match the wildcard pattern given. For example, the command

```
rm ch1*
```

removes all files whose names have the prefix of ch1. In this case, the * character is a special character. Most of the time, this is exactly what you want, but there is a case where you need to use quoting to remove the character's special meaning. Assume you have these files in a directory:

```
ch1      ch1*      ch1a      ch15
```

Notice that the filename ch1* contains the * character. Although this is certainly not recommended, sometimes you encounter files whose names contain strange characters (usually through some accident or mistake). If you only want to delete the file ch1*, don't do so like this:

```
rm ch1*
```

This deletes all your ch1 files. Instead, quote the special character using single quotes, double quotes, or the backslash:

```
rm 'ch1*'
```

Quoting the special character takes away its wildcard meaning and enables you to delete the desired file.

Avoid using special characters in filenames because you have to quote the special character each time you access that file.

Here again is the list of special characters:

* ? [ ] ' " \ $; & ( ) | ^ < > new-line space tab

Quoting Regular Expression Wildcards

In Chapter 16, "Filtering Text Using Regular Expressions," you learn about another type of wildcard called regular expression. Regular expressions use some of the same wildcard characters as filename substitution, as you can see in this grep command (which is covered in Chapter 15, "Text Filters"):

```
grep '[0-9][0-9]*$' report2 report7
```

The quoted string [0-9][0-9]*$ is a regular expression (wildcard) pattern that grep searches for within the contents of files report2 and report7. Wildcards in the grep pattern must be quoted to prevent the shell from erroneously replacing that pattern with a list of filenames that match the pattern.

You should always quote your regular expressions to protect them from shell filename expansion, but sometimes they work even if you don't quote them. The shell only expands the pattern if it finds existing files whose names match the pattern. If you happen to be in a directory where no matching files are found, the pattern is left alone, and grep works fine. Move to another directory, though, and the exact same command might fail.

Quoting the Backslash to Enable echo Escape Sequences

In Chapter 13, "Input/Ouput," you see that echo enables some special characters like \n:

```
echo -e "Line 1\nLine 2"
```

This displays the following:

```
Line 1
Line 2
```

The -e option of echo enables it to interpret echo escape sequences as special, not literal, characters. Some versions of UNIX object to -e as an illegal option to echo. In that case, simply omit -e from your echo command, as it is not required on that system to enable these escape sequences.

The \n option is called an escape sequence because the preceding backslash causes the following n to be treated as a special character. How do the quoting rules apply here? If the backslash takes away the special meaning of its following character, shouldn't you just see n in the output?

Review Table 9.1. It shows that a backslash within double quotes is only special if it precedes these four characters:

- $
- `
- "
- \

\n within double quotes is treated as two normal characters that are passed to the echo command as arguments. The echo command enables its own set of special characters, which are indicated by a preceding backslash. \n passed to echo tells echo to display a newline. In this example, the \n has to be quoted so that the backslash can be passed to echo and not removed before echo can see it. Watch what happens if you don't quote the backslash:

```
echo Line 1\nLine 2
```

This displays:

```
Line 1nLine 2
```

The \n is not quoted, so the shell removed the backslash before echo sees the arguments. Because echo sees n, not \n, it simply displays n, not a newline as desired.

Quote Wildcards for `cpio` and `find`

There are other commands like echo that have their own special characters that must be quoted for the shell to pass them unaltered. cpio is a command that saves and restores files. It enables shell filename wildcards to select the files to restore. These wildcards must be quoted to prevent shell expansion. This enables them to be passed to cpio for interpretation, as in the following example:

```
cpio -icvdum 'usr2/*' < /dev/rmt0
```

-icvdum includes options to cpio to specify how it should restore files from the tape device /dev/rmt0. usr2/* says to restore all files from directory usr2 on tape. Again, this command sometimes works correctly even if the wildcards aren't quoted because shell expansion doesn't occur if matching files aren't found in the current path (in this case, if there is no usr2 subdirectory in the current directory). It is best to quote these cpio wildcards so you can be sure the command works properly every time.

The find command is covered in chapter 18, "Miscellaneous Tools." It supports its own wildcards to look for partial filenames:

```
find / -name 'ch*.doc' -print
```

ch*.doc is a wildcard pattern that tells find to display all filenames that start with ch and end with a .doc suffix. Unlike shell filename expansion, this find command checks all directories on the system for a match. However, the wildcard must be quoted using single quotes, double quotes, or a backslash, so the wildcard is passed to find and not expanded by the shell.

Summary

In this chapter, you looked at three types of quoting and when to use them:

- Backslash
- Single quote
- Double quote

Here is a summary of the quoting rules you learned in this chapter in the order of presentation:

- A backslash takes away the special meaning of the character that follows it.
- The character doing the quoting is removed before command execution.
- Single quotes remove the special meaning of all enclosed characters.
- Quoting regular characters is harmless.
- A single quote can not be inserted within single quotes.
- Double quotes remove the special meaning of most enclosed characters.
- Quoting can ignore word boundaries.
- Different types of quoting can be combined in one command.
- Quote spaces to embed them in a single argument.
- Quote the newline to continue a command on the next line.
- Use quoting to access filenames that contain special characters.
- Quote regular expression wildcards.
- Quote the backslash to enable echo escape sequences.
- Quote wildcards for cpio and find.

Questions

1. Give an `echo` command to display this message:

   ```
   It's <party> time!
   ```

2. Give an `echo` command to display one line containing the following fields:

   - The contents of variable `$USER`
   - A single space
   - The word "owes"
   - Five spaces
   - A dollar sign ($)
   - The contents of the variable `$DEBT` (this variable contains only digits)

   Sample output:

   ```
   fred owes     $25
   ```

Terms

Quoting   Quoting literally encloses selected text within some type of quotation marks. When applied to shell commands, quoting means to disable shell interpretation of special characters by enclosing the characters within single or double quotes or by escaping the characters.

Escaping   Escaping a character means to put a backslash (\) just before that character. Escaping can either remove the special meaning of a character in a shell command, or it can add special meaning as we saw with \n in the `echo` command. The character following the backslash is called an escaped character.

Special characters, metacharacters, wildcards   All these terms indicate characters that are not taken at face value. These characters have an extra meaning or cause some action to be taken by the shell or other UNIX commands.

Literal characters   These characters have no special meaning and cause no extra action to be taken. Quoting causes the shell to treat a wildcard as a literal character.

Newline character   This is literally the linefeed character whose ASCII value is 10. In general, the newline character is a special shell character that indicates a complete command line has been entered and can now be executed.

PS2 variable   This shell variable's content is usually the > character. The content of the PS2 variable is displayed by the shell as a secondary prompt that indicates the previous command was not complete and the current command line is a continuation of that command line.

Shell preprocessing   This describes actions taken by the shell to manipulate the command line before executing it. This is when filename, variable, command, and arithmetic substitution occur (as covered in chapter 8).

9

HOUR 10

Flow Control

The order in which commands execute in a shell script is called the *flow* of the script. In the scripts that you have looked at so far, the flow is always the same because the same set of commands executes every time.

In most scripts, you need to change the commands that execute depending on some condition provided by the user or detected by the script itself. When you change the commands that execute based on a condition, you change the flow of the script. For this reason, the commands discussed in this chapter are called *flow control commands*. You might also see them referred to as *conditional flow control commands* because they change the flow of a script based on some condition.

Two powerful flow control mechanics are available in the shell:

- The `if` statement
- The `case` statement

The `if` statement is normally used for the conditional execution of commands, whereas the `case` statement enables any number of command sequences to be executed depending on which one of several patterns matches a variable first.

In this chapter, I explain how to use flow control in your shell scripts.

The `if` Statement

The `if` statement performs actions depending on whether a given condition is true or false. Because the return code of a command indicates true (return code is zero) or false (return code is nonzero), one of the most common uses of the `if` statement is in error checking. An example of this is covered shortly.

The basic `if` statement syntax follows:

```
if list1
then
    list2
elif list3
then
    list4
else
    list5
fi
```

Both the `elif` and the `else` statements are optional. If you have an `elif` statement, you don't need an `else` statement and vice versa. An `if` statement can be written with any number of `elif` statements.

The flow control for the general `if` statement follows:

1. *list1* is evaluated.
2. If the exit code of *list1* is 0, indicating a true condition, *list2* is evaluated and the `if` statement exits.
3. Otherwise, *list3* is executed and its exit code is checked.
4. If *list3* returns 0, *list4* executes and the `if` statement exits.
5. If *list3* does not return 0, *list5* executes.

Because the shell considers an `if` statement to be a list, you can write it all in one line as follows:

```
if list1 ; then list2 ; elif list3 ; then list4 ; else list5 ; fi ;
```

Usually this form is used only for short `if` statements.

An `if` Statement Example

A simple use of the `if` statement is

```
if uuencode koala.gif koala.gif > koala.uu ; then
    echo "Encoded koala.gif to koala.uu"
else
    echo "Error encoding koala.gif"
fi
```

Look at the flow of control through this statement:

1. First, the command

   ```
   uuencode koala.gif koala.gif > koala.uu
   ```

   executes. This command is *list1* in the general statement.

2. If this command is successful, the command

   ```
   echo "Encoded koala.gif to koala.uu"
   ```

   executes and the `if` statement exits. This command is *list2* in the general statement.

3. Otherwise the command

   ```
   echo "Error encoding koala.gif"
   ```

   executes, and the `if` statement exits. This command is *list5* in the general statement.

You might have noticed in this example that both the `if` and `then` statements appear on the same line. Most shell programmers prefer to write `if` statements this way in order to make the `if` statement more concise. The majority of shell programmers claim that this form looks better.

Common Errors

Three common errors can occur when using the `if` statement:

- Omitting the semicolon (`;`) before the `then` statement in the single line form.
- Using `else if` or `elsif` instead of `elif`.
- Omitting the `then` statement when an `elif` statement is used.
- Writing `if` instead of `fi` at the end of an `if` statement.

As an example of the first type of error, if you leave out the `;` from the previous example

```
if uuencode koala.gif koala.gif > koala.uu then
    echo "Encoded koala.gif to koala.uu"
```

10

```
else
   echo "Error encoding koala.gif"
fi
```

an error message appears:

```
ch11-ex1.sh[2]: Syntax error at line 5 : `else' is not expected.
```

If you see this type of error, make sure that a semicolon precedes the then statement.

The second type of error can be illustrated using the following if statement:

```
if uuencode koala.gif koala.gif > koala.uu ; then
   echo "Encoded koala.gif to koala.uu"
elif rm koala.uu ; then
   echo "Encoding failed, temporary files removed."
else
   echo "An error occured."
fi
```

Here you have an elif statement that removes the intermediate file koala.uu, if the uuencode fails. If the elif is changed to an else if as follows

```
if uuencode koala.gif koala.gif > koala.uu ; then
   echo "Encoded koala.gif to koala.uu"
else if rm koala.uu ; then
   echo "Encoding failed, temporary files removed."
else
   echo "An error occured."
fi
```

an error message similar to the following is generated:

```
./ch11-ex1.sh: ./ch11-ex1.sh: line 8: syntax error: unexpected end of file
```

If the elif statement is changed to elsif as follows

```
if uuencode koala.gif koala.gif > koala.uu ; then
   echo "Encoded koala.gif to koala.uu"
elsif rm koala.uu ; then
   echo "Encoding failed, temporary files removed."
else
   echo "An error occured."
fi
```

an error message similar to the following is generated:

```
./ch11-1.sh: syntax error at line 4: `then' unexpected
```

If the then statement was omitted after the elif statement as follows

```
if uuencode koala.gif koala.gif > koala.uu ; then
   echo "Encoded koala.gif to koala.uu"
elif rm koala.uu
```

```
    echo "Encoding failed, temporary files removed."
else
    echo "An error occured."
fi
```

an error message similar to the following is generated:

```
./ch11-1.sh: syntax error at line 6: `else' unexpected
```

Finally, if the `fi` statement is written as `if`, an error message such as the following is generated:

```
./ch11-1.sh: syntax error at line 8: `end of file' unexpected
```

This indicates that the `if` statement was not closed with a `fi` statement before the end of the script.

Using test

Most often, the list given to an `if` statement is one or more `test` commands, which are invoked by calling the `test` command as follows:

```
test expression
```

Here `expression` is constructed using one of the special options to the `test` command. The `test` command returns either a `0` (true) or a `1` (false) after evaluating an expression.

A shorthand for the `test` command is the `[` command:

```
[ expression ]
```

Here `expression` is any valid expression that the `test` command understands. This shorthand form is the most common form of test that you can encounter.

The types of expressions understood by test can be broken into three types:

- File tests
- String comparisons
- Numerical comparisons

You look at each of these types in turn. You also look at compound expressions, formed by combining two or more test expressions.

When using the `[` shorthand for test, the space after the open bracket (`[`) and the space before the close bracket (`]`) are required.

Without these spaces, the shell cannot tell where the expression begins and ends.

File Tests

File test expressions test whether a file fits some particular criteria. The general syntax for a file test is

```
test option file
```

or

```
[ option file ]
```

Here *option* is one of the options given in Table 10.1 and *file* is the name of a file or directory.

Look at a few examples of if statements that use the test command to perform file tests.

Consider the following if statement:

```
$ if [ -d /home/ranga/bin ] ; then PATH="$PATH:/home/ranga/bin" ; fi
```

Here you are testing whether the directory /home/ranga/bin exists. If it does, append it to the variable PATH. Similar statements are often encountered in shell initialization scripts such as .profile or .kshrc.

Say you want to execute commands stored in the file $HOME/.bash_aliai if it exists. You can use the command

```
$ if [ -f $HOME/.bash_aliai ] ; then . $HOME/.bash_aliai ; fi
```

An improvement on this would be to test whether the file has any content and, if so, run the commands stored in it. You can change the command to use the -s option instead of the -f option to achieve this result:

```
if [ -s $HOME/.bash_aliai ] ; then . $HOME/.bash_aliai ; fi
```

Now the commands stored in the file $HOME/.bash_aliai execute if that file exists and has some content.

TABLE **10.1** FILE TEST OPTIONS FOR THE test COMMAND

Option	Description
-b file	True if file exists and is a block special file.
-c file	True if file exists and is a character special file.
-d file	True if file exists and is a directory.
-e file	True if file exists.
-f file	True if file exists and is a regular file.

Option	Description
-g file	True if file exists and has its SGID bit set.
-h file	True if file exists and is a symbolic link.
-k file	True if file exists and has its "sticky" bit set.
-p file	True if file exists and is a named pipe.
-r file	True if file exists and is readable.
-s file	True if file exists and has a size greater than zero.
-u file	True if file exists and has its SUID bit set.
-w file	True if file exists and is writable.
-x file	True if file exists and is executable.
-O file	True if file exists and is owned by the effective user ID.

10

String Comparisons

The `test` command also supports simple string comparisons. There are two main forms:

1. Checking whether a string is empty
2. Checking whether two strings are equal

A string cannot be compared to an expression using the `test` command. The `case` statement, covered later in this chapter, has to be used instead.

The `test` options relating to string comparisons are given in Table 10.2.

TABLE 10.2   STRING COMPARISON OPTIONS FOR THE `test` COMMAND

Option	Description
-z string	True if string has zero length.
-n string	True if string has nonzero length.
string1 = string2	True if the strings are equal.
string1 != string2	True if the strings are not equal.

Checking Whether a String Is Empty

The syntax of the first form is

test *option string*

or

[*option string*]

Here *option* is either -z or -n and *string* is any valid shell string. The -z (*z* as in *zero*) option checks whether the length of a string is zero, whereas the -n (*n* as in *nonzero*) option is used to check whether the length of a string is nonzero.

For example, the following command

```
if [ -z "$FRUIT_BASKET" ] ; then
    echo "Your fruit basket is empty" ;
else
    echo "Your fruit basket has the following fruit: $FRUIT_BASKET"
fi
```

produces the string

```
Your fruit basket is empty
```

if the string contained in the variable $FRUIT_BASKET has zero length.

If you were to use the -n option instead of the -z option, the example would change as follows:

```
if [ -n "$FRUIT_BASKET" ] ; then
    echo "Your fruit basket has the following fruit: $FRUIT_BASKET"
else
    echo "Your fruit basket is empty" ;
fi
```

Notice that the variable $FRUIT_BASKET is quoted in this example. This is required in the event that the variable is unset. If $FRUIT_BASKET is not quoted, an error message is displayed when it is unset:

```
test: argument expected
```

This error message is presented because the shell does not quote the null value of $FRUIT_BASKET. The resulting test looks like

```
[ -z ]
```

Because the string argument is missing, test complains that a required argument is missing. By quoting $FRUIT_BASKET, the test looks like

```
[ -z "" ]
```

Here the required string argument is "".

Checking Whether Two Strings Are Equal   The test command enables you to determine whether two strings are equal. Two strings are considered equal if they contain exactly the same sequence of characters. For example, the strings

```
"There are more things in heaven and earth"
"There are more things in heaven and earth"
```

are equal, but the strings

```
"than are dreamt of in your philosophy"
"Than are dreamt of in your Philosophy"
```

are not equal because of the differences in capitalization.

The basic syntax for checking whether two strings are equal is

```
test string1 = string2
```

or

```
[ string1 = string2 ]
```

Here *string1* and *string2* are the two strings being compared.

A simple example of using string comparisons is the following:

```
if [ "$FRUIT" = apple ] ; then
    echo "An apple a day keeps the doctor away."
else
    echo "You must like doctors, your fruit $FRUIT is not an apple."
fi
```

If the operator != is used instead of =, test returns true if the two strings are not equal. Using the != operator, you can rewrite the previous command as follows:

```
if [ "$FRUIT" != apple ] ; then
    echo "You must like doctors, your fruit $FRUIT is not an apple."
else
    echo "An apple a day keeps the doctor away."
fi
```

Numerical Comparisons

The test command enables you to compare two integers. The basic syntax is

```
test int1 operator int2
```

or

```
[ int1 operator int2 ]
```

Here *int1* and *int2* can be any positive or negative integers and *operator* is one of the operators given in Table 10.3. If either *int1* or *int2* is a string, not an integer, it is treated as 0.

Among the most common tasks in a shell script are executing a program and checking its return status. By using the numerical comparison operators, you can check the return or

exit status of a command and perform different actions when a command is successful
and when a command is unsuccessful.

For example, consider the following command:

```
ln -s /home/ranga/bin/bash /usr/contrib/bin
```

If you execute this command on the command line, you can see any error messages and
intervene to fix the problem. In a shell script, the error message is ignored and the script
continues to execute. For this reason, it is necessary to check whether a program exited
successfully.

As you saw with the test command, an exit status of 0 is successful, whereas nonzero
values indicate some type of failure. The exit status of the last command is stored in the
variable $?, so you can check whether a command was successful as follows:

```
if [ $? -eq 0 ] ; then
    echo "Command was successful." ;
else
    echo "An error was encountered."
    exit
fi
```

If the command exits with an exit code of 0, issue the "good" message; otherwise, issue
an error message and then exit. This can be simplified as follows:

```
if [ $? -ne 0 ] ; then
    echo "An error was encountered."
    exit
fi
echo "Command was successful."
```

Here you check to see whether the command failed. If so, you echo an error message and
exit: otherwise, the if statement completes and the "good" message is issued. This is
slightly more efficient than using an else clause.

TABLE 10.3 NUMERICAL COMPARISON OPERATORS FOR THE test COMMAND

Operator	Description
int1 -eq int2	True if int1 equals int2.
int1 -ne int2	True if int1 is not equal to int2.
int1 -lt int2	True if int1 is less than int2.
int1 -le int2	True if int1 is less than or equal to int2.
int1 -gt int2	True if int1 is greater than int2.
int1 -ge int2	True if int1 is greater than or equal to int2.

Compound Expressions

NEW TERM So far you have seen individual expressions, but many times you need to combine expressions in order to satisfy a particular expression. When two or more expressions are combined, the result is called a *compound* expression.

You can create compound expressions using the `test` command's built in operators, or you can use the conditional execution operators, && and ¦¦.

Also you can create a compound expression that is the negation of another expression by using the ! operator.

Table 10.4 gives a summary of these operators.

TABLE 10.4 OPERATORS FOR CREATING COMPOUND EXPRESSIONS

Operator	Description
! expr	True if expr is false. The expr can be any valid test command.
expr1 -a expr2	True if both expr1 and expr2 are true.
expr1 -o expr2	True if either expr1 or expr2 is true.

Using the Built-in Operators The syntax for creating compound expressions using the built-in operators is

```
test expr1 operator expr2
```

or

```
[ expr1 operator expr2 ]
```

Here *expr1* and *expr2* are any valid test expression, and *operator* is either –a (*a* as in *and*) or –o (*o* as in *or*).

If the –a operator is used, both *expr1* and *expr2* must be true (evaluate to 0) in order for the compound expression to be true.

If the –o operator is used, either *expr1* or *expr2* must be true (evaluate to 0) in order for the compound expression to be true.

Using the Conditional Operators The syntax for creating compound expressions using the conditional operators is

```
test expr1 operator test expr1
```

or

```
[ expr1 ] operator [ expr2 ]
```

Here *expr1* and *expr2* are any valid test expression, and *operator* is either && (and) or
¦¦ (or).

If the && operator is used, both *expr1* and *expr2* must be true (evaluate to 0) in order for
the compound expression to be true.

If the ¦¦ operator is used, either *expr1* or *expr2* must be true (evaluate to 0) in order for
the compound expression to be true.

A Compound Expression Example   Here are two equivalent examples that demonstrate how to create a compound expression:

```
if [ -z "$DTHOME" ] && [ -d /usr/dt ] ; then DTHOME=/usr/dt ; fi

if [ -z "$DTHOME" -a -d /usr/dt ] ; then DTHOME=/usr/dt ; fi
```

The first version is executed as follows:

1. First the test

   ```
   [ -z "$DTHOME" ]
   ```

   is performed.

2. If this test returns 0, the second test

   ```
   [ -d /usr/dt ]
   ```

   is performed. Otherwise the if statement finishes.

3. If the second test returns 0, the variable assignment

   ```
   DTHOME=/usr/dt
   ```

   is performed. Otherwise the if statement finishes.

Execution of the second version is similar:

1. First the expression

   ```
   -z "$DTHOME"
   ```

   is evaluated.

2. If this expression evaluates to 0, the expression

   ```
   -d /usr/dt
   ```

   is evaluated. Otherwise the if statement finishes.

3. If the second expression evaluates to 0, the variable assignment

   ```
   DTHOME=/usr/dt
   ```

   is performed. Otherwise the if statement finishes.

Some programmers prefer the version that uses the conditional operators because the individual tests are isolated. Other programmers prefer the second form because it invokes the `test` command only once and might be marginally more efficient on older hardware or for large numbers of tests.

If you are interested in maximum portability to older systems, you should use conditional operators. On modern shells both forms work equally well, thus you can use either one.

In this example you used only two expressions. You are not limited to two. In fact any number of expressions can be combined into one compound expression.

Negating an Expression

The final type of compound expression consists of negating an expression. Negation reverses the result of an expression. True expressions are treated as false expressions and vice versa.

The basic syntax of the negation operator is

```
test ! expr
```

or

```
[ ! expr ]
```

Here *expr* is any valid `test` expression.

A simple example is the following command:

```
$ if [ ! -d $HOME/bin ] ; then mkdir $HOME/bin ; fi
```

Here you make the directory `$HOME/bin` if it does not exist. The execution is as follows:

1. First the test

   ```
   -d $HOME/bin
   ```

   is performed.

2. The result of the test is negated because of the `!` operator. If the directory `$HOME/bin` exists, the return value of the compound expression is false (1): otherwise, the return value is true (0).

3. If the result of the previous step is true, the directory `$HOME/bin` is created: otherwise, the `if` statement finishes.

A shorter form of the same command is the following:

```
$ test ! -d $HOME/bin && mkdir $HOME/bin
```

This command achieves the same result because mkdir executes only if test returns true. test returns true only if the directory $HOME/bin does not exist.

The case Statement

The case statement is the other major form of flow control available in the shell. In this section I explain its usage.

The basic syntax is

```
case word in
    pattern1)
            list1
            ;;
    pattern2)
            list2
            ;;
esac
```

go to end of case statement

Here the string *word* is compared against every *pattern* until a match is found. The *list* following the matching *pattern* executes. If no matches are found, the case statement exits without performing any action. There is no maximum number of patterns, but the minimum is one.

When a list executes, the command ;; indicates that program flow should jump to the end of the entire case statement. This is similar to break in the C programming language.

Some programmers prefer to use the form

```
case word in
    pattern1) list1 ;;
    pattern2) list2 ;;
esac
```

This form should be used only if the *list* of commands to be executed is short.

A case Statement Example

Consider the following variable declaration and case statement:

```
FRUIT=kiwi
case "$FRUIT" in
    apple) echo "Apple pie is quite tasty." ;;
    banana) echo "I like banana nut bread." ;;
    kiwi) echo "New Zealand is famous for kiwi." ;;
esac
```

The execution of the `case` statement is as follows:

1. The string contained in the variable `FRUIT` is expanded to `kiwi`.

2. The string `kiwi` is compared against the first pattern, `apple`. Because they don't match, you go to the next pattern.

3. The string `kiwi` is compared against the next pattern, `banana`. Because they don't match, you go to the next pattern.

4. The string `kiwi` is compared against the final pattern, `kiwi`. Because they match, the following message is produced:

   ```
   New Zealand is famous for kiwi.
   ```

Using Patterns

In the previous example, you used fixed strings as the pattern. If used in this fashion the `case` statement degenerates into an `if` statement. For example, the `if` statement

```
if [ "$FRUIT" = apple ] ; then
    echo "Apple pie is quite tasty."
elif [ "$FRUIT" = banana ] ; then
    echo "I like banana nut bread."
elif [ "$FRUIT" = kiwi ] ; then
    echo "New Zealand is famous for kiwi."
fi
```

is more verbose, but the real power of the `case` statement does not lie in simplifying `if` statements. The power lies in the fact that it uses *patterns* to perform matching.

A pattern is a string that consists of regular characters and special wildcard characters. The pattern determines whether a match is present.

The patterns can use the same special characters as patterns for pathname expansion covered in Chapter 8, "Substitution," along with the or operator, ¦. Some default actions can be performed by giving the * pattern, which matches anything.

An example of a simple `case` statement that uses patterns is

```
case "$TERM" in
      *term)
            TERM=xterm ;;
      network¦dialup¦unknown¦vt[0-9][0-9][0-9])
            TERM=vt100 ;;
esac
```

Here the string contained in `$TERM` is compared against two patterns. If this string ends with the string `term`, `$TERM` is assigned the value `xterm`. Otherwise ,`$TERM` is compared against the strings `network`, `dialup`, `unknown`, and `vtXXX`, where *XXX* is some three digit number, such as 102. If one of these strings matches, `$TERM` is set to `vt100`.

Summary

In this chapter, you covered the two main flow control mechanisms available in the shell. You looked at the following topics related to the `if` statement:

- Performing file tests
- Performing string comparisons
- Performing numerical comparisons
- Using compound expressions

You also looked at the basic `case` statement and using *pattern* in conjunction with it.

Starting with the next chapter, you begin to see how you can use flow control while programming.

Questions

1. What is the difference between the following commands?

   ```
   if [ -e /usr/local/bin/bash ] ; then /usr/local/bin/bash ; fi
   if [ -x /usr/local/bin/bash ] ; then /usr/local/bin/bash ; fi
   ```

2. Given the following variable declarations,

   ```
   HOME=/home/ranga
   BINDIR=/home/ranga/bin
   ```

   what is the output of the following `if` statement?

   ```
   if [ $HOME/bin = $BINDIR ] ; then
        echo "Your binaries are stored in your home directory."
   fi
   ```

   home/ranga/bin

3. What `test` command should be used in order to test whether `/usr/bin` is a directory or a symbolic link?

4. Given the following `if` statement, write an equivalent `case` statement:

   ```
   if [ "$ANS" = "Yes" -o "$ANS" = "yes" -o "$ANS" = "y" -o "$ANS" = "Y"
   ] ; then
        ANS="y"
   else
        ANS="n"
   fi
   ```

HOUR 11

Loops

In this chapter, you'll learn how to set up and use loops in your shell scripts. Loops enable you to execute a series of commands multiple times. Two main types of loops are

- The while loop
- The for loop

The while loop enables you to execute a set of commands repeatedly until some condition occurs. It is usually used when you need to manipulate the value of a variable repeatedly.

The for loop enables you to execute a set of commands repeatedly for each item in a list. One of its most common uses is in performing the same set of commands for a large number of files.

In addition to these two types of loops, ksh and bash support an additional type of loop called the select loop. It frequently presents a menu of choices to a shell scripts user.

The first section of this chapter explains the while loop and its uses. The second section of this chapter shows you how to use the for and select loops.

The while Loop

The basic syntax of the while loop is

```
while command
do
     list
done
```

Here *command* is a single command to execute, whereas *list* is a set of one or more commands to execute. Although *command* can be any valid UNIX command, it is usually a test expression of the type covered in the last chapter.

list is commonly referred to as the *body* of the while loop because it contains the heart or guts of the loop. The do and done keywords are not considered part of the body of the loop because the shell uses them only for determining where the while loop begins and ends.

The execution of a while loop proceeds according to the following steps:

1. Execute *command*.
2. If the exit status of *command* is nonzero, exit from the while loop.
3. If the exit status of *command* is zero, execute *list*.
4. When *list* finishes executing, return to Step 1.

If both *command* and *list* are short, the while loop is written in a single line as follows:

```
while command ; do list ; done
```

Here is a simple example that uses the while loop to display the numbers zero to nine:

```
x=0
while [ $x -lt 10 ]
do
     echo $x
      x=`echo "$x + 1" | bc`
done
```

Its output looks like this:

```
0
1
2
3
4
5
6
7
8
9
```

Each time this loop executes, the variable x is checked to see whether it has a value that is less than 10. If the value of x is less than 10, this test expression has an exit status of 0. In this case, the current value of x is displayed and then x is incremented by 1.

This example uses the bc command to increment x each time the loop executes. If you are not familiar with the bc command, it is covered in detail in Chapter 18, "Miscellaneous Tools."

If x is equal to 10 or greater than 10, the test expression returns 1, causing the while loop to exit.

Nesting while Loops

It is possible to use a while loop as part of the body of another while loop as follows:

```
while command1 ; # this is loop1, the outer loop
do
    list1
    while command2 ; # this is loop2, the inner loop
    do
        list2
    done
    list3
done
```

Here *command1* and *command2* are single commands to execute, whereas *list1*, *list2*, and *list3* are a set of one or more commands to execute. Both *list1* and *list3* are optional.

NEW TERM   Here you have two while loops, *loop1* and *loop2*. Usually *loop1* is referred to as the *main loop* or *outer loop*, and *loop2* is referred to as the *inner loop*.

NEW TERM   When describing the inner loop, *loop2*, many programmers say that it is *nested* one level deep. The term *nested* refers to the fact that *loop2* is located in the body of *loop1*. If you had a *loop3* located in the body of *loop2*, it would be nested two levels deep. The level of nesting is relative to the outermost loop.

There are no restrictions on how deeply nested loops can be, but you should try to avoid nesting loops more deeply than four or five levels to avoid difficulties in finding and fixing problems in your script.

As an illustration of loop nesting, let's add another countdown loop inside the loop that you used to count to nine:

```
x=0
while [ "$x" -lt 10 ] ; # this is loop1
do
    y="$x"
    while [ "$y" -ge 0 ] ; # this is loop2
```

11

```
    do
        echo "$y \c"
        y=`echo "$y - 1" | bc`
    done
    echo
    x=`echo "$x + 1" | bc`
done
```

The main change that I have introduced is the variable y. You set it to the value of x-1 before *loop2* executes. Because of this, each time *loop2* executes you display all the numbers greater than 0 and less than x in reverse order. The output looks like the following:

```
0
1 0
2 1 0
3 2 1 0
4 3 2 1 0
5 4 3 2 1 0
6 5 4 3 2 1 0
7 6 5 4 3 2 1 0
8 7 6 5 4 3 2 1 0
9 8 7 6 5 4 3 2 1 0
```

Validating User Input

Say that you need to write a script that needs to ask the user for the name of a directory. You can use the following steps to get information from the users:

1. Ask the user a question.
2. Read the user's response.
3. Check to see whether the user responded with the name of a directory.

What should you do when the user gives you a response that is not a directory?

The simplest choice would be to do nothing, but this is not very user friendly. Your script can be much more user friendly by informing the user of the error and asking for the name of a directory again.

The while loop is perfect for doing this. In fact, one of the most common uses for the while loop is to check whether user input has been gathered correctly. Usually a strategy similar to the following is employed:

1. Set a variable's value to null.
2. Start a while loop that exits when the variable's value is not null.
3. In the while loop, ask the user a question and read in the users response.

4. Validate the response.

5. If the response is invalid the variable's value is set to null. This enables the while loop to repeat.

6. If the response is valid, the variable's value is not changed. It continues to hold the user's response. Because the variable's value is not null, the while loop exits.

In the following example, use the commands

- echo to display a string

- read to read in the user's response

I have not formally introduced these commands, but you might be familiar with them. For readers who are not familiar with these commands, I'll cover them in Chapter 13, "Input/Output."

A while loop follows that solves your problem:

```
RESPONSE=                    string has zero length
while [ -z "$RESPONSE" ] ;
do
    echo "Enter the name of a directory where your files are
    ➡located:\c "                    suppress trailing newline
    read RESPONSE
    if [ ! -d "$RESPONSE" ] ; then
        echo "ERROR: Please enter a directory pathname."
        RESPONSE=
    fi
done                    True if file is a directory
                         not
```

Here you store the user's response in the variable RESPONSE. Initially this variable is set to null, enabling the while loop to begin executing.

When the while loop first executes, the user is prompted as follows:

```
Enter the name of a directory where your files are located:
```

The user can type the name of a directory at this prompt. When the user finishes typing and presses Enter, the read command puts the user's input into the variable RESPONSE. You then check to make sure the input is a directory. If the input is not a directory, issue an error message and the loop repeats. The error message is produced so that the user knows what was wrong with the input.

If the user does not enter any value, the variable RESPONSE is still set to null. In this case the value stored in the variable RESPONSE is not a directory, thus the error message is produced.

11

The until Loop

The while loop is perfect for a situation where you need to execute a set of commands while some condition is true. Sometimes you need to execute a set of commands until a condition is true.

A variation on the while loop available only in ksh and bash, the until loop provides this functionality. Its basic syntax is:

```
until command
do
     list
done
```

Here command is a single command to execute, whereas list is a set of one or more commands to execute. Although command can be any valid UNIX command, it is usually a test expression of the type covered in the last chapter.

The execution of an until loop is identical to that of the while loop and proceeds according to the following steps:

1. Execute command.

2. If the exit status of command is nonzero, exit from the until loop.

3. If the exit status of command is zero, execute list.

4. When list finishes executing, return to Step 1.

If both command and list are short, the until loop can be written on a single line as follows:

```
until command ; do list ; done
```

In most cases the until loop is identical to a while loop with list1 negated using the ! operator. For example, the following while loop

```
x=1
while [ ! $x -ge 10 ]
do
     echo $x
     x=`echo "$x + 1" | bc`
done
```

is equivalent to the following until loop:

```
x=1;
until [ $x -ge 10 ]
do
     echo $x
     x=`echo "$x + 1" | bc`
done
```

The `until` loop offers no advantages over the equivalent `while` loop. Because it isn't supported by all versions of the Bourne shell, programmers do not favor it. I have covered it here because you might run across it occasionally.

The `for` and `select` Loops

Unlike the `while` loop, which exits when a certain condition is false, both the `for` and `select` loops operate on lists of items. The `for` loop repeats a set of commands for every item in a list, whereas the `select` loop enables the user to select an item from a list.

The `for` Loop

The basic syntax is

```
for name in word1 word2 ... wordN
do
    list
done
```

Here *name* is the name of a variable and *word1* to *wordN* are sequences of characters separated by spaces (words). Each time the `for` loop executes, the value of the variable *name* is set to the next word in the list of words, *word1* to *wordN*. The first time, *name* is set to *word1*; the second time, it's set to *word2*; and so on.

This means that the number of times a `for` loop executes depends on the number of words that are specified. For example, if the following words were specified to a `for` loop

```
there comes a time
```

the loop would execute four times.

In each iteration of the `for` loop, the commands specified in *list* are executed.

You can also write the entire loop on a single line as follows:

```
for name in word1 word2 ... wordN ; do list ; done
```

If *list* and the number of words are short, the single line form is often chosen; otherwise, the multiple-line form is preferred.

A simple `for` loop example is

```
for i in 0 1 2 3 4 5 6 7 8 9
do
    echo $i
done
```

11

This loop counts to nine as follows:

```
0
1
2
3
4
5
6
7
8
9
```

Note that although the output is identical to the `while` loop, the `for` loop does something altogether different. In each iteration, `$i` is set to the next item in the list. When the list is finished, the loop exits.

In this example I chose the list to be the numbers from 0 to 9. In the `while` loop, the next number to display was being computed, and it was not part of a predetermined list.

If you change the list slightly, notice how the output changes:

```
for i in 0 1 2 4 3 5 8 7 9
do
      echo $i
done

0
1
2
4
3
5
8
7
9
```

Manipulating a Set of Files

Say that you need to copy a bunch of files from one directory to another and change the permissions on the copy. You could do this by copying each file and changing the permissions manually.

A better solution would be to determine the commands you need to execute in order to copy a file and change its permissions and then have the computer do this for every file you were interested in. In fact this is one of the most common uses of the `for` loop—iterating over a set of file names and performing some operations on those files.

The procedure to do this follows:

1. Create a `for` loop with a variable named `file` or `FILE`. Other favored names include `i`, `j`, and `k`. Usually the name of the variable is singular.

2. Create a list of files to manipulate. This is frequently accomplished using the file-name substitution technique I discussed in Chapter 8, "Substitution."

3. Manipulate the files in the body of the loop.

An example of this is the following `for` loop:

```
for FILE in $HOME/.bash*
do
    cp $FILE ${HOME}/public_html
    chmod a+r ${HOME}/public_html/${FILE}
done
```

substitutes the value of the name [handwritten annotation]

In this loop I use filename substitution to obtain a list of files in my home directory that start with `.bash*`. In the body of the loop, I copy each of these files to my `public_html` directory, and then I make them readable by everyone. This way people stopping by my Web page can see the scripts.

Notice that you are using the name `FILE` for the variable. This is because each time you are dealing with a single file from a list of files. The rationale behind making the `for` loop's variable singular, such as `FILE` instead of `FILES`, is that you are dealing with only one item from a set of items each time the loop executes.

The `select` Loop

The `select` loop provides an easy way to create a numbered menu from which users can select options. It is useful when you need to ask the user to choose one or more items from a list of choices.

This loop was introduced in `ksh` and has been adapted into `bash`. It is not available in `sh`.

The basic syntax of the `select` loop is

```
select name in word1 word2 ... wordN
do
    list
done
```

Here *name* is the name of a variable and *word1* to *wordN* are sequences of characters separated by spaces (words). The set of commands to execute after the user has made a selection is specified by *list*.

The execution process for a `select` loop is as follows:

1. Each item in *list1* is displayed along with a number.

2. A prompt, usually #?, is displayed.

3. When the user enters a value, $REPLY is set to that value.

4. If $REPLY contains a number of a displayed item, the variable specified by *name* is set to the item in *list1* that was selected. Otherwise, the items in *list1* are displayed again.

5. When a valid selection is made, *list2* executes.

6. If *list2* does not exit from the `select` loop using one of the loop control mechanisms such as `break`, the process starts over at step 1.

If the user enters more than one valid value, $REPLY contains all the user's choices. In this case, the variable specified by *name* is not set.

An Example of the `select` Loop

One common use of the `select` loop is in scripts that configure software. The following example is a simplified version of one such script. The actual configuration commands have been omitted because they are not relevant in this discussion.

```
select COMPONENT in comp1 comp2 comp3 all none
do
    case $COMPONENT in
        comp1|comp2|comp3) CompConf $COMPONENT ;;   End of a
                                                     case statement
        all) CompConf comp1
            CompConf comp2
            CompConf comp3
            ;;
        none) break ;;
        *) echo "ERROR: Invalid selection, $REPLY." ;;
    esac
done
```

The menu presented by the `select` loop looks like the following:

```
1) comp1
2) comp2
3) comp3
4) all
5) none
#?   - prompt
```

Here you see that each of the items in the list

```
comp1 comp2 comp3 all none
```

are displayed with a number preceding them. The user can enter one of these numbers to select a particular component.

If a valid selection is made, the select loop executes a case statement contained in its body. This case statement performs the correct action based on the user's input. Here the correct action is either calling a command named CompConf, exiting the loop, or displaying an error message.

Changing the Prompt

You can change the prompt displayed by the select loop by altering the variable PS3. If PS3 is not set, the default prompt, #?, is displayed. Otherwise the value of PS3 is used as the prompt to display. For example, the commands

```
$ PS3="Please make a selection => " ; export PS3
```

change the menu displayed in the previous example to the following:

```
1) comp1
2) comp2
3) comp3
4) all
5) none
Please make a selection =>
```

Notice that the value of PS3 that you used has a space as its last character so that user input does not run into the prompt. You do this in order to make the menu user-friendly.

Loop Control

So far you have looked at creating loops and working with loops to accomplish different tasks. Sometimes you need to stop a loop or skip iterations of the loop. In this section you'll look at the commands used to control loops:

- break

- continue

Infinite Loops and the break Command

When you looked at the while loop earlier in this chapter, it terminated when a particular condition was met. This happened when the task of the while loop completed.

If you make a mistake in specifying the termination condition of a while loop, it can continue forever. For example, say you forgot to specify the $ before the x in the test expression:

```
x=0
while [ x -lt 10 ]
do
    echo $x
    x=`echo "$x + 1" | bc`
done
```

11

NEW TERM This loop would continue to display numbers forever. A loop that executes forever without terminating executes an infinite number of times. For this reason,
such loops are called *infinite* loops.

In most cases infinite looping is not desired and stems from programming errors, but in
certain instances they can be useful. For example, say that you need to wait for a particular event, such as someone logging on to a system, to occur.

You can use an infinite loop to check every few seconds whether the event has occurred.
Because you don't know how many times you need to execute the loop, when the event
occurs, you can exit the infinite loop using the break command.

In sh, you can create infinite loops using the while loop. Because a while loop executes
list while *command* is true, specifying *command* as either : or /bin/true causes the loop
to execute forever.

The basic syntax of the infinite while loop is

```
while :
do
    list
done
```

In most infinite loops, the while loop usually exits from within *list* via the break command, which enables you to exit any loop immediately.

Consider the following interactive script that reads and executes commands:

```
while :
do
    read CMD
    case $CMD in
        [qQ]¦[qQ][uU][iI][tT]) break ;;
        *) process $CMD ;;
      esac
done
```

In this loop you read a command at the beginning of each iteration. If that command is
either q or Quit, the loop exits; otherwise, the loop tries to process the command.

Breaking Out of Nested Loops

The break command also accepts as an argument an integer, greater or equal to 1, indicating the number of levels to break out of. This feature is useful when nested loops are
being used. Consider the following nested for loops:

```
for i in 1 2 3 4 5
do
    mkdir -p /mnt/backup/docs/ch0${i}
```

```
        if [ $? -eq 0 ] ; then
            for j in doc c h m pl sh
            do
                cp $HOME/docs/ch0${i}/*.${j} /mnt/backup/docs/ch0${i}
                if [ $? -ne 0 ] ; then break 2 ; fi
            done
        else
            echo "Could not make backup directory."
        fi
done
```

In this loop, I'm making a backup of several important files from my home directory to the backup directory. The outer loop takes care of creating the backup directory, whereas the inner loop copies the important files based on the extension.

In the inner loop, you have a break command with the argument 2. This indicates that if an error occurs while copying you should break out of both loops, and not just the inner loop.

The `continue` Command

The `continue` command is similar to the `break` command, except that it causes the current iteration of the loop to exit, rather than the entire loop. This command is useful when an error has occurred but you want to try to execute the next iteration of the loop.

As an example, the following loop doesn't exit if one of the input files is bad:

```
for FILE in $FILES ;
do
    if [ ! -f "$FILE" ] ; then
        echo "ERROR: $FILE is not a file."
        continue
    fi
    # process the file
done
```

If one of the filenames in $FILES is not a file, this loop skips it, rather than exiting.

Summary

Loops are a powerful programming tool that enable you to execute a set of commands repeatedly. In this chapter, you have examined the following types of loops available to shell programmers:

- while
- until

11

- for

- select

You have also examined the concept of nested loops, infinite loops, and loop control. In the next chapter, I'll introduce the concept of parameters. Here you'll see one of the most common applications of loops.

Questions

1. What changes are required to the following `while` loop

```
x=0
while [ $x -lt 10 ]
do
      echo "$x \c"
      y=$(($x-1))
      x=$(($x+1))
      while [ $y -ge 0 ] ; do
           y=$(($y-1))
           echo "$y \c"
      done
      echo
done
```

so that the output looks like the following:

```
0
0 1
0 1 2
0 1 2 3
0 1 2 3 4
0 1 2 3 4 5
0 1 2 3 4 5 6
0 1 2 3 4 5 6 7
0 1 2 3 4 5 6 7 8
0 1 2 3 4 5 6 7 8 9
```

2. Write a `select` loop that lists each file in the current directory and enables the user to view the file by selecting its number. In addition to listing each file, use the string `Exit Program` as the key to exit the loop. If the user selects an item that is not a regular file, the program should identify the problem. If no input is given, the menu should be redisplayed.

Terms

Loops   Loops enable you to execute a series of commands multiple times. Two main types of loops are the `while` and `for` loops.

Body   The set of commands executed by a loop.

Iteration   A single execution of the body of a loop.

Nested Loops   When a loop is located inside the body of another loop it is said to be nested within another loop.

Infinite Loops   Loops that execute forever without terminating.

11

HOUR 12

Parameters

As you saw in previous chapters, the general format for the invocation of programs in UNIX is

command options files

Here *command* is the command name, *options* is any option that you need to specify, and *files* is an optional list of files on which the command should operate. Consider the following example:

```
$ ls -l *.doc
```

Here ls is the command, -l is the only option, and *.doc is the list of files for ls to operate on.

Because most UNIX users are familiar with this interface, you should adhere to this format in shell scripts. This means that scripts that can have options specified must be able to read and interpret them correctly.

You have two common methods for the handling options passed to a shell script:

- Handle options manually using a case statement
- Handle options using the getopts command

For scripts that support only one or two options, the first method is easy to implement and works quite well, but many scripts allow any combination of several options to be given. For such scripts, the getopts command is very useful because it affords the maximum flexibility in parsing options.

This chapter looks at both methods but it first covers the topic of special shell variables.

Special Variables

The shell defines several special variables that are relevant to option parsing. In addition to these, a few variables give the status of commands that the script executes. Table 12.1 describes all of the special variables defined by the shell.

In this section you construct a simple yet useful shell script that illustrates the use of these variables.

TABLE 12.1 SPECIAL SHELL VARIABLES

Variable	Description
$0	The name of the command being executed. For shell scripts, this is the path with which it was invoked.
$n	These variables correspond to the arguments with which a script was invoked. Here n is a positive decimal number corresponding to the position of an argument (the first argument is $1, the second argument is $2, and so on).
$#	The number of arguments supplied to a script.
$*	All the arguments are double quoted. If a script receives two arguments, $* is equivalent to $1 $2.
$@	All the arguments are individually double quoted. If a script receives two arguments, $@ is equivalent to $1 $2.
$?	The exit status of the last command executed.
$$	The process number of the current shell. For shell scripts, this is the process ID under which they are executing.
$!	The process number of the last background command.

Using $0

Start by looking at $0. This variable is commonly used to determine the behavior of scripts that can be invoked with more than one name. Consider the following script:

```
#!/bin/sh
case $0 in
```

```
    *listtar) TARGS="-tvf $1" ;;
    *maketar) TARGS="-cvf $1.tar $1" ;;
esac
tar $TARGS
```

You can use this script to list the contents of a tar file (*t* as in *tape* and *ar* as in *archive*, a common format for distributing files in UNIX) or to create a tar file based on the name with which the script is invoked. The tar file to read or create is specified as the first argument, $1.

I called this script mytar and made two symbolic links to it called listtar and maketar as follows:

```
$ ln -s mytar listtar
$ ln -s mytar maketar
```

If the script is invoked with the name maketar and is given a directory or filename, a tar file is created. If you had a directory called fruits with the following contents

```
$ ls fruits
apple   banana  mango   peach   pear
```

you can invoke the script as maketar to obtain a tar file called fruit.tar containing this directory, by issuing the following command:

```
$ ./maketar fruits
```

If you want to list the contents of this tar file, you can invoke the script as follows:

```
$ ./listtar fruits.tar
```

This gives us the following output:

```
rwxr-xr-x 500/100      0 Nov 17 08:48 1998 fruits/
rw-r--r-- 500/100      0 Nov 17 08:48 1998 fruits/apple
rw-r--r-- 500/100      0 Nov 17 08:48 1998 fruits/banana
rw-r--r-- 500/100      0 Nov 17 08:48 1998 fruits/mango
rw-r--r-- 500/100      0 Nov 17 08:48 1998 fruits/pear
rw-r--r-- 500/100      0 Nov 17 08:48 1998 fruits/peach
```

For this example, the output that you encounter depends on the version of tar that is installed on your machine. Some versions include more detail in the output than are shown here.

Usage Statements

NEW TERM   Another common use for $0 is in the *usage statement* for a script, which is a short message informing the user how to invoke the script properly. All scripts used by more than one user should include such a message.

In general, the usage statement is something like the following:

```
echo "Usage: $0 [options][files]"
```

12

> **SIMPLIFYING SCRIPT MAINTENANCE**
>
> Using $0 as I've illustrated is encountered in the install and the uninstall scripts of some software packages.
>
> Because these scripts share many of the same routines and global variables, it is desirable, for ease of maintenance, to merge them into a single script having different behavior depending on the name with which it is invoked.
>
> If you are writing scripts that need to share main routines, consider using such a scheme to simplify maintenance.

If you consider the `mytar` script given previously, a usage statement would be a helpful addition, in case the script was called with some name other than the two names it knows about. To implement this, change the case statement as follows:

```
case $0 in
    *listtar) TARGS="-tvf $1" ;;
    *maketar) TARGS="-cvf $1.tar $1" ;;
    *) echo "Usage: $0 [file¦directory]"
       exit 0
       ;;
esac
```

Thus, if the script is invoked as just `mytar`, you see following message:

```
Usage: mytar [file¦directory]
```

Although this message describes the usage of the script correctly, it does not inform us that the script's name was given incorrectly. There are two possible methods for rectifying this:

- Hard coding the valid names in the "usage statement"
- Changing the script to use its arguments to decide in which mode it should run

To demonstrate the use of options, the next section uses the latter method.

Options and Arguments

Options are given on the command line to change the behavior of a script or program. For example, the –a option of the `ls` command changes the behavior of the `ls` command from listing all visible files to listing all files. This section shows you how to use options to change the behavior of scripts.

NEW TERM   Often you will see or hear options called *arguments*. The difference between the two is subtle. A command's arguments are all of the separate strings or words that appear on the command line after the command name, whereas *options* are only those arguments that change the behavior of the command.

For example, in the following

```
$ ls -aF fruit
```

the command is ls, and its arguments are -aF and fruit. The options to the ls command are -aF.

Dealing with Arguments, an Example

To illustrate the use of options, change the mytar script to use its first argument, $1, as the mode argument and $2 as the tar file to read or create.

To implement this, change the case statement as follows:

```
USAGE="Usage: $0 [-c¦-t] [file¦directory]"
case "$1" in
    -t) TARGS="-tvf $2" ;;
    -c) TARGS="-cvf $2.tar $2" ;;
    *) echo "$USAGE"
        exit 0
        ;;
esac
```

terminal special device

The three major changes are

- All references to $1 have been changed to $2 because the second argument is now the filename.
- listtar has been replaced by -t.
- maketar has been replaced by -c.

Now running mytar produces the correct output:

```
Usage: ./mytar [-c¦-t] [file¦directory]
```

To create a tar file of the directory fruits with this version, use the command

```
$ ./mytar -c fruits
```

To list the contents of the resulting tar file, fruits.tar, use the command

```
$ ./mytar -t fruits
```

Using basename

Currently, the message displays the entire path with which the shell script was invoked, but what is really required is the name of the shell script. You can correct this by using the basename command.

The basename command takes an absolute or relative path and returns the file or directory name. Its basic syntax is

12

```
basename file
```

For example,

```
$ basename /usr/bin/sh
```

prints the following:

```
sh
```

Using `basename`, you can change the variable `$USAGE` in the `mytar` script as follows:

```
USAGE="Usage: `basename $0` [-c¦-t] [file¦directory]"
```

This produces the following output:

```
Usage: mytar [-c¦-t] [file¦directory]
```

You could also have used the `basename` command in the first version of the `mytar` script to avoid using the `*` wildcard character in the case statement as follows:

```
#!/bin/sh
case `basename $0` in
    listtar) TARGS="-tvf $1" ;;
    maketar) TARGS="-cvf $1.tar $1" ;;
esac
tar $TARGS
```

In this version, the `basename` command allows us to match the exact names with which scripts can be called. This simplifies the possible user interactions and is preferred for that reason.

As an illustration of a potential problem with the original version, you can see that if the script is called

```
$ ./makelisttar
```

the original version would use the first case statement, even though it was incorrect, but the new version would fall through and report an error.

Common Argument Handling Problems

Now that the `mytar` script uses options to set the mode in which the script runs, you have another problem to solve. Namely, what should it do if the second argument, $2, is not provided?

You don't have to worry about what happens if the first argument, $1, is not provided because the case statement deals with this situation via the default case, `*`.

The simplest method for checking the necessary number of arguments is to see whether the number of given arguments, $#, matches the number of required arguments. Add this check to the script:

```
#!/bin/sh

USAGE="Usage: `basename $0` [-c|-t] [file|directory]"

if [ $# -lt 2 ] ; then
    echo "$USAGE"
    exit 1
fi

case "$1" in
    -t) TARGS="-tvf $2" ;;
    -c) TARGS="-cvf $2.tar $2" ;;
     *) echo "$USAGE"
        exit 0
        ;;
esac

tar $TARGS
```

Handling Additional Files

This mytar script is mostly finished, but you can still make a few improvements. For example, it only deals with the first file that is given as an argument, and it does not check to see whether the file argument is really a file.

You can add the processing of all file arguments by using the special shell variable $@. Start with the -t (list contents) option. The case statement now becomes

12

```
case "$1" in
    -t) TARGS="-tvf"
        for i in "$@" ; do
            if [ -f "$i" ] ; then tar $TARGS "$i" ; fi ;
        done
        ;;
    -c) TARGS="-cvf $2.tar $2" ;
        tar $TARGS
        ;;
     *) echo "$USAGE" ;
        exit 0
        ;;
esac
```

The main change is that the -t case now includes a for loop that cycles through the arguments and checks to see whether each one is a file. If an argument is a file, tar is invoked on that file.

When examining the arguments passed to a script, two special variables are available for inspection, $* and $@.

The main difference between these two is how they expand arguments. When $* is used, it simply expands each argument without preserving quoting. This can sometimes cause a problem. If your script is given a filename containing spaces as an argument,

```
mytar -t "my tar file.tar"
```

using $* would mean that the for loop would call tar three times for files named my, tar, and file.tar, instead of once for the file you requested: my tar file.tar.

By using $@, you avoid this problem because it expands each argument as it was quoted on the command line.

Some Minor Issues

You should deal with a few more minor issues. Looking closely, you see that all the arguments given to the script, including the first argument, $1, are considered as files. Because you are using the first argument as the flag to indicate the mode in which the script runs, you should not consider it.

Not only does this reduce the number of times the for loop runs, but it also prevents the script from accidentally trying to run tar on a file with the name -t. To remove the first argument from the list of arguments, use the shift command. A similar change to the make mode of the script is also required.

Another issue is what the script should do when an operation fails. In the case of the listing operation, if the tar cannot list the contents of a file, skipping the file and printing an error would be a reasonable operation. Because the shell sets the variable $? to the exit status of the most recent command, you can use that to determine whether a tar operation failed.

Resolving the previous issues, your script is as follows:

```
#!/bin/sh

USAGE="Usage: `basename $0` [-c¦-t] [files¦directories]"

if [ $# -lt 2 ] ; then
    echo "$USAGE" ;
    exit 1 ;
fi

case "$1" in
    -t) shift ; TARGS="-tvf" ;
```

```
       for i in "$@" ; do
           if [ -f "$i" ] ; then
               FILES=`tar $TARGS "$i" 2>/dev/null`
               if [ $? -eq 0 ] ; then
                   echo ; echo "$i" ; echo "$FILES"
               else
                   echo "ERROR: $i not a tar file."
               fi
           else
               echo "ERROR: $i not a file."
           fi
       done
       ;;
   -c) shift ; TARGS="-cvf" ;
       tar $TARGS archive.tar "$@"
       ;;
    *) echo "$USAGE"
       exit 0
       ;;
esac
exit $?
```

Option Parsing in Shell Scripts

You have two common ways to handle the parsing of options passed to a shell script. In the first method, you can manually deal with the options using a case statement. This method was used in the mytar script presented earlier in the chapter. The second method, discussed in this section, is to use the getopts command.

The syntax of the getopts command is

getopts *option-string variable*

Here *option-string* is a string consisting of all the single character options getopts should consider, and *variable* is the name of the variable that the option should be set to. Usually the *variable* used is named OPTION.

The process by which getopts parses the options given on the command line is

1. The getopts option examines all the command line arguments, looking for arguments starting with the – character.
2. When an argument starting with the – character is found, it compares the characters following the – to the characters given in the *option-string*.
3. If a match is found, the specified *variable* is set to the option: otherwise, *variable* is set to the ? character.
4. Steps 1 through 3 are repeated until all the options have been considered.

12

5. When parsing has finished, `getopts` returns a nonzero exit code. This allows it to be easily used in loops. Also, when `getopts` has finished, it sets the variable `OPTIND` to the index of the last argument.

Another feature of `getopts` is the capability to indicate options requiring an additional parameter. You can accomplish this by following the option with a : character in the *option-string*. In this case, after an option is parsed, the additional parameter is set to the value of the variable named `OPTARG`.

Using getopts

To get a feeling for how `getopts` works and how to deal with options, write a script that simplifies the task of uuencoding a file.

For readers who are not familiar with uuencode, it is a program that was originally used to encode binary files (executable files) into ASCII text so that they could be emailed or transferred via FTP. Today, MIME encoding has taken the place of uuencoding for email attachments, but it is still used for posting binaries to newsgroups and transferring them via modem.

You'll first examine the interface of this script, which makes it easier to understand the implementation.

This script should be able to accept the following options:

- `-f` to indicate the input filename
- `-o` to indicate the output filename
- `-v` to indicate the script should be verbose

The `getopts` command to implement these requirements is

```
getopts f:o:v OPTION
```

This indicates that all the options expect for –v to require an additional parameter. The variables you require in order to support this are

- `VERBOSE`, which stores the value of the verbose flag. By default this is false.
- `INFILE`, which stores the name of the input file.
- `OUTFILE`, which stores the name of the output filename. If this value is unset, uudecode uses the name supplied in the input file, and uuencode uses the name of the supplied input file and append to it the `.uu` extension.

The loop to implement the preceding requirements is as follows:

```
VERBOSE=false
```

```
while getopts f:o:v OPTION ;
do
    case "$OPTION" in
        f)  INFILE="$OPTARG" ;;
        o)  OUTFILE="$OPTARG" ;;
        v)  VERBOSE=true ;;
        \?) echo "$USAGE" ;
            exit 1
            ;;
    esac
done
```

Now that you have dealt with option parsing, you need to deal with still other error conditions. For example, what should your script do if the input file is not specified?

The simplest answer would be to exit with an error, but with a little more work, you can make the script much more user-friendly. If you use the fact that getopts sets the variable OPTIND to the value of the last option that it scanned, you can have the script assume that the first argument after this is the input filename. If no additional arguments remain, you should exit. Your error checking consists of the following lines:

```
shift `echo "$OPTIND - 1" | bc`
if [ -z "$1" -a -z "$INFILE" ] ; then
    echo "ERROR: Input file was not specified."
    exit 1
fi
if [ -z "$INFILE" ] ; then INFILE="$1" ; fi
```

Here you use the shift command to discard the arguments given to the script by one minus the last argument processed by getopts. The exact number of arguments to shift is calculated by the bc command, which is a command line calculator. Its usage is explained in detail in Chapter 18, "Miscellaneous Tools."

Strictly speaking, you do not have to shift the arguments. It simplifies the if statement.

After shifting the arguments, check whether the new $1 contains some value. If it does not, print and exit. Otherwise, set INFILE to the filename specified by $1.

You also need to set the output filename, in case the -o option was not specified. You can use variable substitution to accomplish this:

```
: ${OUTFILE:=${INFILE}.uu}
```

Here the name of the output file is set to the input file plus the .uu extension, if an output file is not given. Note that you use the : command to prevent the shell from trying to execute the result of the variable substitution.

12

true regular file

When you have made sure that all the inputs are correct, the actual work is quite simple. The uuencode command that you use is:

```
uuencode $INFILE $INFILE > $OUTFILE ;
```

You should also check whether the input file is really a file before doing this command, so the actual body is

```
if [ -f "$INFILE" ] ; then uuencode $INFILE $INFILE > $OUTFILE ; fi
```

At this point the script is fully functional, but you still need to add the verbose reporting. This changes the preceding if statement to the following:

```
if [ -f "$INFILE" ] ; then
    if [ "$VERBOSE" = "true" ] ; then
        echo "uuencoding $INFILE to $OUTFILE... \c"     suppress trailing line
    fi
    uuencode $INFILE $INFILE > $OUTFILE ; RET=$? ;
    if [ "$VERBOSE" = "true" ] ; then
        MSG="Failed" ;
        if [ $RET -eq 0 ] ; then MSG="Done." ; fi
        echo $MSG
    fi
fi
```

You could simplify the verbose reporting to print a statement after the uuencode completes, but issuing two statements, one before the operation starts and one after the operation completes, is much more user-friendly. This method clearly indicates that the operation is being performed.

The complete script is as follows:

```
#!/bin/sh

USAGE="Usage: `basename $0` [-v] [-f] [filename] [-o] [filename]";
VERBOSE=false

while getopts f:o:v OPTION ; do
    case "$OPTION" in
        f) INFILE="$OPTARG" ;;          End of case statement
        o) OUTFILE="$OPTARG" ;;
        v) VERBOSE=true ;;
        \?) echo "$USAGE" ;
            exit 1
            ;;
    esac
done

shift `echo "$OPTIND - 1" | bc`
```

```
if [ -z "$1" -a -z "$INFILE" ] ; then
    echo "ERROR: Input file was not specified."
    exit 1
fi
if [ -z "$INFILE" ] ; then INFILE="$1" ; fi

: ${OUTFILE:=${INFILE}.uu}

if [ -f "$INFILE" ] ; then
    if [ "$VERBOSE" = "true" ] ; then
        echo "uuencoding $INFILE to $OUTFILE... \c"
    fi
    uuencode $INFILE $INFILE > $OUTFILE ; RET=$?
    if [ "$VERBOSE" = "true" ] ; then
        MSG="Failed" ; if [ $RET -eq 0 ] ; then MSG="Done." ; fi
        echo $MSG
    fi
fi
exit 0
```

With this script you can uuencode files in all of the following ways (assuming the script is called uu):

```
uu ch11.doc
uu -f ch11.doc
uu -f ch11.doc -o ch11.uu
```

In each of the preceding examples, file ch11.doc is uuencoded. The last one places the result into the file ch11.uu instead of the default ch11.doc.uu, which might be required if the document needs to be used on a DOS or Windows system.

Because this script uses getopts any of the commands given previously can run in verbose mode by simply specifying the -v option.

Conclusion

In this chapter you examined how to deal with arguments and options in shell script. Specifically you looked at the following methods:

- Manually handling arguments and options using a case statement
- Handling options using getopts

You worked through two examples that illustrate the implementation and rationale behind each method. In addition, you saw several special variables that pertain to arguments and command execution.

As you will see in later chapters, using options greatly increases the flexibility and the reusability of your shell scripts.

12

Questions

1. Add `tar` file extraction to the `mytar` script.

   Assume that the -x option indicates that the user wants to extract `tar` files and that the correct value of TARGS for extracting `tar` files is `-xvf`.

2. Add the extract option to the uu script. Assume that the -x option indicates that the file should be extracted, and that the command

   `uudecode $INFILE`

   is used to extract a uuencoded file.

HOUR 13

Input/Output

Until now you have been looking at commands that print out messages. When a command prints a message, the message is called *output*. In this chapter, you will look at the different types of output available to shell scripts. This chapter also introduces the mechanisms used to obtain *input* from users.

Specifically, the areas that you will cover are

- Output to the screen
- Output to a file
- Input from a file
- Input from users

Output

As you have seen in previous chapters, most commands produce output. For example, the command

```
$ date
```

produces the current date in the terminal window:

```
Thu Nov 12 16:32:35 PST 1998
```

NEW TERM   When a command produces output that is written to the terminal, we say that the program has printed its output to the *Standard Output*, or STDOUT. When you run the date command, it prints the date to STDOUT.

You might have also seen commands produce error messages, such as:

```
$ ln -s ch01.doc ch01-01.doc
ln: cannot create ch01-1.doc: File Exists
```

NEW TERM   Error messages are not written to STDOUT, but instead they are written to a special type of output called *Standard Error* or STDERR, which is reserved for error messages. Most commands use STDERR for error messages and STDOUT for informational messages.

You will look at STDERR later in this chapter. In this section you will look at how shell scripts can use STDOUT to output messages to each of the following:

- The terminal (STDOUT)
- A file
- The terminal and a file

Output to the Terminal

Two common commands print messages to the terminal (STDOUT):

- echo
- printf

The echo command is mostly used for printing strings that require simple formatting. The printf command is the shell version of the C language function printf. It provides a high degree of flexibility in formatting output.

You first look at echo and then printf.

echo

The most common command used to output messages to the terminal is the echo command. Its syntax is

echo *string*

Here *string* is the string you want printed. For example, the command

$ echo Hi

produces the following output:

Hi

You can also embed spaces in the output as follows:

```
$ echo Safeway has fresh fruit
Safeway has fresh fruit
```

In addition to spaces, you can embed each of the following in the *string*:

- Punctuation marks
- Variable substitutions
- Formatting escape sequences

Embedding Punctuation Marks   Punctuation marks are used when you need to ask the user a question, complete a sentence, or issue a warning. For example the following echo statement might be the prompt in an install script:

```
echo Do you want to install?
```

Usually, significant error messages are terminated with the exclamation point. For example, the echo command

```
echo ERROR: Could not find required libraries! Exiting.
```

might be found in a script that configures a program for execution.

You can also use any combination of the punctuation marks. For example, the following command uses the comma (,), question mark (?), and exclamation point(!) punctuation marks:

```
$ echo Eliza, where the devil are my slippers?!?
Eliza, where the devil are my slippers?!?
```

Embedding Variable Substitution   Chapters 7, "Variables," and 8, "Substitution," cover variable substitution, which is the process that the shell uses to substitute in the *value* of a variable where that variable's *name* occurs. Often variable substitution is embedded in an echo command, where part or all of the text of the message that is displayed depends on the value of a variable.

A common use of this technique is in the display of pathnames:

```
echo Your home directory is $HOME
Your home directory is /home/ranga
```

In this example, you used the simplest form of variable substitution, the $ character, but you can use any form of variable substitution.

13

NEW TERM **Formatting with Escape Sequences** In the previous examples, the output consisted of single lines with words separated by spaces. Frequently, output needs to be formatted into columns or multiple lines. By using escape sequences you can format the output of echo. An *escape sequence* is a special sequence of characters that represents another character. When the shell encounters an escape sequence, it substitutes the escape sequence with a different character. The echo command understands several formatting escape sequences, the most common of which are given in Table 13.1.

TABLE 13.1 ESCAPE SEQUENCES FOR THE echo COMMAND

Escape Sequence	Description
\n	Prints a newline character
\t	Prints a tab character
\c	Prints a string without a default trailing newline

The \n escape sequence is usually used when you need to generate more than one line of output using a single echo command. You usually use this when you need to print a list preceded by a description of the list. For example, the command

```
$ FRUIT_BASKET="apple orange pear"
$ echo "Your fruit basket contains:\n$FRUIT_BASKET"
Your fruit basket contains:
apple orange pear
```

generates a list of fruit preceded by a description of the list.

This example illustrates two important aspects of using escape sequences:

- The entire string is quoted.
- The escape sequence appears in the middle of the string and is not separated by spaces.

Whenever an escape sequence is used in the input string of an echo command, the string must be quoted to prevent the shell from expanding the escape sequence on the command line.

Also, whenever an escape sequence is used in the input string of an echo command, the string is a specification of how the output should look. Spaces should not be used to separate the escape sequences unless that is how the output needs to be formatted.

You can always rewrite any echo command that uses the \n escape sequence as several echo commands. For example, you can generate the same output as in the previous example using the echo command:

```
$ echo "Your fruit basket contains:"
$ echo $FRUIT_BASKET
```

Another commonly used escape sequence is the \t sequence, which generates a tab in the output. Usually it is used when you need to make a small table or generate tabular output that is only a few lines long. As an example, the following echo command generates a small table of two users and their usernames:

```
$ echo "Name \tUser Name\nSriranga\tranga\nSrivathsa\tvathsa"
Name    User Name
Sriranga        ranga
Srivathsa       vathsa
```

As you can see, the heading User Name is not centered over its column. You can change this by adding another tab:

```
$ echo "Name\t\tUser Name\nSriranga\tranga\nSrivathsa\tvathsa"
Name            User Name
Sriranga        ranga
Srivathsa       vathsa
```

For generating large tables, the printf command, covered in the next section, is preferred because it provides a greater degree of control over the size of each column in the table.

Another commonly used escape sequence is the \c sequence, which is frequently used in shell scripts that need to generate user prompts or diagnostic output.

As you have seen in the previous example, the default behavior of echo is to add a newline at the end of its output. When you are generating a prompt, this is not the most user-friendly behavior. When the \c escape sequence is used, echo does not output a newline when it finishes printing its input string.

As an example of its use, this excerpt from a shell script

```
echo "Making directories, please wait...\t\c"
for i ${DIRS_TO_MAKE} ; do mkdir -p $I ; done
echo "Done."
```

produces diagnostic output that looks like the following:

```
Making directories, please wait...      Done.
```

Without the \c escape at the end of the first echo statement, the output looks like the following:

```
Making directories, please wait...
Done.
```

As you can see, the previous version of the output is more user-friendly, especially if you have several such lines in sequence.

Another possible use is shown in the following example:

13

```
echo "Copying files, please wait\t\c"
for i in ${FILES} ; do cp $i $DEST && echo ".\c" ; done
echo "\tDone."
```

The output is similar to the following:

```
Copying files, please wait      .......      Done
```

Here a single . is printed for each file that is copied.

> Some newer versions of sh, ksh, and bash include a version of echo as a
> built-in command that does not understand the \c escape sequence. On
> these shells, you might see output like the following:
>
> ```
> $ echo "Please enter your name \c"
> echo Please enter your name \c
> $
> ```
>
> Because these versions of echo print a newline after printing the \c escape
> sequence literally, they defeat the purpose of using this escape sequence. If
> you are using such a version of echo, you can switch to using either
> /bin/echo or /usr/bin/echo, which handle the \c escape sequence correctly.

printf

The printf command is similar to the echo command, in that it enables you to print
messages to STDOUT. In its most basic form, its usage is identical to echo. For example,
the following echo command:

```
$ echo "Is that a mango?"
```

is identical to the printf command:

```
$ printf "Is that a mango?\n"
```

The only major difference is that the string specified to printf explicitly requires the \n
escape sequence at the end of a string, in order for a newline to print. The echo command prints the newline automatically.

> The printf command is located in the directory /usr/bin on Linux, Solaris,
> and HP-UX machines. In addition, the printf command is a built-in
> command in bash.

The power of `printf` comes from its capability to perform complicated formatting by using format specifications. The basic syntax for this is

```
printf format arguments
```

NEW TERM Here, *format* is a string that contains one or more of the formatting sequences, and *arguments* are strings that correspond to the formatting sequences specified in *format*. For those who are familiar with the C language `printf` function, the formatting sequences supported by the `printf` command are identical.

The formatting sequences have the form:

`%[-]m.nx`

Here `%` starts the formatting sequence and *x* identifies the formatting sequences type. Table 13.2 gives possible values of *x*.

TABLE 13.2 FORMATTING SEQUENCE TYPES

Letter	Description
s	String
c	Character
d	Decimal (integer) number
x	Hexadecimal number
o	Octal number
e	Exponential floating-point number
f	Fixed floating-point number
g	Compact floating-point number

Depending on the value of *x*, the integers *m* and *n* are interpreted differently. Usually *m* is the minimum length of a field, and *n* is the maximum length of a field. If you specify a real number format, *n* is treated as the precision that should be used.

The hyphen (-) left justifies a field. By default, all fields are right justified.

Look at a few examples to see how to use `printf` in practice.

Consider the following shell script written with only `echo` commands:

```
#!/bin/sh

echo "File Name\tType"

for i in *;
do
```

13

```
        echo "$i\t\c"
        if [ -d $i ]; then
            echo "directory"
        elif [ -h $i ]; then
            echo "symbolic link"
        elif [ -f $i ]; then
            echo "file"
        else
            echo "unknown"
        fi
done
```

This script produces a table that lists all the visible files in the current directory along with their file type. The output looks similar to the following:

```
File Name        Type
RCS      directory
dev      directory
humor    directory
images   directory
index.html        file
install directory
java     directory
```

As you can see, the items in the table's rows are not lined up with the table headings. You could fix this using spaces and tabs in conjunction with the echo command, but using the printf command makes the task extremely easy.

First, you must determine the format sequence to use. Because the filenames and the column headings are both strings, you need the %s format sequence for formatting. Then you need to pick a maximum size for the filenames. If you pick 32 as the maximum size of your format sequence, the first column becomes %32s. Because you don't really care about the size of the second column, you can stick with %s for that column. With these changes your script becomes

```
#!/bin/sh

printf "%32s %s\n" "File Name" "File Type"

for i in *;
do
    printf "%32s " "$i"
    if [ -d "$i" ]; then
        echo "directory"
    elif [ -h "$i" ]; then
        echo "symbolic link"
    elif [ -f "$i" ]; then
        echo "file"
    else
```

```
        echo "unknown"
    fi;
done
```

The output now changes as follows:

```
 File Name File Type
       RCS directory
       dev directory
     humor directory
    images directory
index.html file
   install directory
      java directory
```

As you can see, the columns line up but the justification of the first column is incorrect. By adding the - character to the first format sequence, you get the correct sequence %-32s. The script now looks like:

```
#!/bin/sh

printf "%-32s %s\n" "File Name" "File Type"
                 left justify
for i in *;
do
    printf "%-32s " "$i"
    if [ -d "$i" ]; then
        echo "directory"
    elif [ -h "$i" ]; then
        echo "symbolic link"
    elif [ -f "$i" ]; then
        echo "file"
    else
        echo "unknown"
    fi;
done
```

The output is now formatted nicely:

```
File Name                       File Type
RCS                             directory
dev                             directory
humor                           directory
images                          directory
index.html                      file
install                         directory
java                            directory
```

13

One thing that you might have noticed about this script is that it uses both printf and echo. Because the printf statements used in this example do not explicitly specify the \n escape sequence, these commands do not produce a newline. To print the newline at the end of each output line, you use echo.

To format numbers, specify a number formatting sequence, such as %f, %e, or %g, instead of the string formatting sequence, %s. One of the questions at the end of this chapter familiarizes you with using number formats.

Output Redirection

In the process of developing a shell script, you often need to capture the output of a command and store it in a file. When the output is in a file, you can edit and modify it easily.

NEW TERM   In UNIX, the process of capturing the output of a command and storing it in a file is called *output redirection* because it redirects the output of a command into a file instead of the screen. To redirect the output of a command or a script to a file, instead of STDOUT, use the output redirection operator, >, as follows:

```
command > file
list > file
```

The first form redirects the output of the specified *command* to a specified *file*, whereas the second redirects the output of a specified *list* to a specified *file*. If *file* exists, its contents are overwritten; if *file* does not exist, it is created.

For example, the command

```
date > now
```

redirects the output of the date command into the file now. The output does not appear on the terminal, but it is placed into the file instead. If you view the file now, you find the output of the date command:

```
$ cat now
Sat Nov 14 11:14:01 PST 1998
```

You can also redirect the output of lists as follows:

```
{ date; uptime; who ; } > mylog
```

Here the output of the commands date, uptime, and who is redirected into the file mylog.

When you redirect output to a file using the output redirection operator, the shell overwrites the data in that file with the output of the command you specified. For example, the command

```
$ date > now
```

overwrites all the data in the file now with the output of the date command. For this reason, you should take extra care and make sure the file you specified does not contain important information.

Appending to a File

Overwriting a file simply by redirecting output to it is often undesirable. Fortunately, the shell provides a second form of output redirection with the >> operator, which appends output to a file. The basic syntax is

```
command >> file
list >> file
```

In these forms, output is appended to the end of the specified `file`, or the specified `file` is created if it does not exist. For example, you can prevent the loss of data from the file `mylog` each time a date is added, by using the following command:

```
{ date; uptime; who ; } >> mylog
```

If you view the contents of `mylog`, now you find that it contains the output of both lists:

```
11:15am  up 79 days, 14:48,  5 users,  load average: 0.00, 0.00, 0.00
ranga     tty1       Aug 26 14:12
ranga     ttyp2      Aug 26 14:13 (:0.0)
ranga     ttyp0      Oct 27 19:42 (:0.0)
amma      ttyp3      Oct 30 08:20 (localhost)
ranga     ttyp4      Nov 14 11:13 (rishi.bosland.u)
Sat Nov 14 11:15:54 PST 1998
 11:16am  up 79 days, 14:48,  5 users,  load average: 0.00, 0.00, 0.00
ranga     tty1       Aug 26 14:12
ranga     ttyp2      Aug 26 14:13 (:0.0)
ranga     ttyp0      Oct 27 19:42 (:0.0)
amma      ttyp3      Oct 30 08:20 (localhost)
ranga     ttyp4      Nov 14 11:13 (rishi.bosland.u)
```

Redirecting Output to a File and the Screen

In certain instances, you need to direct the output of a script to a file and onto the terminal. An example of this is shell scripts that are required to produce a log file of their activities. For interactive scripts, the log file cannot just contain the script's output redirected to a file.

To redirect output to a file and the screen, use the `tee` command. The basic syntax is as follows:

```
command ¦ tee file
```

Here `command` is the name of a command, such as `ls`, and `file` is the name of the file where you want the output written. For example, the command

```
$ date ¦ tee now
```

produces the following output on the terminal:

13

```
Sat Nov 14 19:50:16 PST 1998
```

The same output is written to the file now.

For shell scripts that require all their output to be logged, the following `if` statement is often used:

```
if [ "$LOGGING" != "true" ] ; then
    LOGGING="true" ; export LOGGING ;
    exec $0 | tee $LOGFILE
fi
```

[handwritten margin note: name of a command currently being executed / script]

Here you check to see whether a variable, `$LOGGING`, indicates that logging is turned on. If it is, the script continues; otherwise, the script reruns, and `tee` sends the output to a log file. To record all the output from a script, this `if` statement is usually one of the first commands in a script.

Input

Many UNIX programs are interactive and read input from the user. To use such programs in shell scripts, you need to provide them with input in a noninteractive manner. Also, scripts often need to ask the user for input in order to execute commands correctly.

To provide input to interactive programs or to read input from the user, you need to use input redirection. In this section, you will look at the following two methods in detail:

- Input redirection from files
- Reading input from a user
- Redirecting the output of one command to the input of another

Input Redirection

When you need to use an interactive command such as `mail` in a script, you need to provide the command with input. One method for doing this is to store the input of the command in a file and then tell the command to read input from that file. You accomplish this using input redirection.

The input can be redirected in a manner similar to output redirection. In general, input redirection is

```
command < file
```

Here the contents of `file` become the input for `command`. For example, the following would be an excellent use of redirection:

```
Mail ranga@soda.berkeley.edu < Final_Exam_Answers
```

Here the input to the `Mail` command, which becomes the body of the mail message, is the file `Final_Exam_Answers`. In this particular example, a professor might perform this function, and the file might contain the answers to a current final exam.

Here Documents

NEW TERM An additional use of input redirection is in the creation of *here documents*. A common use of here documents is in the generation of email messages within scripts and in the generation of files containing the values of all the variables in the script. Also, here documents store temporary information. Say you need to send a list of phone numbers or URLs to the printer. By using a here document, you can enter the information that you want to send to the printer into the here document and then send that here document to the printer. This is much simpler than using a temporary file, which needs to be created and then deleted.

The general form for a here document is

```
command << delimiter
document
delimiter
```

NEW TERM Here the shell interprets the << operator as an instruction to read input until it finds a line containing the specified `delimiter`. All the input lines up to the line containing the `delimiter` are then fed into the standard input of the `command`.

The `delimiter` tells the shell that the here document has completed. Without it, the shell continues to read input forever. The `delimiter` must be a single word that does not contain spaces or tabs.

For example, to print a quick list of URLs, you could use the following here document:

```
lpr << MYURLS
        http://www.csua.berkeley.edu/~ranga/
        http://www.cisco.com/
        http://www.marathon.org/story/
        http://www.gnu.org/
MYURLS
```

To strip the tabs in this example, you can give the << operator a - option.

You can also combine here documents with output redirection as follows:

```
command > file << delimiter
document
delimiter
```

If used in this form, the output of `command` is redirected to the specified `file`, and the input of `command` becomes the here document.

13

the contains URL's
the following

For example, you can use the following command to create a file with the short list of URLs given previously:

```
cat > urls << MYURLS
http://www.csua.berkeley.edu/~ranga/
     http://www.cisco.com/
     http://www.marathon.org/story/
     http://www.gnu.org/
MYURLS
```

Reading User Input

A common task in shell scripts is to prompt users for input and then read their responses. To do this, use the `read` command to set the value of a variable and then evaluate the value of the variable with a `case` statement.

The `read` command works as follows:

```
read name
```

It reads the entire line of user input until the user presses return and makes that line the value of the variable specified by `name`.

An example of this is

```
YN=yes
printf "Do you want to play a game [$YN]? "
read YN
: ${YN:=yes}
case $YN in
    [yY]¦[yY][eE][sS]) exec xblast ;;
    *) echo "Maybe later." ;;
esac
```

Here you prompt the user and provide a default response. Then you read and evaluate the user's answer using a `case` statement.

A common use of input redirection in conjunction with the `read` command is the reading of a file one line at a time using the `while` loop. The basic syntax is

```
while read LINE
do
: # manipulate file here
done < file
```

In the body of the `while` loop, you can manipulate each line of the specified `file`. A simple example of this is

```
while read LINE
do
    case $LINE in
```

```
   *root*) echo $LINE ;;
esac
done < /etc/passwd
```

Here only the lines that contain the string `root` in the file `/etc/passwd` are displayed. On my system, the output looks like:

```
root:x:0:1:Super-User:/:/sbin/sh
```

In Chapters 16, "Filtering Text Using Regular Expressions," 17, "Filtering Text with awk," and 18, "Miscellaneous Tools," I will show you how to use more powerful filters in place of the `case` statement used here.

Pipelines

Most commands in UNIX that are designed to work with files can also read input from STDIN. This enables you to use one program to filter the output of another. This is one of the most common tasks in shell scripting: having one program manipulate the output of another program.

You can redirect the output of one command to the input of another command using a *pipeline*, which connects several commands together with *pipes* as follows:

```
command1 ¦ command2 ¦ ...
```

The pipe character, ¦, connects the standard output of *command1* to the standard input of *command2*, and so on. The commands can be as simple or complex as are required.

Here are some examples of pipeline commands:

```
tail -f /var/adm/messages ¦ more
```

```
ps -ael ¦ grep "$UID" ¦ more
```

In the first example, the standard output of the `tail` command is piped into the standard input of the `more` command, which enables the output to be viewed one screen at a time.

In the second example, the standard output of `ps` is connected to the standard input of `grep`, and the standard output of `grep` is connected to the standard input of `more`, so that the output of `grep` can be viewed one screen at a time. For now, simply be aware of this technique of redirection. I show you how to use it to filter text in Chapters 16, 17, and 18.

13

> One important thing about pipelines is that each command is executed as a separate process, and the exit status of a pipeline is the exit status of the last command.
>
> It is vital to remember this fact when writing scripts that must do error handling.

File Descriptors

NEW TERM   When you issue any command, three files are opened and associated with that command. In the shell, each of these files is represented by a small integer called a file descriptor. A *file descriptor* is a mechanism by which you can associate a number with a filename and then use that number to read and write from the file. Sometimes file descriptors are called *file handles*.

The three files opened for each command along with their corresponding file descriptors are

- Standard Input (STDIN), 0
- Standard Output (STDOUT), 1
- Standard Error (STDERR), 2

The integer following each of these files is its file descriptor. Usually, these files are associated with the user's terminal, but they can be redirected into other files.

In the previous examples in this chapter, you have used input and output redirection using the default file descriptors. This section introduces the general form of input and output redirection.

First you examine associating files with a file descriptor.

Associating Files with a File Descriptor

By default, the shell provides you with three standard file descriptors for every command. With it, you can also associate any file with file descriptors using the exec command.

Associating a file with a file description is useful when you need to redirect output or input to a file many times but you don't want to repeat the filename several times.

To open a file for writing, use one of the following forms:

```
exec n>file
exec n>>file
```

Here *n* is an integer, and `file` is the name of the file you want to open for writing. The first form overwrites the specified `file` if it exists. The second form appends to the specified `file`. For example, the following command

```
$ exec 4>fd4.out
```

associates the file `fd4.out` with the file descriptor 4.

To open a file for reading, you use the following form:

```
exec n<file
```

Here *n* is an integer, and `file` is the name of the file you want to open for reading.

General Input/Output Redirection

You can perform general output redirection by combining a file descriptor and an output redirection operator. The general forms are

```
command n> file
command n>> file
```

Here `command` is the name of a command, such as `ls`, *n* is a file descriptor (integer), and `file` is the name of the file. The first form redirects the output of `command` to the specified `file`, whereas the second form appends the output of `command` to the specified `file`.

For example, you can write the standard output redirection forms in the general form as

```
command 1> file
command 1>> file
```

Here the 1 explicitly states that STDOUT is being redirected into the given file.

General input redirection is similar to general output redirection. It is performed as follows:

```
command n<file
```

Here `command` is the name of a command, such as `ls`, *n* is a file descriptor (integer), and `file` is the name of the file. For example, the standard input redirection forms can be written in the general form as

```
command 0<file
```

Redirecting STDOUT and STDERR to Separate Files

One of the most common uses of file descriptors is to redirect STDOUT and STDERR to separate files. The basic syntax is

```
command 1> file1 2> file2
```

13

Here the STDOUT of the specified *command* is redirected to *file1*, and the STDERR (error messages) is redirected to *file2*.

Often the STDOUT file descriptor, 1, is not written, so a shorter form of the basic syntax is

```
command > file1 2> file2
```

You can also use the append operator in place of either standard redirect operator:

```
command >> file1 2> file2
command > file1 2>> file2
command >> file1 2>> file2
```

The first form appends STDOUT to *file1* and redirects STDERR to *file2*. The second form redirects STDOUT to *file1* and appends STDERR to *file2*. The third form appends STDOUT to *file1* and appends STDERR to *file2*.

In the following example, I will illustrate using *form1* because you are interested in only the output of the command:

```
for FILE in $FILES
do
    ln -s $FILE ./docs >> /tmp/ln.log 2> /dev/null
done
```

Here the STDOUT of ln is appended to the file /tmp/ln.log, and the STDERR is redirected to the file /dev/null, in order to discard it.

> The file /dev/null is a special file available on all UNIX systems used to discard output. It is sometimes referred to as the *bit bucket*.
>
> If you redirect the output of a command into /dev/null, it is discarded. You see it used for this purpose often. For example, the command
>
> ```
> rm file > /dev/null
> ```
>
> discards the output of the rm command.
>
> If you use cat to display the contents of /dev/null to a *file*, the file's contents are erased:
>
> ```
> $ cat /dev/null > file
> ```
>
> After this command, the *file* still exists, but its size is zero.

Redirecting STDOUT and STDERR to the Same File

You looked at how to use file descriptors to redirect STDOUT and STDERR to different files, but sometimes you need to redirect both to the same file. In general, you do this by

```
command > file 2>&1
list > file 2>&1
```

Redirects stand error to where ever standard out is going

Here STDOUT (file description 1) and STDERR (file descriptor 2) are redirected into the specified `file`.

Here is a situation where it is necessary to redirect both the standard output and the standard error:

```
rm -rf /tmp/my_tmp_dir > /dev/null 2>&1 ; mkdir /tmp/my_tmp_dir
```

Here, you are not interested in the error message or the informational message printed by the `rm` command. You only want to remove the directory, thus its output or any error message it prints are redirected to `/dev/null`.

If you had one command that should append its standard error and standard output to a file, you use the following form:

```
command >> file 2>&1
list >> file 2>&1
```

An example of a command that might require this is

```
rdate -s ntp.nasa.gov >> /var/log/rdate.log 2>&1
```

Here you are using the `rdate` command to synchronize the time of the local machine to an Internet time server and you want to keep a log of all the messages.

Printing a Message to STDOUT   You can also use this form of output redirection to output error messages on STDERR. The basic syntax is

```
echo string 1>&2
printf format args 1>&2
```

redirect standard out as standard error

You might also see these commands with the STDOUT file descriptor, 1, omitted:

```
echo string >&2
printf format args >&2
```

As an example, say that you need to display an error message if a directory is given instead of a file. You can use the following `if` statement:

```
if [ ! -f $FILE ] ; then echo "ERROR: $FILE is not a file" >&2 ; fi
```

Redirecting Two File Descriptors

You can redirect STDOUT and STDERR to a single file by using the general form for redirecting the output of one file descriptor to another:

```
n>&m
```

Here *n* and *m* are file descriptors (integers). If you let *n*=2 and *m*=1, you see that STDERR

13

is redirected to STDOUT. By redirecting STDOUT to a file, you also redirect STDERR.

If *m* is a hyphen (-) instead of a number, the file corresponding to the file descriptor *n* is closed. When a file descriptor is closed, trying to read or write from it results in an error.

Reading Files, Another Look   One of the most common uses of this form of redirection is for reading files one line at a time. You already looked at using a while loop to perform this task:

```
while read LINE
do
: # manipulate file here
done < file
```

The main problem with this loop is that it is executed in a subshell, thus changes to the script environment, such as exporting variables and changing the current working directory, does not apply to the script after the while loop changes. As an example, consider the following script:

```
#!/bin/sh
if [ -f "$1" ] ; then
    i=0
    while read LINE
    do
        i=`echo "$i + 1" | bc`
    done < "$1"
    echo $i
fi
```

This script tries to count the number of lines in the file specified to it as an argument. Executing this script on the file

```
$ cat dirs.txt
/tmp
/usr/local
/opt/bin
/var
```

produces the following output:

```
0
```

Although you are incrementing the value of $i using the command

```
i=`echo "$i + 1" | bc`
```

when the while loop exits, the value of $i is not preserved. In this case, you need to change a variable's value inside the while loop and then use that value outside the loop. You can accomplish this by redirecting the STDIN prior to entering the loop and then restoring STDIN to the terminal after the while loop. The basic syntax is

```
exec n<&0 < file
while read LINE
do
: # manipulate file here
done
exec 0<&n n<&-          close file descriptor N
```

Here *n* is an integer greater than 2, and `file` is the name of the file you want to read. Usually *n* is chosen as a small number such as 3, 4, or 5.

As an example, you can construct a shell version of the `cat` command:

```
#!/bin/sh
if [ $# -ge 1 ] ; then            list of command line arguments
    for FILE in $@
        do          file
            exec 5<&0 < "$i"
            while read LINE ; do echo $LINE ; done
            exec 0<&5 5<&-          closes file
        done
fi
```

Summary

In this chapter, I formally introduced the concept of input and output. I covered the `echo` and `printf` commands that are used to produce messages from within shell scripts.

I also introduced output redirection, covering the methods of redirecting and appending the output of a command to a file. In addition, I discussed reading input for the first time. I also covered reading in files and reading input from users.

Finally, I introduced the concept of a file descriptor and showed several aspects of its use, including opening files for reading and writing, closing files, and redirecting the output of two file descriptors to one source.

In the subsequent chapters, I will expand on the material covered here, and you will see many more applications of both input and output redirection along with the use of file descriptors.

13

Questions

1. Complete the script using the appropriate `printf` commands to perform the specified numeric conversions. Assume that the input is always a number:

```sh
#!/bin/sh

if [ $# -lt 2 ] ; then
    echo "ERROR: Insufficient arguments." ;
    exit 1 ;
fi

case "$1" in
    -o) : # convert the number stored in "$2" into octal
        ;;
    -x) : # convert the number stored in "$2" into hexadecimal
        ;;
    -e) : # convert the number stored in "$2" into scientific
➥notation
        ;;
    *) echo "ERROR: Unknown conversion, $1!" ;;
esac
```

2. Rewrite the error messages in the previous script to redirect their output to STDERR instead of STDOUT.

Terms

File Descriptor An integer that is associated with a file. Enables you to read and write from a file using the integer instead of the file's name.

STDIN Standard Input. User input is read from STDIN. The file descriptor for STDIN is 0.

STDOUT Standard Output. The output of scripts is usually to STDOUT. The file descriptor for STDOUT is 1.

STDERR Standard Error. A special type of output used for error messages. The file descriptor for STDERR is 2.

Escape Sequence An escape sequence is special sequence of characters that represents another character.

Output Redirection In UNIX, the process of capturing the output of a command and storing it in a file is called *output redirection* because it redirects the output of a command into a file instead of the screen.

Input Redirection In UNIX the process of sending input to a command from a file is called input redirection.

HOUR 14

Functions

Shell functions provide a way of mapping a name to a list of commands. Shell functions are similar to subroutines, procedures, and functions in other programming languages.

Think of them as miniature shell scripts that enable a name to be associated with a set of commands. The main difference is that a new instance of the shell begins in order to run a shell script, whereas functions run in the current shell.

Creating and Using Functions

The formal definition of a shell function is as follows:

```
name () { list ; }
```

A function binds a *name* to the *list* of commands that composes the body of the function. The (and) characters are required at the function definition.

The following examples illustrate valid and invalid function definitions:

```
lsl() { ls -l ; }    # valid
lsl { ls -l ; }        # invalid
```

In this example, the first definition is valid but the second one is not because it omits the parentheses after the string ls1.

This example also demonstrates a common use of functions. Because the original shell, sh, did not have the `alias` keyword common to more recent shells, all aliases were defined in terms of shell functions. A frequently encountered example of this is the source command. The sh equivalent is the . command. Many converts from csh use the following function to simulate the source command:

```
source() { . "$@" ; }
```

As this example shows, shell functions have a separate set of arguments than the shell script to which they belong. You explore this feature later in the chapter.

An important feature of shell functions is that you can use them to replace binaries or shell built-ins of the same name.

An example of this is

```
cd () { chdir ${1:-$HOME} ; PS1="`pwd`$ " ; export PS1 ; }
```

This function replaces the cd command with a function which changes directories but also sets the primary shell prompt, $PS1, to include the current directory.

Invoking a Function

To invoke a function, only its name is required, thus typing

```
$ ls1
```

on the command line executes the ls1() function, but typing

```
$ ls1()
```

does not work because sh interprets this as a redefinition of the function by the name ls1. In most versions of the shell, typing ls1() results in a prompt similar to the following:

```
>
```

This is a prompt produced by the shell when it expects you to provide more input. Here the input it expects is the body of the function ls1.

Function Examples

In this section you will look at two examples of how functions are used to gain a better understanding of their role in shell scripting.

Listing Your Path

A simple task that is well-suited to a function is listing the current value of your PATH, with each directory listed on a single line. The basic shell code is

```
OLDIFS="$IFS"
IFS=:
for DIR in $PATH ; do echo $DIR ; done
IFS="$OLDIFS"
```

Here you save the value of IFS in the variable OLDIFS and then set IFS to :. Because IFS is the Internal Field Separator for the shell, you can use the for loop to cycle through the individual entries in PATH. When you are finished, restore the value of IFS.

> The shell uses the value of the variable IFS to split up a string into separate words. Normally it is set to the space and tab character, enabling the shell to figure out that the following string
>
> ```
> this is a string
> ```
>
> contains four words. The shell uses the value of IFS to determine how many options are supplied to a command, script, or shell function and how many items are specified to a for loop.
>
> In the previous example, you set the value of IFS to be the colon character. This means that the shell sees four words in the following string:
>
> ```
> this:is:a:string
> ```

To wrap this up in a function, insert the function name and the brackets as follows:

```
lspath() {
    OLDIFS="$IFS"
    IFS=:
    for DIR in $PATH ; do echo $DIR ; done
    IFS="$OLDIFS"
}
```

Now you can run the function as follows:

```
$ lspath
```

On my system the output is

```
/sbin
/bin
/usr/bin
/usr/sbin
/opt/bin
/usr/ucb
/usr/ccs/bin
/usr/openwin/bin
```

14

One of the main uses of this function is to check whether a particular directory is in your PATH. For example, to check whether /usr/dt/bin is in my path, I can do the following:

```
$ lspath ¦ grep "/usr/dt/bin"
```

Tailoring Your Path

At many companies and schools, a user's home directory is accessible from many machines running different versions of UNIX. A problem that I face every day is using my shell initialization script, .profile, on Linux, Solaris, FreeBSD, and HP-UX machines.

Although many issues arise involving cross-platform initialization scripts, one of the largest issues is getting your PATH variable set correctly. Because each different UNIX platform stores commands in different directories, your initialization script must be able to tailor the value of the variable PATH. This problem has four possible solutions:

- Maintain UNIX version-specific initialization files.
- Maintain UNIX version-specific sections in your initialization files.
- Use the same PATH on all versions of UNIX, by having it include all possible directories of interest on all versions. This solution relies on the fact that the shell ignores directories in the path that do not exist.
- Set a different PATH depending on the existence of individual directories.

The first two solutions are difficult to maintain. Each change or new UNIX version that you have to work with means that you have to create either a new initialization file or a new section on your initialization file. The complexity of your shell initialization process increases drastically with either of these approaches.

The third option is easy to implement and maintain, but it results in a PATH that is extremely long and hard to restructure. If you have more than one or two machines, PATH can grow to contain dozens of entries.

The fourth option is the easiest to maintain and extend, so how do you implement it?

The simplest way is to have a for loop that checks each directory and includes it if it exists:

```
PATH=
for DIR in /bin /sbin /usr/bin /usr/sbin /usr/ccs/bin /usr/ucb ;
do
    if [ -d "$DIR" ] ; PATH="$PATH:$DIR" ; fi
done
export PATH
```

At this point you might wonder why I am discussing this problem in this chapter and not in a previous chapter. The reason is that the complete problem is more than simply tailoring PATH on a per-UNIX-version basis. The complete problem requires you to tailor PATH for both interactive shells and for different user IDs.

You can solve these problems by including several case statements with different for loops in them, or you can write one function and reuse it. Because this chapter covers functions, I will show you how to do the latter.

The function that you need is quite simple. Rewrite the for loop to use the functions' arguments rather than a list of directories:

```
SetPath() {
    for _DIR in "$@"
    do
        if [ -d "$_DIR" ] ; then PATH="$PATH":"$_DIR" ; fi
    done
    export PATH
    unset _DIR
}
```

> → use for local variables

This function has three important points:

- **This function exports the PATH variable before it finishes.** This is required to ensure that the child process started by the shell can access the value of the variable.

- **This function unsets its internal variable _DIR.** It is a good habit to unset all variables that should not be exported. In some languages, this is not an issue because local variables disappear after execution leaves the scope of the function. In other languages, variables can be marked for local scope only, but in shell all variables are of global scope. This means that the programmer must take care in managing variables.

- **The local variable, _DIR, starts with the underscore _ character.** You do this to avoid name conflicts with variables set by other functions. It is not required, but it is good practice to name your local function variables differently than global variables.

There is only one additional thing to add to this function, and that is to check to see whether PATH is set. Without this check, you can potentially end up with a PATH set to

```
PATH=:/usr/bin:/usr/sbin:/usr/local/bin
```

The problem here is that the first entry in the variable PATH appears to be a null string. Some versions of the shell cannot deal with this entry, so you need to prevent this from happening.

14

You can do this check using variable substitution. The complete function is

```
SetPath() {
    PATH=${PATH:="/sbin:/bin"};
    for _DIR in "$@"
    do
        if [ -d "$DIR" ] ; then PATH="$PATH":"$DIR" ; fi
    done
    export PATH
    unset _DIR
}
```

Here you set PATH to /sbin:/bin if it is unset. You can invoke this function as follows:

```
SetPath /sbin /usr/sbin /bin /usr/bin /usr/ccs/bin
```

It checks to see whether each of its arguments is a directory, and if a directory exists, it is added to PATH.

Sharing Data Between Functions, an Example

The functions seen thus far operate independently of one another, but in most shell scripts functions either depend on or share data with other functions.

In this section you will look at an example where three functions work together and share data.

Moving Around the File System

The C shell, csh, provides three commands for quickly moving around in the UNIX file system:

- popd
- pushd
- dirs

These commands maintain a stack of directories internally and enable the user to add and remove directories from the stack and list the contents of the stack.

For those readers who are not familiar with the programming concept of a *stack*, you can think of it as a stack of plates: you can add or remove a plate only at the top of the stack. You can access only the top plate, not any of the middle plates in the stack. A stack in programming terms is similar. You can add or remove an item only at the top of the stack.

In csh, the stack is maintained within the shell, but in your shell function–based implementation you have to maintain the stack as an exported environment variable so that all three functions have access to it.

Use the variable _DIR_STACK to store the directory stack. Each entry in the stack is separated by the : character similar to the PATH variable. By using this character rather than a space or tab, you increase the flexibility of the directory names that you can handle.

Implementing dirs

Now you'll look at the simplest of the three functions, the dirs() function, which lists the directory stack:

```
dirs() {

    # save IFS, then set it to : to access the
    # the items in _DIR_STACK individually.

    OLDIFS="$IFS"
    IFS=:

    # print each directory followed by a space

    for i in $_DIR_STACK
    do
        echo "$i \c"
    done

    # add a new line after all entries in _DIR_STACK
    # have been printed

    echo

    # restore IFS

    IFS="$OLDIFS"
}
```

[handwritten annotation: internal field separator]

Here you use the same trick as you used in the lspath() function: save IFS and then set it to :, enabling you to list each of the items individually. The final echo is required to add a new line after all the entries are printed. Finally you restore IFS.

Implementing pushd

The pushd function is slightly more complicated than the dirs function. It needs to change to a requested directory and then add that directory to the top of the stack.

Your implementation is as follows:

14

```
pushd() {

        # set the requested directory, $REQ, to the first argument
        # If no argument is given, set REQ to .

        REQ="$1";
        if [ -z "$REQ" ] ; then REQ=. ; fi

        # if $REQ is a directory, cd to the directory
        # if the cd is successful update $_DIR_STACK
        # otherwise issue the appropriate error messages

        if [ -d "$REQ" ] ; then
            cd "$REQ" > /dev/null 2>&1
            if [ $? -eq 0 ] ; then
                _DIR_STACK="`pwd`:$_DIR_STACK" ; export _DIR_STACK ;
                dirs
            else
                echo "ERROR: Cannot change to directory $REQ." >&2
            fi
        else
            echo "ERROR: $REQ is not a directory." >&2
        fi

        unset REQ

}
```

(handwritten margin notes: "Test it string to empty"; "Test it directory"; "numeric exit status of last command"; "if [-d "$REQ"] ; then cd "$REQ"" pointer; "Standard error & O/P going to dev/null"; "Standard error")

First check to see whether an argument was given by setting REQ to the value of $1. If no argument was given, assume that the user means the current directory.

Then check to see whether the requested directory is really a directory. If it is, change to that directory and then update the directory stack with the full path of the new directory. You cannot use the value in $REQ because it could be a relative path.

Finally print the contents of the stack by calling the dirs function. By doing this, this function does not have to know how to print the stack. You have to know that dirs prints the stack.

This enables you to change the implementation of a function, such as dirs, without affecting the other functions. The one thing to keep in mind is that if you change the arguments that a function, such as dirs, expects to receive, you must change all the other functions that use it. Otherwise, you might encounter strange errors and bugs.

The three important points here are

- Setting a default value if an expected argument is not given.
- Using other functions to perform your tasks.

- Producing error messages when something goes wrong. If your script does not tell users what went wrong, they will be extremely confused and might not use your script again.

Implementing popd

The popd() function is far more complicated than the other two. First look at the operations that it performs:

1. Removes the first entry from the directory stack variable
2. Updates the directory stack to reflect the removal
3. Changes to the directory indicated by the entry that was removed from the stack
4. Displays the full path of the current directory

In order to make the first and second operations easy, implement a helper function for popd() called _popd_helper(). This function performs all the work; popd() is simply a wrapper around it. Frequently, you need to write functions in this manner: one function that simplifies the interface and one that performs the work.

The Helper Function

Look at _popd_helper first to see how the directory stack is manipulated:

```
_popd_helper() {

    # set the directory to pop to the first argument, if
    # this directory is empty, issue an error and return 1
    # otherwise get rid of POPD from the arguments

    POPD="$1"
    if [ -z "$POPD" ] ; then
        echo "ERROR: The directory stack is empty." >&2
        return 1
    fi
    shift          discards $1 r shifts all possible parameters up one to take its place

    # if any more arguments remain, reinitalize the directory
    # stack, and then update it with the remaining items,
    # otherwise set the directory stack to null

    if [ -n "$1" ] ; then
        _DIR_STACK="$1" ;
        shift ;
        for i in $@ ; do _DIR_STACK="$_DIR_STACK:$i" ; done
    else
        _DIR_STACK=
    fi
```

14

```
        # if POPD is a directory cd to it, otherwise issue
        # an error message

        if [ -d "$POPD" ] ; then
            cd "$POPD" > /dev/null 2>&1
            if [ $? -ne 0 ] ; then
                echo "ERROR: Could not cd to $POPD." >&2
            fi
            pwd
        else
            echo "ERROR: $POPD is not a directory." >&2
        fi

        export _DIR_STACK
        unset POPD
}
```

This function expects the directory stack to be given to it as arguments, so the first thing that it checks is whether $1, the first argument, has any value. Do this by setting the variable POPD equal to $1 and then checking the contents of POPD.

If the directory stack is empty, issue an error message; otherwise, shorten the stack by using shift. At this point, you have taken care of the first operation.

Now, you have to check to see whether the directory stack is empty. Because the individual items in the stack are arguments to this function, you need to check whether $1, the new first argument, has any content. If it does, reinitialize the directory stack with this value and proceed to add all the remaining values back onto the stack. At this point, you have taken care of the second operation.

The last two operations are fairly trivial, and the last if statement takes care of them.

The Wrapper Function

Now that you know that the helper function expects all the directories on the stack to be given to it as arguments, you can write the wrapper function that translates the value of _DIR_STACK into separate arguments.

This process is fairly easy, thanks to the IFS trick. The popd() function is the following:

```
popd() {
    OLDIFS="$IFS"
    IFS=:
    _popd_helper $_DIR_STACK
    IFS="$OLDIFS"
}
```

Conclusion

In this chapter you looked at creating and calling functions. Some of the major topics that you covered are

- Creating a function
- Using functions to replace built-in commands
- Using IFS to simplify parsing
- Using arguments with functions
- Sharing data between functions
- Calling a function from within another function

Part III introduces the concept of function libraries and presents a set of functions that you can use in your scripts.

Questions

1. Write a function to make a directory (and all its parents) change to that directory and then print the full path of that directory. Please include error checking at all levels. Make sure that all error messages are generated by your script, not the commands that you execute.

2. Chapter 13, "Input/Output," introduced the concept of prompting the user from a shell script. Write a function that can be used to prompt the user for a response. This function should take a single argument that is the prompt, and it should place the user's response in the variable RESPONSE. Please include error checking at all levels.

14

HOUR 15

Text Filters

Shell scripts are often called on to manipulate and reformat the output from commands that they execute. Sometimes this task is as simple as displaying only part of the output by filtering out certain lines. In most instances, the processing required is much more sophisticated.

In this chapter, you will look at several commands that are used heavily as text filters in shell scripts. These commands include

- head
- tail
- grep
- sort
- uniq
- tr

I will also show you how to combine these commands to filter text in extremely powerful ways.

The head and tail Commands

In Chapter 3, "Working with Files," you looked at viewing the contents of a file using the cat command. This command enables you to view an entire file, but often you need more control over lines that are displayed. The head and tail commands provide some of this control.

The head Command

The basic syntax for the head command is

```
head [-n lines] files
```

Here *files* is the list of the files you want the head command to process. Without the -n *lines* option, the head command shows the first 10 lines of its standard input. This option shows the specified number of *lines* instead.

Although this command is useful for viewing the tops of large README files, its real power happens in daily applications. Consider the following problem. I need to generate a list of the five most recently accessed files in my public HTML files directory. What is the easiest solution?

It's easy to devise a solution by breaking the problem down. First, I generate a list of my public HTML files using the following command:

```
$ ls -1 /home/ranga/public_html
```

In my case, this generates the following list of files and directories:

```
RCS
cgi-bin
downloads
humor
images
index.html
misc
projects
school
```

Next, I need to sort the list by the date of the last access. I can do this by specifying the -ut (sort by last accessed time) option to the ls command:

```
$ ls -1ut /home/ranga/public_html
```

The output now changes as follows:

```
RCS
humor
misc
```

```
downloads
images
resume
projects
school
cgi-bin
index.html
```

To retrieve a list of the five most recently accessed files, I can pipe the output of the `ls` command into a `head` command:

```
ls -1ut /home/ranga/public_html ¦ head -5
```

This produces the following list:

```
index.html
RCS
humor
misc
downloads
```

The `tail` Command

The basic syntax for the `tail` command is similar to that of the `head` command:

```
tail [-n lines] files
```

Here *files* is the list of the files the `tail` command should process. Without the `-n` *lines* option, the `tail` command shows the last 10 lines of its standard input. With this option it shows the specified number of *lines* instead.

To illustrate the use of the `tail` command, consider the problem of generating a list of the five oldest mail spools on my system.

I can start with `ls -1` command again, but this time I'll use the `-t` (sort by last modified time) option instead:

```
$ ls -1t /var/spool/mail
```

To get the bottom five, I'll use `tail` instead of `head`:

```
$ ls -1t /var/spool/mail ¦ tail -5
```

On my system the following list is generated:

```
anna
root
amma
vathsa
ranga
```

In this list, the files are listed from newest to oldest. To reverse the order, I can also specify the `-r` option to the `ls` command:

```
ls -1rt /var/spool/mail ¦ tail -5
```

On my system, I get this list:

```
ranga
vathsa
amma
root
anna
```

The `follow` Option

An extremely useful feature of the `tail` command is the `-f` (*f* as in *follow*) option:

```
tail -f file
```

Specifying the `-f` option enables you to examine the specified *file* while programs are writing to it.

Often I have to look at the log files generated by programs that I am debugging, but I don't want to wait for the program to finish, so I can start the program and then use `tail -f` for the log file.

Some Web administrators use a command such as the following to watch the HTTP requests made for their system:

```
$ tail -f /var/log/httpd/access_log
```

Using grep

The `grep` command lets you locate the lines in a file that contain a particular word or a phrase. The word *grep* stands for *globally regular expression print*. The command is derived from a feature of the original UNIX text editor, `ed`. To find a word in `ed`, the following command was used:

```
g/word/p
```

Here *word* is a regular expression. For those readers who are not familiar with regular expressions, Chapter 16, "Filtering Text Using Regular Expressions," discusses them in detail.

This particular `ed` command was used widely in shell scripts, thus it was factored into its own command called `grep`. In this section, you will look at the `grep` command and some of its most commonly used options.

Looking for Words

The basic syntax of the grep command is

`grep word file`

15

Here *file* is the name of a file in which you want to search for *word*. The grep command displays every line in *file* that contains *word*. When you specify more than one file, grep precedes each of the output lines with the name of the file that contains that line.

As an example, the following command locates all the occurrences of the word pipe in file ch15.doc (this chapter):

```
$ grep pipe ch15.doc
I've broken the command into two lines, with the pipe character
➥as the
the right thing and use the next line as the command to pipe to. It's
The first few lines look like (ten actually, I piped the output to
```

If I specify more than one file the output changes as follows:

```
$ grep pipe ch15.doc ch15-01.doc
ch15.doc:I've broken the command into two lines, with the pipe
➥character as the
ch15.doc:the right thing and use the next line as the command to
➥pipe to. It's
ch15.doc:The first few lines look like (ten actually, I piped the
➥output to
ch15-01.doc:I've broken the command into two lines, with the pipe
➥character as the
ch15-01.doc:the right thing and use the next line as the command to
➥pipe to.  It's
ch15-01.doc:The first few lines look like (ten actually, I piped
➥the output to
```

As you can see, the name of the file precedes each line that contains the word *pipe*.

If grep cannot find a line in any of the specified files that contains the requested *word*, no output is produced. For example,

`$ grep utilities ch16.doc`

produces no output because the word *utilities* does not appear in the file ch16.doc.

Case Independent Matching

One of the features of grep is that it matches the specified word according to the case that you specify. In grep, the word *Apple* is different than the word *apple*.

Sometimes you want to match words regardless of the case that you specify. To do this, use the -i option. For example, the command

```
$ grep unix ch16.doc
```

produces the output:

```
all unix users.  The GNU versions of these commands support all the
unix has several additional pieces of information associated with it.
unix counterparts, but implement a few nice options which makes their
unix files names, but they are, and handling them correctly is
```

On the other hand, the command

```
$ grep UNIX ch16.doc
```

produces different output:

```
GNU stands for GNU's not Unix and is the name of a Unix-compatible
Project utilities are the GNU implementation of familiar Unix
➥programs
```

By using the -i option, you get the sum of both of these commands:

```
$ grep -i unix ch16.doc
GNU stands for GNU's not Unix and is the name of a Unix-compatible
Project utilities are the GNU implementation of familiar Unix
➥programs
all unix users.  The GNU versions of these commands support all the
unix has several additional pieces of information associated with it.
unix counterparts, but implement a few nice options which makes their
unix files names, but they are, and handling them correctly is
```

Reading From STDIN

When no files are specified, grep looks for matches on the lines that are entered on STDIN. This makes it perfect for attaching to pipes.

For example, the following command looks for all users named ranga in the output of the who command:

```
$ who ¦ grep ranga
ranga      tty1      Aug 26 14:12
ranga      ttyp2     Nov 23 14:15 (rishi.bosland.u)
```

The -v Option

Most of the time you use grep to search through a file looking for a particular *word*, but sometimes you want to acquire a list of all the lines that do not match a particular *word*.

Using grep, this is simple—specify the -v option. For example, the following command produces a list of all the lines in /etc/passwd that do not contain the word *home*:

```
$ grep -v home /etc/passwd
```

15

On my system, the output looks like the following:

```
root:*:0:3::/:/sbin/sh
daemon:*:1:5::/:/sbin/sh
bin:*:2:2::/usr/bin:/sbin/sh
sys:*:3:3::/:
adm:*:4:4::/var/adm:/sbin/sh
uucp:*:5:3::/var/spool/uucppublic:/usr/lbin/uucp/uucico
lp:*:9:7::/var/spool/lp:/sbin/sh
nobody:*:-2:-2::/:
```

Active processes

One common use of the -v option is to parse the output of the ps command. For example, if I were looking for all instances of bash that were running on a system, I could use the following command:

```
$ /bin/ps -ef ¦ grep bash
```

Sometimes the output looks like the following:

```
ranga  3277  3276  2 13:41:45 pts/t0    0:02 -bash
ranga  3463  3277  4 18:38:26 pts/t0    0:00 grep bash
```

The second process in this list is the grep that I just ran. Because it is not really an instance of bash, I can get rid of it as follows:

```
$ /bin/ps -ef ¦ grep bash ¦ grep -v grep
```

This removes the extraneous output:

```
ranga  3277  3276  0 13:41:45 pts/t0    0:02 -bash
```

Line Numbers

As grep looks through a file for a given *word*, it keeps track of the line numbers that it has examined. You can have grep list the line numbers along with the matching lines by specifying the -n option. With this option the output format is

```
file:line number:line
```

Here *file* is the name of the file in which the match occurs, *line number* is the line number in the file on which the matching line occurs, and *line* is the complete line that contains the specified word. For example, the command

```
$ grep -n pipe ch15.doc ch15-01.doc
```

produces the following output:

```
ch15.doc:969:I've broken the command into two lines, with the pipe
➥character as the
ch15.doc:971:the right thing and use the next line as the command
➥to pipe to.  It's
ch15.doc:1014:The first few lines look like (ten actually, I piped
```

```
➥the output to
ch15-01.doc:964:I've broken the command into two lines, with the
➥pipe character as the
ch15-01.doc:966:the right thing and use the next line as the command
➥to pipe to.  It's
ch15-01.doc:1009:The first few lines look like (ten actually, I
➥piped the output to
```

As you can see, the lines might be the same in both files, but the line numbers are different.

Listing Filenames Only

Sometimes you don't really care about the actual lines in a file that match a particular word. You want a list of all the files that contain that word.

For example, the following command looks for the word *delete* in all the files in my projects directory:

```
$ grep delete /home/ranga/docs/projects
```

In my case, it produces the following output:

```
pqops.c:/* Function to delete a node from the heap. Adapted from
➥Introduction
pqops.c:void heap_delete(binary_heap *a,int i) {
pqops.c:  node deleted;
pqops.c:  /* return with an error if the input is invalid, ie trying
➥to delete
pqops.c:   sprintf(messages,"heap_delete(): %d, no such element.",i);
pqops.c:  /* switch the item to be deleted with the last item, and
➥then
pqops.c:  deleted = a->elements[i];
pqops.c:  /* (compare_priority(a->elements[i],deleted)) ? heap_
➥up(a,i) : heap_down(a,i); */
pqops.h:extern void        heap_delete(binary_heap *a,int i);
scheduler.c:    /* if the requested id is in the heap, delete it */
scheduler.c:    heap_delete(&my_heap,node_num);
```

As you look at the output, you see that only three files—pqops.c, pqops.h, and scheduler.c—contain the word *delete*.

Here you had to generate a list of matching lines and then manually look at the filenames in which those lines were contained. By using the -l option of the grep command, you reach this conclusion much faster. For example, the following command

```
$ grep -l delete *
pqops.c
pqops.h
scheduler.c
```

produces the list you wanted.

Counting Words

15

Counting words is an essential capability in shell scripts. There are many ways to do it, with the easiest being the wc command. Unfortunately, it displays only the number of characters, words, or lines.

What about when you need to count the number of occurrences of *word* in a file? The wc command falls short. In this section, you will solve this problem using the following commands:

- tr
- sort
- uniq

The tr command (*tr* for *transliterate*) changes all the characters in one set into characters in a second set. Sometimes it deletes sets of characters.

The sort command sorts the lines in an input file. If you don't specify an input file, it sorts the lines given on STDIN.

The uniq command (*uniq* for *unique*) prints all the unique lines in a file. If a line occurs multiple times, only one copy of the line is printed out. It can also list the number of times a particular line was duplicated.

I will use the text of this chapter, ch15.doc, as the input file for this example.

The tr Command

First, you need to eliminate all the punctuation and delimiters in the input file because the word end. and the word end are the same. You accomplish this task using the tr command. Its basic syntax is

```
tr 'set1' 'set2'
```
Replaces characters in set 1 with set 2

Here tr takes all the characters in *set1* and transliterates them to the characters in *set2*. Usually, the characters themselves are used, but the standard C language escape sequences also work.

To accomplish my first task, I used the following command:

```
$ tr '!?":;\[\]{}(),.' ' ' < /home/ranga/docs/ch15.doc
```
ESCAPES

all special character here will change to space

Here I specified *set2* as the space character because words separated by the characters in *set1* need to remain separate after the punctuation is removed.

Notice that the characters [and] are given as \[and \]. As you will see later in this chapter, these two characters have a special meaning in tr and need to be escaped using the backslash character (\) in order to be handled correctly.

At this point most of the words are separated by spaces, but some of the words are separated by tabs and newlines. To get an accurate count, all the words should be separated by spaces, so you need to covert all tabs and newlines to spaces:

```
$ tr '!?":;\[\]{}(),.\t\n' ' ' < /home/ranga/docs/ch15.doc
```

The next step is to transliterate all capitalized versions of words to a lowercase version because the words *To* and *to*, *The* and *the*, and *Files* and *files* are really the same word. To do this, you tell tr to change all the capital characters 'A-Z' into lowercase characters 'a-z' as follows:

```
$ tr '!?":;\[\]{}(),.\t\n' ' ' < /home/ranga/docs/ch15.doc |
tr 'A-Z' 'a-z'
```

I broke the command into two lines, with the pipe character as the last character in the first line so that the shell does the right thing and uses the next line as the command to pipe to. This makes it easier to read and cut and paste, also.

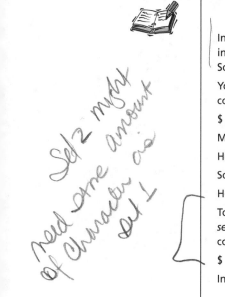

Differences between tr versions

In this example, you are using a single space for *set2*. Most versions of tr interpret this to mean transliterating all the characters in *set1* to a space. Some versions of tr do not do this.

You can determine whether your tr works in this manner using the test code:

```
$ echo "Hello, my dear!" | tr ',!' ' '
```

Most versions of tr produce the following output:

Hello my dear

Some versions produce the following output instead:

Hello my dear!

To obtain the desired behavior from these versions of tr, make sure that *set1* and *set2* have the same number of characters. In this case, *set2* needs to contain two spaces:

```
$ echo "Hello, my dear!" | tr ',!' '  '
```

In the case of the sample problem, *set2* would need to contain 15 spaces.

(handwritten margin note: Set2 might need some amount of character set 1)

Squeezing Out Spaces

At this point, several of the lines have multiple spaces separating the words. You need to reduce or squeeze these multiple spaces into single spaces to avoid problems with counting later in this example. To do this, you need to use the -s (*s* as in *squeeze*) option to the tr command. The basic syntax is

15

```
tr -s 'set1'
```

When `tr` encounters multiple consecutive occurrences of a character in *set1*, it replaces these with only one occurrence of the character. For example,

```
$ echo "feed me" | tr -s 'e'
```

produces the output

```
fed me
```

Here the two *e*'s in *feed* were reduced to a single *e*.

If you specify more than one character in *set1*, the replacement is character specific. For example:

```
$ echo "Shell Programming" | tr -s 'lm'
```

produces the following output:

```
Shel Programing
```

As you can see the two *l*'s in *Shell* were reduced to a single *l*. Also, the two *m*'s in *Programming* were reduced to a single *m*.

Now you can squeeze multiple spaces in the output into single spaces using the command:

```
$ tr '!?":;\[\]{}(),.\t\n' ' ' < /home/ranga/docs/ch15.doc |
tr 'A-Z' 'a-z' | tr -s ' '
```

The sort Command

To get a count of how many times each word is used, you need to sort the file using the `sort` command. In its simplest form, the `sort` command sorts each of its input lines. Thus you need to have only one word per line. You can do this changing all the spaces into new lines as follows:

```
$ tr '!?":;\[\]{}(),.\t\n' ' ' < /home/ranga/docs/ch15.doc |
tr 'A-Z' 'a-z' | tr -s ' ' | tr ' ' '\n'
```

Now you can sort the output, by adding the `sort` command:

```
$ tr '!?":;\[\]{}(),.\t\n' ' ' < /home/ranga/docs/ch15.doc |
tr 'A-Z' 'a-z' | tr -s ' ' | tr ' ' '\n' | sort
```

The uniq Command

At this point, you can eliminate all the repeated words by using the -u (*u* as in *unique*) option of the `sort` command. Because you need a count of the number of times a word is repeated, you should use the `uniq` command.

By default, the `uniq` command discards all but one of the repeated lines. For example, the commands

```
$ echo '
peach
peach
peach
apple
apple
orange
' > ./fruits.txt
$ uniq fruits.txt
```

produce the output

```
peach
apple
orange
```

As you can see, `uniq` discarded all but one of the repeated lines.

The `uniq` command produces a list of the `uniq` items in a file by comparing consecutive lines. To function properly, its input needs to be a sorted file. For example, if you change `fruits.txt` as follows

```
$ echo '
peach
peach
orange
apple
apple
peach
' > ./fruits.txt
$ uniq fruits.txt
```

the output is incorrect for your purposes:

```
peach
orange
apple
peach
```

Returning to the original problem, you need `uniq` to print not only a list of the unique words in this chapter but also the number of times a word occurs. You can do this by specifying the `-c` (*c* as in *count*) option to the `uniq` command:

```
$ tr '!?":;\[\]{}(),.\t\n' ' ' < /home/ranga/docs/ch15.doc ¦
tr 'A-Z' 'a-z' ¦ tr -s ' ' ¦ tr ' ' '\n' ¦ sort ¦ uniq -c
```

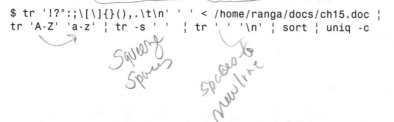

Squeeze
Spaces

Spaces to
new line

Sorting Numbers

15

At this point the output is sorted alphabetically. Although this output is useful, it is much easier to determine the most frequently used words if the list is sorted by the number of times a word occurs.

To obtain such a list, you need sort to sort by numeric value instead of string comparison. It would also be nice if the largest number was printed first. By default, sort prints the largest number last. To satisfy both of these requirements, you specify the -n (*n* as in *numeric*) and -r (*r* as in *reverse*) options to the sort command:

```
$ tr '!?":;\[\]{}(),.\t\n' ' ' < /home/ranga/docs/ch15.doc |
tr 'A-Z' 'a-z' | tr -s ' ' | tr ' ' '\n' | sort | uniq -c |
sort -rn
```

[handwritten: to produce desired list]
[handwritten: for uniq command]

By piping the output to head, you can get an idea of what the ten most repeated words are:

```
$ tr '!?":;\[\]{}(),.\t\n' ' ' < /home/ranga/docs/ch15.doc |
tr 'A-Z' 'a-z' | tr -s ' ' | tr ' ' '\n' | sort | uniq -c |
sort -rn | head
389 the
164 to
127 of
115 is
115 and
111 a
 80 files
 70 file
 69 in
 65 '
```

[handwritten: prints first 10 in file]

Sorting Numbers in a Different Column

In the preceding output, you used the sort -rn command to sort the output by numbers because the numbers occurred in the first column instead of the second column. If the numbers occurred in any other column, this would not be possible.

Suppose the output looked like the following:

```
$ cat switched.txt
files 80
file 70
is 115
and 115
a 111
in 69
' 65
the 389
to 164
of 127
```

Now you need to tell sort to sort on the second column, and you cannot simply use the -r and -n options. You need to use the -k (*k* as in *key*) option also.

The sort command constructs a key for each line in the file, and then it arranges these keys into sorted order. By default, the key spans the entire line. The -k option gives you the flexibility of telling sort where the key should begin and where it should end, in terms of columns.

The number of columns in a line is the number of individual words on that line. For example, the following line contains three columns:

```
files 80 100
```

The basic syntax of the -k option is

```
sort -k start,end files
```

Here *start* is the starting column for the key, and *end* is the ending column for the key. The first column is 1, the second column is 2, and so on.

For the switched.txt file, *start* and *end* are both 2 because there are only two columns and you want to sort on the second one. The command you use is

```
$ sort -rn -k 2,2 switched.txt
the 389
to 164
of 127
is 115
and 115
a 111
files 80
file 70
in 69
' 65
```

Because there are only two columns, you can omit the ending column as follows:

```
$ sort -rn -k 2 switched.txt
```

Using Character Classes with tr

Take a look at the output of the command:

```
$ tr '!?":;\[\]{}(),.\t\n' ' ' < /home/ranga/docs/ch15.doc ¦
tr 'A-Z' 'a-z' ¦ tr -s ' ' ¦ tr ' ' '\n' ¦ sort ¦ uniq -c ¦
sort -rn ¦ head
389 the
164 to
127 of
115 is
```

```
115 and
111 a
 80 files
 70 file
 69 in
 65 '
```

You might have noticed that the tenth most common word in this chapter is the single quote character. You might be wondering what's going on because I said you took care of the punctuation with the very first `tr` command.

Well, I lied (sort of). You took care of all the characters that would fit between quotes, and a single quote won't fit.

So why not backslash escape that sucker? Well, not all versions of the shell handle that properly.

So what's the solution?

The solution is to use the predefined character sets in `tr`. The `tr` command knows several character classes, and the punctuation class is one of them. Table 15.1 gives a complete list of the character class names.

TABLE 15.1   CHARACTER CLASSES UNDERSTOOD BY THE TR COMMAND

Class	Description
alnum	Letters and digits
alpha	Letters
blank	Horizontal whitespace
cntrl	Control characters
digit	Digits
graph	Printable characters, not including spaces
lower	Lowercase letters
print	Printable characters, including spaces
punct	Punctuation
space	Horizontal or vertical whitespace
upper	Uppercase letters
xdigit	Hexadecimal digits

The way to invoke `tr` with one of these character classes is

```
tr '[:classname:]' 'set2'
```

Here *classname* is the name of one of the classes given in Table 15.1, and *set2* is the set of characters you want the characters in *classname* to be transliterated to.

For example, to get rid of punctuation and spaces, you use the punct and space classes:

```
$ tr '[:punct:]' ' ' < /home/ranga/docs/ch15.doc ¦ tr
➥'[:space:]' ' ' ¦
tr 'A-Z' 'a-z' ¦ tr -s ' ' ¦ tr ' ' '\n' ¦ sort ¦ uniq -c ¦
sort -rn ¦ head
```

Here's some of the new output:

```
405 the
170 to
136 a
134 of
122 and
119 is
 80 files
 74 file
 72 in
 67 or
```

The numbers are different for some of the words because I ran the commands and wrote the chapter at the same time.

I could also have replaced 'A-Z' and 'a-z' with the upper and lower classes, but there is no real advantage to using the classes. In most cases the ranges are much more illustrative of your intentions.

Summary

In this chapter you looked at some of the commands that are heavily used for filtering text in scripts. These commands include:

- head
- tail
- grep
- sort
- uniq
- tr

I also covered how to combine these commands together to solve problems such as counting the number of times a word was repeated in a text file. In Chapter 16 I will introduce two more text filtering commands, awk and sed, that give you much more control over editing lines and printing specific columns of your output.

15

Questions

1. Given the following shell function

   ```
   lspids() { /bin/ps -ef ¦ grep "$1"¦ grep -v grep ; }
   ```

   make the necessary changes so that when the function is executed as follows

   ```
   $ lspid -h ssh
   ```

   the output looks like this:

   ```
   UID   PID PPID  C    STIME TTY       TIME COMMAND
   root  2121    1  0   Nov 16  ?       0:14 /opt/bin/sshd
   ```

   Also, when the function executes as

   ```
   $ lspid ssh
   ```

   the output looks like this:

   ```
   root  2121    1  0   Nov 16  ?              0:14 /opt/bin/sshd
   ```

   Here you are using ssh as the *word* specified to grep, but your function should be able to use any *word* as an argument.

   Also, validate that you have enough arguments before executing the ps command.

   If you are using a Linux or FreeBSD-based system, please use the following version of the function lspids as a starting point instead of the version given previously:

   ```
   lspids() { /bin/ps -auwx 2> /dev/null ¦ grep "$1"¦ grep -v
   ➥grep ; }
   ```

   (HINT: The header that you are using is the first line in the output from the /bin/ps -ef command.)

2. Take the function you wrote in question 1 and add a -s option that sorts the output of the ps command by process ID. The process IDs, or pids, do not have to be arranged from largest to smallest.

   If you are using a Linux or FreeBSD system, you need to sort on column 1. On other systems you need to sort on column 2.

HOUR **16**

Filtering Text Using Regular Expressions

NEW TERM
The most powerful text filtering tools in the UNIX environment are a pair of oddly named programs, awk and sed. They let shell programmers easily edit text files and filter the output of other commands using regular expressions. A *regular expression* is a string that can be used to describe several sequences of characters.

sed (which stands for *stream editor*) was created as an editor exclusively for executing scripts. As its name implies, sed is stream oriented, thus all the input you feed into it passes through and goes to STDOUT. It does not change the input file. In this chapter I will show you how to use sed in shell scripts.

I will cover awk programming in Chapter 17, "Filtering Text with awk," but I'll discuss some of the many similarities between awk and sed at the beginning of this chapter.

The Basics of awk and sed

There are many similarities between awk and sed:

- They have similar invocation syntax.
- They enable you to specify instructions that execute for every line in an input file.
- They use regular expressions for matching patterns.

For those readers who are not familiar with patterns and regular expressions, I will explain them shortly.

Invocation Syntax

The invocation syntax for awk and sed is as follows:

```
command 'script' filenames
```

Here command is either awk or sed, script is a list of commands understood by awk or sed, and filenames is a list of files that the command acts on.

The single quotes around script are required to prevent the shell from accidentally performing substitution. The actual contents of script differ greatly between awk and sed. The commands understood by awk and sed are covered in separate sections later in this chapter.

If filenames are not given, both awk and sed read input from STDIN. This enables them to be used as output filters on other commands.

Basic Operation

When an awk or sed command runs, it performs the following operations:

1. Reads a line from an input file
2. Makes a copy of this line
3. Executes the given script on this line
4. Repeats step 1 for the next line

These operations illustrate the main feature of awk and sed—they provide a method of acting on every record or line in a file using a single script. When every record has been read, the input file is closed. If the input file is the last file specified in filenames, the command exits.

Script Structure and Execution

The script specified to awk or sed consists of one or more lines of the following form:

```
/pattern/ action
```

Here `pattern` is a regular expression, and `action` is the action that either `awk` or `sed` should take when the `pattern` is encountered. Regular expressions will be covered shortly. The slash characters (`/`) that surround the `pattern` are required because they are used as delimiters.

When `awk` or `sed` is executing a script, it uses the following procedure on each record:

1. Sequentially searches each `pattern` until a match is found.
2. When a match is found, the corresponding `action` is performed on the input line.
3. When the `action` is completed, it goes to the next `pattern` and repeats step 1.
4. When all patterns have been exhausted, it reads in the next line.

Just before step 4 is performed, `sed` displays the modified record. In `awk` you must manually display the record.

The actions taken in `awk` and `sed` are quite different. In `sed`, the actions consist of commands that edit single letters, whereas in `awk` the action is usually a set of programming statements.

Regular Expressions

The basic building blocks of a regular expression are

- Ordinary characters
- Metacharacters

Ordinary characters are

- Uppercase and lowercase letters such as *A* or *b*
- Numerals such as *1* or *2*
- Characters such as a space or an underscore

NEW TERM *Metacharacters* are characters that have a special meaning inside a regular expression: They are expanded to match ordinary characters. By using metacharacters, you need not explicitly specify all the different combinations of ordinary characters that you want to match. The basic set of metacharacters understood by both `sed` and `awk` is given in Table 16.1.

NEW TERM Frequently regular expressions are referred to as *patterns*. In Chapter 8, "Substitution," I described the shell feature know as filename substitution, which uses a subset of regular expressions to produce lists of files.

16

In the context of filename substitution, I referred to metacharacters as *wild-cards*. You might see these two terms used interchangeably in books and reference materials.

TABLE 16.1 METACHARACTERS USED IN REGULAR EXPRESSIONS

Character	Description
.	Matches any single character except a newline.
*	Matches zero or more occurrences of the character immediately preceding it.
[chars]	Matches any one of the characters given in chars, where chars is a sequence of characters. You can use the - character to indicate a range of characters. If the ^ character is the first character in chars, one occurrence of any character that is not specified by chars is matched.
^	Matches the beginning of a line.
$	Matches the end of a line.
\	Treats the character that immediately follows the \ literally. This is used to specify patterns that contain one of the preceding wildcards.

Regular Expression Examples

As I stated before, a regular expression is a string that can represent many sequences of characters. Thus the simplest regular expression is one that exactly represents the sequence of characters that you need to match. For example, the following expression

```
/peach/
```

matches the string peach exactly. If this expression was used in awk or sed, any line that contains the string peach is selected by this expression. This includes lines such as the following:

```
We have a peach tree in the backyard
I prefer peaches to plums
```

Matching Characters   Look at a few more expressions to demonstrate the use of the metacharacters. For example, the following pattern

```
/a.c/
```

matches lines that contain strings such as a+c, a-c, abc, match, and a3c, whereas the pattern

`/a*c/`

matches the same strings along with strings such as ace, yacc, and arctic. It also matches the following line:

`close the window`

Notice that there is no letter *a* in this sentence. The * metacharacter matches zero or more occurrences of the character immediately preceding it. In this case it matched zero occurrences of the letter *a*.

Another important thing to note about the * is that it tries to make the longest possible match. For example, consider the pattern

`/a*a/`

and the following line

`able was I, ere I saw elba`

Here you have asked to match lines that contain a string that starts with the letter *a* and ends with the letter *a*. In the sample line, there are several possibilities:

```
able wa
able was I, ere I sa
able was I, ere I saw elba
```

Because you used the * metacharacter, the last possibility is selected.

You can combine the . and the * metacharacters to obtain behavior equivalent to the * filename expansion wildcard. For example, the following expression

`/ch.*doc/`

matches the strings ch01.doc, ch02.doc, and chdoc. The shell's * wildcard matches files by the same names.

Specifying Sets of Characters

One of the major limitations with the . operator is that it does not enable you to specify which characters you want to match. It matches all characters. To specify a particular set of characters in a regular expression, use the bracket characters, ([and]), as follows:

`/[chars]/`

Here a single character in the set given by chars is matched. The use of sets in regular expression is almost identical to the shell's use of sets in filename substitution.

Here is an example of using sets. The following expression matches the string *The* and *the*:

```
/[tT]he/
```

Table 16.2 shows some frequently used sets of characters.

TABLE 16.2 COMMON CHARS SETS

Set	Description
[a-z]	Matches a single lowercase letter
[A-Z]	Matches a single uppercase letter
[a-zA-Z]	Matches a single letter
[0-9]	Matches a single number
[a-zA-Z0-9]	Matches a single letter or number

Sometimes is it hard to determine the exact set of characters that you need to match. Say that you needed to match every character except the letter *T*. In this case, constructing a set of characters that includes every character except the letter *T* is error prone. You might forget a space or a punctuation character while trying to construct the set.

Fortunately, you can specify a set that is the negation of the set that matches *T* as follows:

```
[^T]
```

Here the ^ character precedes the letter T. When the ^ character is the first character in the set, any character not given in the set is matched. This is called *reversing* or *negating* a set. Any set, including those given in Table 16.2, can be reversed or negated if you give ^ as the first character. For example, the following pattern

```
/ch[^0-9]/
```

matches the beginnings of the strings chapter and chocolate, but not the strings ch01 or ch02.

You can combine the sets with the * character to extend their functionality. For example, the following expression

```
/ch0[0-9]*doc/
```

matches the strings ch01.doc and ch02.doc but not the strings chdoc or changedoc.

Anchoring Patterns Now say that you are looking for lines that start with the word *the*, such as the following:

```
the plains were rich with crops
```

If you use the following pattern

```
/the/
```

it matches the line given previously along with the following lines:

```
there were many orchards of fruit tree
in the dark it was like summer lightning
```

The two main problems are

- Only the word *the* should be matched. Lines starting with words such as *there* should not be matched.

- The string *the* should be at the beginning of the line.

To solve the first problem, add a space as follows:

```
/the /
```

NEW TERM   To solve the second problem you need the ^ metacharacter, which matches the beginning of a line. In a regular expression, it *anchors* the expression to the beginning of the line. By *anchor*, I mean that an expression matches a line only if that line starts with this expression. Normally, any line that contains an expression is matched.

By adding the ^ metacharacter as follows

```
/^the /
```

you cause this expression to match only those lines that start with the word *the*. Some examples are

```
the forest of oak trees on the mountain
the hillside where the chestnut forest grew
```

You can also anchor expressions to the end of the line using the $ metacharacter. For example, the following expression

```
/friend$/
```

matches this line:

```
I have been and always will be your friend
```

But it doesn't match this line:

```
What are friends for
```

You can combine the ^ and the $ metacharacters along with sets of characters and the other metacharacters to match lines according to an expression. For example, the following expression

```
/^Chapter [1-9]*[0-9]$/
```

matches lines such as

```
Chapter 1
Chapter 20
```

but it does not match lines such as

```
Chapter 00 Introduction
Chapter 101
```

Because the ^ and $ metacharacters anchor the expression to the beginning and end of a line, you match empty lines as follows:

```
/^$/
```

Escaping Metacharacters

Many times you need to match strings such as

```
Peaches $0.89/lbs
Oil $15.10/barrel
```

This string contains three characters with special meanings in regular expressions:

- The dollar character, $
- The decimal point character, .
- The per character, /

If you use an ordinary expression such as the following

```
/$[0-9].[0-9][0-9]/[a-zA-Z]*/
```

you are unable to match any string because the expression is garbled. The two main problems are:

- The first character in this expression is the $ character. Because the $ matches the end of the line, this expression tries to look for characters after the end of the line. This is an impossible pattern to match.
- There are three slashes. The first two slashes are used as the delimiters for the pattern. The [a-zA-Z]*/ that occurs after this pattern confuses awk and sed.

The third problem is related to the .. Because this metacharacter matches a single occurrence of any one character, it can match the following strings in addition to the strings you want:

```
0x00
12345
```

NEW TERM You can solve all these problems using the backslash metacharacter (\). The character immediately following the backslash is always treated literally. When an ordinary character is preceded by a backslash, it has no effect. For example, \a and a are both treated as a lowercase *a*. When the backslash precedes a metacharacter, the special meaning of that metacharacter is "deactivated."

NEW TERM The process of using the backslash to deactivate a metacharacter is called *escaping* it. For example,

```
$
```

matches the end of a line, but

```
\$
```

matches the dollar sign ($) literally.

By using escaping, you can use the following expression to solve your problems:

```
/\$[0-9]*\.[0-9][0-9]\/[a-zA-Z]*/
```

If you need to match the \ literally, you can match it by escaping itself, \\.

Sometimes the process of escaping a metacharacter with the backslash is called *backslash escaping*.

Useful Regular Expressions Table 16.3 provides some useful regular expressions.

TABLE 16.3 SOME USEFUL REGULAR EXPRESSIONS

String Type	Expression
Blank lines	/^$/
An entire line	/^.*$/
One or more spaces	/ */
HTML (or XML) Tags	/<[^>][^>]*>/
Valid URLs	/[a-zA-Z][a-zA-Z]*:\/\/[a-zA-Z0-9][a-zA-Z0-9\.]*.*/
Formatted dollar amounts	/\$[0-9]*\.[0-9][0-9]/

Using sed

sed is a stream editor that you can use as a filter. It reads each line of input and then performs a set of requested actions. The basic syntax of a sed command is

```
sed 'script' files
```

Here files is a list of one or more files, and script is one or more commands of the form:

```
/pattern/ action
```

Here, pattern is a regular expression, and action is one of the commands given in Table 16.4. If pattern is omitted, action is performed for every line.

TABLE 16.4 SOME OF THE ACTIONS AVAILABLE IN sed

Action	Description
p	Prints the line
d	Deletes the line
s/pattern1/pattern2/	Substitutes the first occurrence of pattern1 with pattern2.

Printing Lines

Start with the simplest feature available in sed—printing a line that matches a pattern.

Consider the price list for a small fruit market. The list is stored in the file fruit_prices.txt:

```
$ cat fruit_prices.txt
Fruit           Price/lbs
Banana          0.89
Paech           0.79
Kiwi            1.50
Pineapple       1.29
Apple           0.99
Mango           2.20
```

Here you list the name of a fruit and its price per pound.

Say you want to print out a list of those fruits that cost less than $1 per pound. You need to use the sed command p (p as in *print*):

```
/pattern/p
```

Here pattern is a regular expression.

Try the following sed command:

```
$ sed '/0\.[0-9][0-9]$/p' fruit_prices.txt
```

Here you tell sed to print all the lines that match the pattern:

```
/0\.[0-9][0-9]$/
```

This means that lines that end in prices such as 0.89 and 0.99 should be printed. You don't want lines that end in prices such as 2.20 to be printed.

Now, look at the output:

```
Fruit           Price/lbs
Banana          0.89
Banana          0.89
Paech           0.79
Paech           0.79
Kiwi            1.50
Pineapple       1.29
Apple           0.99
Apple           0.99
Mango           2.20
```

You find that the lines for fruit with prices less than a dollar are printed twice, whereas lines for fruit with prices greater than a dollar are printed only once.

This demonstrates the default behavior of sed—it prints every input line to the output. To avoid this behavior, you can specify the -n option to sed as follows:

```
$ sed -n '/0\.[0-9][0-9]$/p' fruit_prices.txt
```

This changes the output as follows:

```
Banana          0.89
Paech           0.79
Apple           0.99
```

Deleting Lines

Say that you run out of mangos and you need to delete them from the list. To accomplish this task, you need to use the sed command d (*d* as in *delete*):

```
/pattern/d
```

Here pattern is a regular expression.

In this case you can use the following sed command:

```
$ sed '/^[Mm]ango/d' fruit_prices.txt
```

Here you request all lines that start with the words *mango* or *Mango* to be deleted. The output is as follows:

```
Fruit           Price/lbs
Banana          0.89
Paech           0.79
Kiwi            1.50
Pineapple       1.29
Apple           0.99
```

Notice that in this case you did not have to specify the -n option to sed to get the correct output. The p command tells sed to produce additional output, whereas the d command tells sed to modify the regular output.

Now that you have modified the output, you need to update the file. You can do this with the help of the shell:

```
$ mv fruit_prices.txt fruit_prices.txt.$$
$ sed '/^[Mm]ango/d' fruit_prices.txt.$$ > fruit_prices.txt
$ cat fruit_prices.txt
```

First, you rename the file fruit_prices.txt to fruit_prices.txt.$$. The value of the variable $$ is the process ID of the current shell. Appending this value to the end of a file is a common practice for creating temporary files.

Next, you use sed to delete the lines starting with *Mango* or *mango* from the temporary file. The output of the sed command is redirected into the file fruit_prices.txt.

The final cat command shows us that the update was successful:

```
Fruit           Price/lbs
Banana          0.89
Paech           0.79
Kiwi            1.50
Pineapple       1.29
Apple           0.99
```

At this point you can remove the temporary file as follows:

```
$ rm fruit_prices.txt.$$
```

Performing Substitutions

By now you might have noticed that *Peach* is misspelled as *Paech* in the file fruit_prices.txt. You can fix this misspelling by substituting *Paech* with the correct spelling *Peach*. To do this, use the sed command s (*s* as in *substitute*):

/pattern/s/pattern1/pattern2/

Here `pattern`, `pattern1`, and `pattern2` are regular expressions. In the `s` command `pattern1` is replaced with `pattern2` on any line that matches `pattern`.

Frequently `pattern` is omitted, so you see the `s` command used as follows:

`s/pattern1/pattern2/`

Here the `s` command executes for every input line.

To fix the spelling of *Paech*, you can use the following `sed` command:

```
$ sed 's/Paech/Peach/' fruit_prices.txt
```

The output looks like the following:

```
Fruit          Price/lbs
Banana         0.89
Peach          0.79
Kiwi           1.50
Pineapple      1.29
Apple          0.99
```

Notice that in this case you did not have to specify the `-n` option to `sed` to get the correct output. The `s` command is similar to the `d` command in that it tells `sed` to modify the regular output.

Common Errors

A common error with the `s` command is forgetting one or more of the `/` characters. For example, say you were to issue the command

```
$ sed 's/Paech/Peach' fruit_prices.txt
```

An error message similar to the following is produced:

```
sed: command garbled: s/Paech/Peach
```

This is the standard style of `sed` error messages:

```
sed: command garbled: command
```

Here `sed` could not understand the `command`. No additional error messages or information are produced. You have to determine what went wrong yourself.

Performing Global Substitutions

Consider the following line:

```
$ cat nash.txt
things that are eqal to the same thing are eqal to each other
```

Here the word *equal* is misspelled as *eqal*. Try to fix this using the s command as
follows:

```
$ sed 's/eqal/equal/' nash.txt
```

This produces the output:

```
things that are equal to the same thing are eqal to each other
```

As you can see, the first misspelling was fixed, but the second one was not. This is the
default behavior of the s command: it only performs one substitution on a line. To perform more than one substitution, you need to use the g (*g* as in *global*) operator as follows:

```
s/pattern1/pattern2/g
```

Here pattern1 and pattern2 are regular expressions. The g operator tells the s command to substitute every occurrence of pattern1 with pattern2.

In this case, you use it as follows:

```
$ sed 's/eqal/equal/g' nash.txt
```

This produces the correct output:

```
things that are equal to the same thing are equal to each other
```

Reusing an Expressions Value

Now say that you want to change the list to reflect that the prices are in dollars by
appending the $ character in front of each of the prices. You know that by using the fol-
lowing expression, you can match all the lines that end with a price:

```
/ *[0-9][0-9]*\.[0-9][0-9]$/
```

The problem, though, is replacing the existing price with a price that is preceded by the $
character. Apparently, you would need to write a separate s command for each fruit in
the file.

Fortunately, the s command provides us with the & operator, which enables us to reuse
the string that matched pattern1 in pattern2. In this case you need to reuse the price
that was matched:

```
$ sed 's/ *[0-9][0-9]*\.[0-9][0-9]$/\$&/' fruit_prices.txt
Fruit           Price/lbs
Banana          $0.89
Paech           $0.79
Kiwi            $1.50
Pineapple       $1.29
Apple           $0.99
```

Using Multiple `sed` Commands

As you can see from the last example, you were able to update the prices, but *Paech* is still misspelled. Say that you need to update `fruit_prices.txt` with both changes. This means that you have to perform more than one `sed` command on the file. You can do this in two ways:

- Perform the first change and then update the file. Perform the second change command and then update the file.
- Perform both changes using a single `sed` command and then update the file once.

16

As you can guess, the second method is much more efficient and less prone to error because the file is updated only once. You can perform both changes using a single `sed` command as follows:

```
sed -e 'command1' -e 'command2' ... -e 'commandN' files
```

Here `command1` through `commandN` are `sed` commands of the type discussed previously. These commands are applied to each of the lines in the list of files given by `files`.

In this case you can perform both updates using either of the following commands:

```
$ sed -e 's/Paech/Peach/' -e 's/ *[0-9][0-9]*\.[0-9][0-9]$/\$&/'
➥fruit_prices.txt

Fruit          Price/lbs
Banana         $0.89
Peach          $0.79
Kiwi           $1.50
Pineapple      $1.29
Apple          $0.99
```

To update the file you use the same procedure as before: *— appends process id*

```
$ mv fruit_pieces.txt fruit_pieces.txt.$$
$ sed -e 's/Paech/Peach/' -e 's/ *[0-9][0-9]*\.[0-9][0-9]$/\$&/'
➥fruit_prices.txt.$$ > fruit_pieces.txt
$ cat fruit_pieces.txt
Fruit          Price/lbs
Banana         $0.89
Peach          $0.79
Kiwi           $1.50
Pineapple      $1.29
Apple          $0.99
```

Using `sed` in a Pipeline

As I have mentioned before, if `sed` does not receive a list of files, it acts on its STDIN. This enables us to use it in pipelines.

I will demonstrate sed's usage in this manner by using it to solve the problem of determining the user's numeric user ID (uid).

On all UNIX systems the /usr/bin/id command prints the current users uid and gid information. In my case, the output of id looks like the following:

```
$ /usr/bin/id
uid=500(ranga) gid=100(users)
```

As you can tell from the output, my numeric uid is 500. You need to modify this output so that only this number is printed. Using sed makes this task quite easy.

First you need to eliminate everything following the first parenthesis. You can do that as follows:

```
$ /usr/bin/id ¦ sed 's/(.*$//'
```

Now the output looks like the following:

```
uid=500
```

If you eliminate the uid= portion at the beginning of the line, you are finished. You can do this as follows:

```
$ /usr/bin/id ¦ sed -e 's/(.*$//' -e 's/^uid=//'
```

Now the output is

```
500
```

This is what you want. Notice that when you added the second s command, you changed from the single command form for sed to the multiple command form that uses the -e option.

Summary

In this chapter you looked at filtering text using regular expressions. Some of the major topics that you covered are

- Matching characters
- Specifying sets of characters
- Anchoring patterns
- Escaping metacharacters

You also covered the similarities between the two most powerful text filtering programs available on UNIX systems, awk and sed. Finally, you looked at using the sed command. Some of the uses that you covered are

- Printing lines
- Deleting lines
- Performing substitution

In the next chapter I will introduce the awk command and its programming language. Using the material covered in this chapter, you will be able to use awk to easily perform difficult text manipulations.

Questions

1. Using sed, write a shell function that searches for a word or simple expression in a list of files, printing out a list of matches. This is similar to the grep program.

   You do not have to support all possible sed expressions. Your function should take the word to look for as its first argument. It should treat its other arguments as a list of files.

   HINT: Use double quotes (") instead of single quotes (') to surround your sed script.

2. Write a sed command that takes as its input the output of the uptime command and prints only the last three load averages. The uptime command's output looks like the following:

   ```
   $ uptime
   6:34pm  up 2 day(s), 49 min(s),  1 user,  load average:
   0.00, 0.00, 0.02
   ```

   Your output should look like the following:

   ```
   load average: 0.05, 0.01, 0.03
   ```

3. Write a sed command that takes as its input the output of the command df -k and prints only those lines that start with a /. The output of the df -k command looks like the following:

   ```
   Filesystem          kbytes   used   avail capacity  Mounted on
   /dev/dsk/c0t3d0s0   739262 455143 224979    67%     /
   /proc                    0      0      0     0%     /proc
   fd                       0      0      0     0%     /dev/fd
   /dev/dsk/c0t3d0s1   123455   4813 106297     5%     /var
   /dev/dsk/c0t3d0s5   842150 133819 649381    18%     /opt
   swap                366052  15708 350344     5%     /tmp
   kanchi:/home       1190014 660165 468363    59%     /users
   ```

On HP-UX use the command `df -b` instead of `df -k`.

4. Write a `sed` command that takes as its input the output of the `ls -l` command and prints the permissions and the filename for regular files. Directories, links, and special files should not appear in the output. The output of `ls -l` should look similar to the following:

```
-rw-r--r--  1 ranga users  85 Nov 27 15:34 fruit_prices.txt
-rw-r--r--  1 ranga users  80 Nov 27 13:53 fruit_prices.txt.7880
lrwxrwxrwx  1 ranga users   8 Nov 27 19:01 nash -> nash.txt
-rw-r--r--  1 ranga users  62 Nov 27 16:06 nash.txt
lrwxrwxrwx  1 ranga users   8 Nov 27 19:01 urls -> urls.txt
-rw-r--r--  1 ranga users 180 Nov 27 12:34 urls.txt
```

Your output should look like:

```
-rw-r--r-- fruit_prices.txt
-rw-r--r-- fruit_prices.txt.7880
-rw-r--r-- nash.txt
-rw-r--r-- urls.txt
```

HOUR 17

Filtering Text with awk

In Chapter 16, "Filtering Text Using Regular Expressions," you looked at the sed command and used regular expressions to filter text. In this chapter you will look at another powerful text filtering command called awk.

The awk command is a complete programming language that enables you to search many files for patterns and conditionally modify files without having to worry about opening files, reading lines, or closing files. It's found on all UNIX systems and is quite fast, easy to learn, and extremely flexible.

This chapter concentrates on the awk elements that are most commonly used in shell scripts. Specifically these features are

- Field editing
- Variables
- Flow control statements

What is awk?

The awk command is a programming language that enables you to search through files and modify records with these files based on patterns. The name *awk* comes from the last names of its creators Alfred *A*ho, Peter *W*einberger, and Brian *K*ernighan. It has been a part of UNIX since 1978, when it was added to UNIX Version 7.

Currently three main versions are available:

- The original awk
- A newer version nawk
- The POSIX/GNU version gawk

The original awk has remained almost the same since its first introduction to UNIX in 1978. Originally it was intended to be a small programming language for filtering text and producing reports.

By the mid-1980s, people were using awk for large programs, so in 1985 its authors decided to extend it. This version, called nawk (as in *new awk*), was released to the public in 1987 and became a part of SunOS 4.1.*x*. Its developers intended for nawk to replace awk eventually. This has yet to happen. Most commercial UNIX versions such as HP-UX and Solaris still ship with both awk and nawk.

In 1992 the Institute of Electrical and Electronics Engineers (IEEE) standardized awk as part of its Portable Operating Systems Interface standard (POSIX). gawk, the GNU version of awk, is based on this standard. All Linux systems ship with gawk.

The examples in this chapter work with any version of awk.

Basic Syntax

The basic syntax of an awk command is

```
awk 'script' files
```

Here *files* is a list of one or more files, and *script* is one or more commands of the form:

```
/pattern/ { actions }
```

Here *pattern* is a regular expression, and *actions* is one or more of the commands that are covered later in this chapter. If *pattern* is omitted, awk performs the specified *actions* for each input line.

Look at the simplest task in awk, displaying all the input lines from a file. In this case you use a modified version of the file fruit_prices.txt from the previous chapter:

```
$ awk '{ print ; }' fruit_prices.txt
Fruit           Price/lbs       Quantity
Banana          $0.89           100
```

```
Peach           $0.79           65
Kiwi            $1.50           22
Pineapple       $1.29           35
Apple           $0.99           78
```

Here you use the awk command print to print each line of the input. When the print command is given without arguments, it prints the input line exactly as it was read.

Notice that there is a semicolon (;) after the print command. This semicolon is required to let awk know that the command has concluded. Strictly speaking, some older versions of awk do not require this, but it is good practice to include it anyway.

Field Editing

NEW TERM One of the nicest features available in awk is that it automatically divides input lines into *fields*. A field is a set of characters that are separated by one or more field separator characters. The default field separator characters are tab and space.

When a line is read, awk places the fields that it has parsed into the variable 1 for the first field, 2 for the second field, and so on. To access a field, use the field operator, $. Thus, the first field is $1.

> The use of the $ in awk is slightly different than in the shell. The $ is required only when accessing the value of a field variable; it is not required when accessing the values of other variables. I will explain creating and using variables in awk in depth later in this chapter.

As an example of using fields, you can print only the name of a fruit and its quantity using the following awk command:

```
$ awk '{ print $1 $3 ; }' fruit_prices.txt
```
1st & 3ed field in the file

Here you use awk to print two fields from every input line:

- The first field, which contains the fruit name
- The third field, which contains the quantity

The output looks like the following:

```
FruitQuantity
Banana100
Peach65
Kiwi22
Pineapple35
Apple78
```

Notice that in the output there is no separation between the fields. This is the default behavior of the `print` command. To print a space between each field you need to use the `,` operator as follows:

```
$ awk '{ print $1 , $3 ; }' fruit_prices.txt
Fruit Quantity
Banana 100
Peach 65
Kiwi 22
Pineapple 35
Apple 78
```

You can format the output by using the awk `printf` command instead of the `print` command as follows:

```
$ awk '{ printf "%-15s %s\n" , $1 , $3 ; }' fruit_prices.txt
Fruit           Quantity
Banana          100
Peach           65
Kiwi            22
Pineapple       35
Apple           78
```

All the features of the `printf` command discussed in Chapter 13, "Input/Output," are available in the awk command `printf`.

Taking Pattern-Specific Actions

Say that you want to highlight those fruits that cost more than a dollar by putting a * at the end of the line for those fruits. This means that you need to perform different actions depending on the pattern that was matched for the price.

Start with the following script:

```
#!/bin/sh
awk '
    / *\$[1-9][0-9]*\.[0-9][0-9] */ { print $1,$2,$3,"*"; }
    / *\$0\.[0-9][0-9] */ { print ; }
' fruit_prices.txt
```

Here you have two patterns: The first one looks for fruit priced higher than a dollar, and the second one looks for fruit priced lower than a dollar. When a fruit priced higher than a dollar is encountered, the three fields are output with a * at the end of the line. For all other fruit, the line is printed exactly as it was read. The output looks like the following:

```
Banana          $0.89           100
Peach           $0.79           65
Kiwi $1.50 22 *
Pineapple $1.29 35 *
Apple           $0.99           78
```

The main problem here is that the lines you wanted to flag with the * in are no longer formatted in the same manner as the other lines. You could solve this using `printf`, but a much nicer and simpler solution is to use the `$0` field. The variable `0` is used by `awk` to store the entire input line as it was read. Change the script as follows:

```
#!/bin/sh
awk '
    / *\$[1-9][0-9]*\.[0-9][0-9] */ { print $0,"*"; }
    / *\$0\.[0-9][0-9] */ { print ; }
' fruit_prices.txt
```

This changes the output so that all the lines are formatted identically:

```
Banana        $0.89         100
Peach         $0.79         65
Kiwi          $1.50         22 *
Pineapple     $1.29         35 *
Apple         $0.99         78
```

Comparison Operators

Say that you have to flag all the fruit whose quantity is less than 75 for reorder by appending the string REORDER to the end of their line. In this case you have to check whether the third field, which holds the quantity, is less than or equal to 75.

To solve this problem, you need to use a comparison operator. In `awk`, comparison operators compare the values of numbers and strings. Their behavior is similar to operators found in the C language or the shell.

When you use a comparison operator, the syntax of an `awk` command changes to the following:

```
expression { actions; }
```

Here *expression* is constructed using one of the comparison operators given in Table 17.1

TABLE 17.1 COMPARISON OPERATORS IN awk

Operator	Description
<	Less than
>	Greater than
<=	Less than or equal to
>=	Greater than or equal to
==	Equal to

continues

17

TABLE 17.1 COMPARISON OPERATORS IN awk

Operator	Description
!=	Not equal to
value ~ /pattern/	True if *value* matches *pattern*
value !~ /pattern/	True if *value* does not match *pattern*

You can solve your problem using the following script:

```
#!/bin/sh
awk '
    $3 <= 75 { printf "%s\t%s\n",$0,"REORDER" ; }
    $3 > 75 { print $0 ; }
' fruit_prices.txt
```

Here you check to see whether the third field contains a value less than or equal to 75. If it does, you print out the input line followed by the string REORDER. Next you check to see whether the third field contains a value greater than 75 and, if it does, you print the input line unchanged.

The output from this scripts looks like the following:

```
Fruit          Price/lbs      Quantity
Banana         $0.89          100
Peach          $0.79          65      REORDER
Kiwi           $1.50          22      REORDER
Pineapple      $1.29          35      REORDER
Apple          $0.99          78
```

Compound Expressions

NEW TERM Often you need to combine two or more expressions to check for a particular condition. When you combine two or more expressions, the result is called a *compound expression*.

Compound expressions are constructed by using either the && (and) or the ¦¦ (or) compound operators. The syntax is

```
(expr1) && (expr2)
(expr2) ¦¦ (expr2)
```

Here *expr1* and *expr2* are expressions constructed using the conditional operators given in Table 17.1. The parentheses surrounding *expr1* and *expr2* are required.

When the && operator is used, both *expr1* and *expr2* must be true for the compound expression to be true. When the ¦¦ operator is used, the compound expression is true if either *expr1* or *expr2* is true.

As an example of using a compound expression, you can use the compound operators to obtain a list of all the fruit that cost more than a dollar and of which there are less than 75:

```
awk '
    ($2 ~ /^\$[1-9][0-9]*\.[0-9][0-9]$/) && ($3 < 75) {
        printf "%s\t%s\t%s\n",$0,"*","REORDER" ;
    }
' fruit_prices.txt ;
```

The output looks like the following

```
Kiwi            $1.50           22        *        REORDER
Pineapple       $1.29           35        *        REORDER
```

THE COMPOUND EXPRESSION OPERATORS

You might hear the && operator called the *and-and operator* because it consists of two ampersands (*and* characters). Similarly, the ¦¦ operator might be referred to as the *or-or operator*.

The next Command

Consider the following script:

```
#!/bin/sh
awk '
    $3 <= 75 { printf "%s\t%s\n",$0,"REORDER" ; }
    $3 > 75 { print $0 ; }
' fruit_prices.txt
```

Clearly it is performing more work than it needs to. For example, when the input line is

```
Kiwi            $1.50           22
```

the execution of the script is as follows:

1. Check whether the value of the third column, 22, is less than 75. Because the value is less than 75, the script proceeds to step 2.
2. Prints the input line followed by REORDER.
3. Checks whether the value of the third column, 22, is greater than 75. Because the value is not greater than 75, the script reads the next line.

As you can see, you have no real need to execute step 3 because step 2 has already printed a line. To prevent step 3 from executing, you can use the next command. The next command tells awk to skip all the remaining patterns and expressions and instead read the next input line and start from the first pattern or expression.

Change your script to use it:

```
#!/bin/sh
awk '
    $3 <= 75 { printf "%s\t%s\n",$0,"REORDER" ; next ; }
    $3 > 75 { print $0 ; }
' fruit_prices.txt ;
```

Reads next input line

Now the execution of the script is as follows:

1. Checks whether the value of the third column, 22, is less than 75. Because the value is less than 75, the script proceeds to step 2.

2. Prints the input line followed by REORDER.

3. Reads the next input line and starts over with the first pattern.

As you can see, the second comparison ($3 > 75) is never performed for this input line.

Using STDIN as Input

Recall that the basic form of an awk command is

```
awk 'script' files
```

If *files*, the list of files, is omitted, awk reads its input from STDIN. This enables us to use it to filter the output of other commands. For example, the command

```
$ ls -l
```

produces output formatted similar to the following:

```
total 64
-rw-r--r--  1 ranga  users  635 Nov 29 11:10 awkfruit.sh
-rw-r--r--  1 ranga  users  115 Nov 28 14:07 fruit_prices.txt
-rw-r--r--  1 ranga  users   80 Nov 27 13:53 fruit_prices.txt.7880
lrwxrwxrwx  1 ranga  users    8 Nov 27 19:01 nash -> nash.txt
-rw-r--r--  1 ranga  users   62 Nov 27 16:06 nash.txt
-rw-r--r--  1 ranga  users   11 Nov 29 10:38 nums.txt
lrwxrwxrwx  1 ranga  users    8 Nov 27 19:01 urls -> urls.txt
-rw-r--r--  1 ranga  users  180 Nov 27 12:34 urls.txt
```

You can use awk to manipulate the output of the ls -l command so that only the name of a file and its size are printed. Here, the name of the file is in field 9, and the size is in field 5. The following command prints the name of each file along with its size:

```
$ /bin/ls -l | awk '$1 !~ /total/ { printf "%-32s %s\n",$9,$5 ; }'
```

Col 1 Value not word total   *Col 9 Col 5*

The output looks like the following:

```
awkfruit.sh                 635
fruit_prices.txt            115
fruit_prices.txt.7880       80
nash                        8
nash.txt                    62
nums.txt                    11
urls                        8
urls.txt                    180
```

Using awk Features

You have seen some of the basics of using awk, and you'll now look at some of the more powerful features that it provides. The main topics are

- Variables
- Flow control
- Loops

These features let you fully exploit the power of awk.

Variables

Variables in awk are similar to variables in the shell: They are words that refer to a value. The basic syntax of defining a variable is

name=value

Here *name* is the name of the variable, and *value* is the value of that variable. For example, the following awk command

```
fruit="peach"
```

creates the variable `fruit` and assigns it the value `peach`. There is no need to initialize a variable: the first time you use it, it is initialized.

Like the shell, the name of a variable can contain only letters, numbers, and underscores. A variable's name cannot start with a number.

You can assign both numeric and string values to a variable in the same script. For example, consider the following awk commands:

```
fruit="peach"
fruit=100
```

The first command assigns the value peach to the variable fruit. The second command assigns the value 100 to the variable fruit.

The value that you assign a variable can also be the value of another variable or a field. For example, the following awk commands

```
fruit=peach
fruity=fruit
```

set the value of the variables fruit and fruity to peach.

In order to set the value of a variable to one of the fields parsed by awk, you need to use the standard field access operator. For example, the following awk command

```
fruit=$1
```

sets the value of the variable fruit to the first field of the input line.

Using Numeric Expressions

NEW TERM   You can also assign a variable the value of a *numeric expression*. Numeric expressions are commands used to add, subtract, multiply, and divide two numbers. Numeric expressions are constructed using the numeric operators given in Table 17.2. The numeric expressions are of the form

```
num1 operator num2
```

Here *num1* and *num2* can be constants, such as 1 or 2, or variable names. A numeric expression performs the action specified by operator on *num1* and *num2* and returns the answer. For example, the following awk commands

```
a=1
b=a+1
```

assign the value 2 to the variable b.

TABLE 17.2   NUMERIC OPERATORS IN awk

Operator	Description
+	Add
-	Subtract
*	Multiply
/	Divide
%	Modulo (Remainder)
^	Exponentiation

As an example of using numeric expressions, look at the following script that counts the number of blank lines in a file:

```
#!/bin/sh
for i in $@ ;
do
    if [ -f $i ] ; then
        echo $i
        awk ' /^ *$/ { x=x+1 ; print x ; }' $i
    else
        echo "ERROR: $i not a file." >&2
    fi
done
```

[handwritten note: line that starts & ends with space]

In the awk command, you increment the variable x and print it each time a blank line is encountered. Because a new instance of the awk command runs for each file, the count is unique of each file.

Consider the file urls.txt, which contains four blank lines:

```
$ cat urls.txt
http://www.cusa.berkeley.edu/~ranga

http://www.cisco.com

ftp://prep.ai.mit.edu/pub/gnu/
ftp://ftp.redhat.com/

http://www.yahoo.com/index.html
ranga@kanchi:/home/ranga/pub

ranga@soda:/home/ranga/docs/book/ch01.doc
```

For urls.txt, the output of this script looks like the following:

```
urls.txt
1
2
3
4
```

There are two important things to keep in mind about numeric expressions:

- If either *num1* or *num2* is the name of a variable whose value is a string rather than a number, awk uses the value 0 rather than the string.
- If you use a variable that has not yet been created in a numeric expression, awk creates the variable and assigns it a value of 0.

[sidebar: 17]

The Assignment Operators   In the previous example, the awk command:

```
awk ' /^ *$/ { x=x+1 ; print x ; }' $i
```

Uses the assignment:

```
x=x+1
```

In awk this can be written in a more concise fashion using the addition assignment operator:

```
x += 1
```

In general the assignment operators have the syntax

```
name operator= num
```

Here *name* is the name of a variable, *operator* is one of the operators specified in Table 17.2, and *num* is either the name of a variable or a numeric constant such as 1 or 2. A list of the assignment operators is given in Table 17.3.

TABLE 17.3   ASSIGNMENT OPERATORS IN awk

Operator	Description
+=	Add
-=	Subtract
*=	Multiply
/=	Divide
%=	Modulo (Remainder)
^=	Exponentiation

Using an assignment operator is shorthand for writing a numeric expression of the form:

```
name=name operator num
```

Many programmers prefer using the assignment operators because they are slightly more concise than a regular numeric expression.

In the case of

```
x += 1
```

the assignment operator += takes the value of x, adds 1 to it, and then assigns the result to x.

The Special Patterns: BEGIN and END

In the awk command

```
awk ' /^ *$/ { x=x+1 ; print x ; }' $i
```

you print out the value of x each time it is incremented. Thus the output looks like this:

```
urls.txt
1
2
3
4
```

It would be much nicer if you could print the total number of empty lines. You can do this by using the special patterns BEGIN and END.

As I stated before, the general syntax of a command in an awk script is

```
/pattern/ { actions }
```

Usually *pattern* is a regular expression, but *pattern* can also be one of the two special patterns BEGIN and END. When these patterns are used, the general form of an awk command becomes

```
awk '
    BEGIN { actions }
    /pattern/ { actions }
    /pattern/ { actions }
    END { actions }
' files
```

The BEGIN pattern must be the first pattern that is specified, and the END pattern must be the last pattern that is specified. Between the BEGIN and END patterns you can have any number of the following pairs:

```
/pattern/ { action ; }
```

Both the BEGIN and the END pattern are optional, so

- When the BEGIN pattern is specified, awk executes its *action*s before reading any input.
- When the END pattern is specified, awk executes its *action*s before it exits.

If a program consists of only a BEGIN pattern, awk does not read any lines before exiting.

When these patterns are given the execution of an awk, the script is as follows:

1. If a BEGIN pattern is present, the script executes the *action*s it specifies
2. Reads an input line and parses it into fields

17

3. Compares each of the specified *patterns* against the input line, until it finds a match. When it does find a match, the script executes the *actions* specified for that *pattern*. This step is repeated for all available *patterns*.

4. Repeats steps 2 and 3 while input lines are present

5. After the script reads all the input lines, if the END pattern is present, it executes the *actions* that the pattern specifies.

To solve your problem, you can use the END pattern to print out the value of x. The modified script is as follows:

```
#!/bin/sh
for i in $@ ;
do
    if [ -f "$i" ] ; then
        echo "$i\c"
        awk '
            /^ *$/ { x+=1 ; }
            END { printf " %s\n",x; }
        ' "$i"
    else
        echo "ERROR: $i not a file." >&2
    fi
done
```

Suppresses trailing newline

Now the output looks like

```
urls.txt 4
```

Built-in Variables

In addition to the variables that you can define, awk predefines several variables that are available for your use. The complete list of these variables is given in Table 17.4. Unless otherwise noted, you can safely change the values of any of these variables.

TABLE 17.4 BUILT-IN VARIABLES IN awk

Variables	Description
FILENAME	The name of the current input file. You should not change the value of this variable.
NR	The number of the current input line or record in the input file. You should not change the value of this variable.
NF	The number of fields in the current line or record. You should not change the value of this variable.
OFS	The output field separator (default is space).

Variables	Description
FS	The input field separator (default is space and tab).
ORS	The output record separator (default is newline).
RS	The input record separator (default is newline).

Using FILENAME and NR   In the previous example you used the shell to print the name of the input file. By using the variable FILENAME in conjunction with the BEGIN statement, you can do this all in awk.

While you're at it, change the previous script to print the percentage of lines in the file that were blank. To accomplish this, you need to use the following expression in the END pattern:

```
100*(x/NR)
```

Because awk does all its numeric computation in floating point, you get a correct answer. Here you are using the variable NR, which stores the current record or line number.

In the END pattern, the value of NR is the line number of the last line that was processed, which is the same as the total number of lines processed.

With these changes, the script is

```
#!/bin/sh
for i in $@ ;
do
    if [ -f "$i" ] ; then
        awk 'BEGIN { printf "%s\t",FILENAME ; }
            /^ *$/ { x+=1 ; }
            END { ave=100*(x/NR) ; printf " %s\t%3.1f\n",x,ave; }
        ' "$i"
    else
        echo "ERROR: $i not a file." >&2
    fi
done
```

The new output looks like

```
urls.txt        4       36.4
```

Changing the Input Field Separator   The input field separator, FS, controls how awk breaks up fields in an input line. The default value for FS is space and tab. Because most commands, such as ls or ps, use spaces or tabs to separate columns, this default value enables you to easily manipulate their output using awk.

17

You can manually set FS to any other characters in order to influence how awk breaks up an input line. Usually, this character is changed when you look through system databases, such as /etc/passwd. The two mechanisms available for changing FS are

- Manually resetting FS in a BEGIN pattern
- Specifying the -F option to awk

As an example, set FS to a colon (:). You can use the following BEGIN pattern

```
BEGIN { FS=":" ; }
```

or the following awk invocation:

```
awk -F: '{ ... }'
```

The major difference between the two is that the -F option enables you to use a shell variable to specify the field separator dynamically as follows

```
$ MYFS=: ; export MYFS ; awk -F${MYFS} '{ ... }'
```

whereas the BEGIN block forces you to hard code the value of the field separator.

A simple example that demonstrates the use of changing FS is the following:

```
$ awk 'BEGIN { FS=":" ; } { print $1 , $6 ; }' /etc/passwd
```

This command prints each user's username and home directory. It can also be written as follows:

```
$ awk -F: '{ print $1, $6 ; }' /etc/passwd
```

A short excerpt of the output on my system is as follows:

```
root /
daemon /
bin /usr/bin
sys /
adm /var/adm
ranga /home/ranga
```

Allowing awk to Use Shell Variables

Most versions of awk have no direct way of accessing the values of environment variables that are set in the shell. In order for awk to use these variables, you have to convert them to awk variables on the command line.

The basic syntax for setting variables on the command line is

```
awk 'script' awkvar1=value awkvar2=value ... files
```

Here, *script* is the awk script that you want to execute. The variables *awkvar1*, *awkvar2*, and so on are the names of awk variables that you want to set. As usual, *files* is a list of files.

Say that you want to generate a list of all the fruit in fruit_prices.txt that are less than or equal to some number x, where x is supplied by the user. In order to make this possible, you need to forward to awk the value of x that the user gives your script.

Assuming that the user-supplied value for x is given to your script as $1, you can make the following changes:

```
#!/bin/sh
NUMFRUIT="$1"
if [ -z "$NUMFRUIT" ] ; then NUMFRUIT=75 ; fi

awk '
    $3 <= numfruit  { print ; }
' numfruit="$NUMFRUIT" fruit_prices.txt
```

Here, you only print those lines that have less than the specified number of fruit.

Assuming this script is called reorder.sh, executing the script as follows

```
$ ./reorder.sh 25
```

produces the output

```
Kiwi            $1.50           22
```

Flow Control

There are three main forms for flow control in awk:

- The if statement
- The while statement
- The for statement

The if and while statements are similar to the versions in the shell, whereas the for statement is much closer to the version found in the C language version.

You will look at each of these statements in turn.

The if Statement

The if statement enables you to make tests before executing some awk command.

The pattern matching and expressions that you have used in the previous examples are essentially if statements that affect the overall execution of the awk program. The if statement should be used within an action rather than in the main input processing loop.

17

The basic syntax of the if statement is

```
if (expression1) {
    action1
} else if (expression2) {
    action2
} else {
    action3
}
```

Here *expression1* and *expression2* are expressions created using the conditional operators. They are identical to expressions you looked at earlier in the chapter. The parentheses surrounding *expression1* and *expression2* are required.

The actions—*action1*, *action2,* and *action3*—can be any sequence of valid awk commands. The braces surrounding these actions are required only when an action contains more than one statement, but I recommend that you always use them for the sake of clarity and maintainability.

Both the `else if` and the `else` statements are optional. There is no limit on the number of `else if` statements that can be given.

The execution is as follows:

1. Evaluate *expression1* (if).
2. If *expression1* is true, execute *action1* and exit the if statement.
3. If *expression1* is false, evaluate *expression2* (else if).
4. If *expression2* is true, execute *action2* and exit the if statement.
5. If *expression2* is false, execute *action3* and exit the if statement (else).

As a simple example, write a script that prints a list of fruit in `fruit_prices.txt` highlighting the following facts:

- Whether an item costs more than a dollar
- Whether you need to reorder the item

Fruit that costs more than a dollar is highlighted with the * character. Fruit that needs to be reordered because its quantity is less than 75 is highlighted with the string REORDER.

Using the `if` statement, the script becomes

```
#!/bin/sh

awk '{
    printf "%s\t",$0;
```

```
if ( $2 ~ /\$[1-9][0-9]*\.[0-9][0-9]/ ) {

    printf " * ";
    if ( $3 <= 75 ) {
        printf "REORDER\n" ;
    } else {
        printf "\n" ;
    }

} else {

    if ( $3 < 75 ) {
        printf "    REORDER\n" ;
    } else {
        printf "\n" ;
    }

}
}' fruit_prices.txt ;
```

The output looks like the following

```
Fruit           Price/lbs       Quantity
Banana          $0.89           100
Peach           $0.79           65           REORDER
Kiwi            $1.50           22         * REORDER
Pineapple       $1.29           35         * REORDER
Apple           $0.99           78
```

This example also shows you how to nest if statements.

The while Statement

The while statement executes awk commands while an expression is true. The basic syntax is

```
while (expression) {
    actions
}
```

Here *expression* is an expression created using the conditional operators. It is identical to expressions you looked at earlier in the chapter. The parentheses surrounding *expression* are required.

The actions that should be performed, *actions*, are any sequence of valid awk commands. The braces surrounding the *actions* are required only for actions containing more than one statement, but I recommend that you always use them for the sake of clarity and maintainability.

Here is a simple example of the `while` loop that counts from one to five:

```
$ awk 'BEGIN{ x=0 ; while (x < 5) { x+=1 ; print x ; } }'
```

The output looks like the following:

```
1
2
3
4
5
```

The `do` Statement   A variation on the `while` statement is the `do` statement. It also performs some actions while an expression is true.

The basic syntax is

```
do {
    actions
} while (expression)
```

Here *expression* is an expression created using the conditional operators. It is identical to expressions you looked at earlier in the chapter. The parentheses surrounding *expression* are required.

The actions that should be performed, *actions*, are any sequence of valid awk commands. The braces surrounding the *actions* are required only for actions containing more than one statement, but I recommend that you always use them for the sake of clarity and maintainability.

The main difference is that the do statement executes at least once, whereas the `while` statement might not execute at all. For example, you can write the `while` loop in the previous example as the following do loop:

```
$ awk 'BEGIN { 'BEGIN{ x=0 ; do { x+=1 ; print x ; } while (x < 5) }'
```

There are slight variations between nawk, gawk, and awk with regard to this do statement. If you want to use the statement, you should stick to nawk or gawk because older versions of awk might have trouble with it. If you are concerned with portability to older versions of UNIX, you should avoid using the do statement.

The `for` Statement

The `for` statement enables you to repeat commands a certain number of times. The `for` loop in awk is similar to the `for` loop in the C language.

The idea behind the `for` loop is that you keep a counter and that you test in each iteration of the loop. Every time the loop executes, the counter is incremented. This is quite different from the `for` loop in the shell, which executes a set of commands for each item in a list.

The basic syntax of the for loop is

```
for (initialize_counter; test_counter; increment_counter) {
    action
}
```

Here *initialize_counter* initializes the counter variable, *test_counter* is an expression that tests the counter variable's value, and *increment_counter* increments the value of the counter. The parentheses surrounding the expression used by the for loop are required.

The actions that should be performed, *action*, are any sequence of valid awk commands. The braces surrounding the *action* are required only for actions containing more than one statement, but I recommend that you always use them for the sake of clarity and maintainability.

A common use of the for loop is to iterate through the fields in a record and output them, possibly modifying each record in the process. The following for loop prints each field in a record separated by two spaces:

```
#!/bin/sh
awk '{
    for (x=1;x<=NF;x+=1) {
        printf "%s  ",$x ;
    }
    printf "\n" ;
}' fruit_prices.txt
```

Here you use NF to access the number of fields in the current record. You also use the field access operator, $, in conjunction with the variable x to access the value stored at a particular field.

Summary

In this chapter I have introduced programming in awk. It is one of the most powerful text filtering tools available in UNIX. By using awk, you can often modify and transform text in ways that are difficult or impossible using only the shell.

Some of the important topics that I have covered are

- Field editing
- Pattern specific actions
- Using STDIN as input
- Variables

17

- Numeric and assignment expressions
- Using flow control

In addition to these topics, awk offers features such as multiple line editing, arrays, and functions. If you are interested in learning more about these topics, consult one of the following sources:

The UNIX Programming Environment by Brian Kernighan and Rob Pike (Prentice-Hall, 1984)

The AWK Programming Language by Alfred Aho, Peter Weinberger, and Brian Kernighan (Addison-Wesley, 1984)

The GNU Awk User's Guide by Arnold Robbins (SCC, 1996)

Questions

1. Write an awk script that prints each of the fields in a record in reverse order. The output for the file `fruit_prices.txt` should look like the following:
   ```
   Quantity Price/lbs Fruit
   100 $0.89 Banana
   65 $0.79 Peach
   22 $1.50 Kiwi
   35 $1.29 Pineapple
   78 $0.99 Apple
   ```

   (HINT: Use the `for` statement and `NF`)

2. Write an awk script that balances a checking account. Your program needs to print the balance in the account every time the user makes a transaction.

   The transactions are stored in a file. Each line or record in the file has the following format:

   `command:date:comment:amount`

   Here `date` is the date on which the transaction was made, `comment` is a string (including embedded spaces) describing the transaction, and `amount` is the amount of the transaction. The `command` determines what should be done to the balance with `amount`. The valid `commands` are

   - `B`, indicates balance. When this command is encountered, the balance in the account should be set to the transaction `amount`.
   - `D`, indicates a deposit. When this command is encountered, the transaction `amount` should be added to the balance.

- C, indicates a check. When this command is encountered, the transaction *amount* should be subtracted from the balance.

- W, indicates a withdrawal. When this command is encountered, the transaction *amount* should be subtracted from the balance.

The main difference between the C (check) and the W (withdrawal) commands is that the C (check) command adds an extra field to its records:

command:date:comment:check number:amount

In addition, the B (balance) command uses only two fields:

B:*amount*

Here *amount* is the balance amount in the account.

For the purposes of this problem, you need to be concerned with the first field, which contains the command; the second field, which contains the transaction date; and the last field, which contains the transaction amount.

The sample input file looks like the following:

```
$ cat account.txt
account.txt
B:0
D:10/24/97:inital deposit:1000
C:10/25/97:credit card:101:100
W:10/30/97:gas:21.43
W:10/30/97:lunch:11.34
C:11/02/97:toner:41.45
C:11/04/97:car payment:347.23
D:11/06/97:dividend:687.34
W:11/10/97:emergency cash:200
```

Your output should look like the following:

```
10/24/97     1000.00
10/25/97      900.00
10/30/97      878.57
10/30/97      867.23
11/02/97      825.78
11/04/97      478.55
11/06/97     1165.89
11/10/97      965.89
```

3. Modify the program you wrote for question 2 to print the ending (total) balance after all input records have been considered. Your output should now look like the following:

```
10/24/97     1000.00
10/25/97      900.00
10/30/97      878.57
10/30/97      867.23
```

```
11/02/97      825.78
11/04/97      478.55
11/06/97     1165.89
11/10/97      965.89
-
Total         965.89
```

(HINT: Use the END pattern)

4. Modify the program you wrote in question 3 to support a new command:

- M, indicates the minimum balance. When the balance drops below this minimum balance, a warning should be printed at the end of the output line.

The M (minimum balance) command uses only two fields:

M:*amount*

Here *amount* is the balance amount in the account.

The input file changes as follows:

```
$ cat account.txt h
B:0
M:500
D:10/24/97:inital deposit:1000
C:10/25/97:credit card:101:100
W:10/30/97:gas:21.43
W:10/30/97:lunch:11.34
C:11/02/97:toner:41.45
C:11/04/97:car payment:347.23
D:11/06/97:dividend:687.34
W:11/10/97:emergency cash:200
```

Your output should be similar to the following:

```
10/24/97     1000.00
10/25/97      900.00
10/30/97      878.57
10/30/97      867.23
11/02/97      825.78
11/04/97      478.55 * Below Min. Balance
11/06/97     1165.89
11/10/97      965.89
-
Total         965.89
```

Terms

Field   A set of characters that are separated by one or more field separator characters. The default field separator characters are tab and space.

Numeric expressions   Commands used to add, subtract, multiply, and divide two numbers. Numeric expressions are constructed using the numeric operators + (add), - (subtract), * (multiply), and / (divide).

Field separator   The field separator controls the manner in which an input line is broken into fields. In the shell, the field separator is stored in the variable IFS. In awk, the field separator is stored in the awk variable FS. Both the shell and awk use the default value of space and tab for the field separator.

17

HOUR **18**

Miscellaneous Tools

by Frank Watson

NEW TERM In this chapter, you will look at several miscellaneous UNIX commands that you often encounter in shell scripts and can use in your own programs. The first of these tools includes *built-in* shell commands, which means that the shell can execute them without reading a separate utility from disk:

- eval
- :
- type

Then you will cover several external commands that exist as binary programs on disk:

- sleep
- find and xargs
- bc and expr
- remsh (sometimes called rsh, rcmd, or remote)

Built-in tools run slightly more efficiently than external programs because they do not need to be read from the disk. Unless you are looping thousands of times, you usually do not need to be concerned if the tool you use is built in or external.

The `eval` Command

The `eval` command can be used when you want the shell to reprocess the command line a second time. The basic syntax is

```
eval any-UNIX-command
```

Insert the `eval` command at the start of any UNIX shell command. This is needed when shell special characters are inserted via variable substitution or command substitution (refer to Chapter 8, "Substitution"). For example,

```
OUTPUT="> out.file"
echo hello $OUTPUT
```

The `OUTPUT` variable contains the > sign to redirect standard output to a file called `out.file`. However, when you try to use the `OUTPUT` variable in the `echo` statement, you find there is a problem. This is what appears on the screen when you run this code:

```
hello > out.file
```

The output went to the screen, but not to the file because the > sign was not present when the shell first looked for redirection signs in the original command line. You can fix this problem by inserting the `eval` command at the start of the `echo` command:

```
OUTPUT="> out.file"
eval echo hello $OUTPUT
```

Now when you run this code, it simply returns to the shell prompt without displaying any text on the screen. It does create a file called `out.file` that contains the word *hello* and this is the desired result. You might ask: Why is this useful? The answer is that later you can change the initial definition of `OUTPUT`, and it affects all later lines that start with `eval` and end with `$OUTPUT`. For example,

```
OUTPUT=" >> out.file"
```

appends to `out.file` instead of overwriting it.

`OUTPUT=` causes output to go to the screen instead of to a file.

The `eval` command is not used frequently in script writing. It is useful for those occasions where you want to compose a shell command line using shell special characters that are contained in variables or produced by command substitution. (Shell special characters were discussed in Chapter 9, "Quoting.")

The : Command

NEW TERM The : character is actually a complete shell command that does nothing but return a zero completion code, which indicates the command has completed successfully. It can be used as a *no-op*, which is a command that does nothing and thus can be safely inserted anywhere a command is needed for purely syntactical reasons:

```
if [ -x $CMD ]
then :
else
    echo Error: $CMD is not executable >&2
fi
```

In this example, assume you are not quite ready to write the code to follow the `then` statement. The shell flags a syntax error if you leave that code out completely, so you insert the : command as a temporary no-op command that can be replaced by the desired code later.

Because the : always returns a successful result, it is sometimes used to create an infinite loop:

```
while :
do
    echo "Enter some input: \c"
    read INPUT
    [ "$INPUT" = stop ] && break
done
```

Because the : always returns a successful or true result, the `while` loop will continue forever or until a `break` is executed within the loop. Sometimes you might find that `while true` used in place of `while :` but using the : is more efficient because it is a shell built-in command, whereas `true` is a command that must be read from a disk file, if you are in the Bourne shell.

You might sometimes find the : used as the first line of a shell script. You sometimes find this in older scripts written when programmers used the C shell but wrote scripts for the Bourne shell. If you start a script from the C shell and the first character of the script is a # sign, it assumes that this script uses C shell syntax, not Bourne shell syntax. Thus it was important to start Bourne shell scripts with something other than a # sign, and the : no-op was often used.

Another use of the : command takes advantage of the fact that the shell evaluates arguments to it. This is a useful way to invoke variable substitution as covered in Chapter 8:

```
: ${LINES:=24} ${TERM:?"TERM not set"}
```

The : is a no-op, but the shell still evaluates its arguments. Thus LINES is set to 24 if LINES is empty or undefined. If TERM is empty or undefined, the whole script aborts with the error message "TERM not set".

The type Command

The type command tells you the full pathname of a given UNIX command.

The basic syntax is

```
type command1 command2 ...
```

If the command given is not a utility that exists as a separate disk file, type tells you whether it is one of the following:

- A shell built-in command
- A shell keyword or reserved word
- An alias

If the given command is an alias for another command, type also gives the command that is actually invoked when you run the alias.

For example,

```
$ type true vi case ulimit history
true is /bin/true
vi is /usr/bin/vi
case is a keyword
ulimit is a shell builtin
history is an exported alias for fc -l
$
```

Different types of UNIX systems can implement the same command in different ways. For example, true is a shell included on some UNIX systems and in some UNIX shells and therefore is as efficient to use as the : command. You can check whether true is built into your system by using the type command.

The sleep Command

The sleep command pauses for a given number of seconds. The basic syntax is

```
sleep n
```

where n is the number of seconds to sleep or pause. Some types of UNIX enable other time units to be specified. It is usually recommended that n not exceed 65,534.

sleep can be used to give a user time to read an output message before clearing the screen. It can also be used when you want to give a series of beeps:

```
echo -e "A value must be input!\a"
sleep 1
echo -ne "\a"
sleep 1
echo -ne "\a"
```

\a causes echo to output an audible beep. -e is required on some UNIX systems for \a to sound a beep. -n suppresses the newline that echo normally prints. The sleep command is used in the previous example to give a sequence of beeps, spaced one second apart.

sleep can be used in a loop to repeat a job periodically:

```
while :
do
    date
    who
    sleep 300
done >> logfile
```

This code enables a list of who is logged into the system to be appended to logfile every 5 minutes (300 seconds).

> If you want to leave this code running all the time, you must clear logfile periodically so that it does not eat up all your disk space.

The find Command

The find command is a very powerful, very flexible way to create a list of files that match given criteria. The basic syntax is

```
find start-dir options actions
```

Here is a simple find example:

```
find / -name alpha -print
```

This example looks for all files named *alpha* and displays the full pathname to the screen (standard output). It is a useful command to know about when you are sure you have a file named *alpha* but can't remember what directory it is in or want to know whether it exists in more than one directory. Here is some possible output from that command:

```
/reports/1998/alpha
/reports/1998/region2/alpha
/tmp/alpha
```

I will shortly cover the elements of the find command in detail. Files can be selected not only by name but also by size, last modification date, last access date, and so on. First let me give you a more complex example with a brief explanation of each part of the example, so you get a sense of what options and actions look like:

```
find /reports/1998 -name alpha -type f -print -exec lp {} \;
```

Table 18.1 provides a breakdown of these elements.

TABLE 18.1   A SAMPLE find COMMAND

Command Element	Description
/reports/1998	The starting directory. find looks only in this directory and its subdirectories for files that match the following criteria.
-name alpha	An option that says you are looking only for files whose name is *alpha*—/reports/1998/region2/alpha, for example. find does not check any words in the directory portion of a filename for *alpha*. It checks only the filename itself, which is also called the file basename.
-type f	An option that says you are looking only for files of type f, which means regular or normal files, and not directories, device files, and so on. Any files selected must match both conditions: they must have the name *alpha* and they must be a regular file.
-print	An action that says to display to standard output the pathname for any files that match the criteria given by the options.
-exec lp {} \;	An action that says to use the lp command to print a hard copy of any files that match the criteria. Multiple actions can be specified.

find: Starting Directory

A UNIX system can contain a huge number of files, often so many that find can take several minutes or more to complete. For this reason, find enables specifying a starting directory to narrow down the number of files it has to search. Only files in this directory and all its subdirectories are checked. find enables either an absolute or relative pathname for the starting directory. If you specify an absolute pathname such as /reports,

```
find /reports -name alpha -print
```

then all the files found are specified as absolute pathnames, as in this sample output:

```
/reports/1998/alpha
/reports/1998/region2/alpha
```

If you specify a relative pathname to `find`,

```
cd /reports
find ./1998 -name alpha -print
```

all the files are displayed relative to the starting directory. For example,

```
./1998/alpha
./1998/region2/alpha
```

To search the whole system, specify / as the starting directory. This indicates the system root directory that includes all other files and directories:

```
find / -name alpha -print
```

To search the entire system and still display all found files as relative pathnames, use the following:

```
cd /
find . -name alpha -print
```

Sample output:

```
./reports/1998/alpha
./reports/1998/region2/alpha
```

18

This point about relative versus absolute pathnames is important if you are using `find` to generate a list of files to be backed up. It is better to back up using relative pathnames that enable the files to be restored to a temporary directory.

Some versions of UNIX let you search multiple directories with one `find` command:

```
find dir1 dir2 -name alpha -print
```

Refer to the `man` page about `find` on your UNIX system to see whether it enables multiple directories.

find: -name Option

The `-name` option enables us to specify either an exact or partial filename for `find` to match. `find` checks for a match only in the filename and not in the directory portion of the pathname.

```
find / -name alpha -print
```

`/tmp/alpha` has a matching filename and would be displayed by this command. `/reports/alpha/file2` would not be displayed because `find` ignores the directory portion of the pathname.

To specify a partial pathname, use filename substitution wildcards (refer to Chapter 8).
For instance,

```
find / -name '*alpha*' -print
```

This displays all files that contain *alpha* anywhere within the filename. Here is some
sample output:

```
/reports/1998/alpha
/reports/1998/alpha2
/reports/1998/old-alpha
/reports/1998/region2/alpha
/tmp/alpha
/usr/fredp/ralphadams
```

All the wildcards covered in Chapter 8 can be used:

```
* ? [characters] [!characters]
```

(handwritten annotations: "multiple", "- 1 char", "1 chae not in list")

You must enclose the filename containing these wildcards within single quotes (see
Chapter 9); otherwise, your `find` command does not always give you the desired results.

find: -type Option

The `-type` option enables us to specify the type of file to search for, as in this example:

```
find / -type d -print
```

`-type d` indicates directories, so only files that are directories are displayed. In this
example, all directories in the whole system are displayed. Notice that no `-name` option
has been given, so you display all directories regardless of their names. Table 18.2 lists
other types that are available.

TABLE 18.2   TYPES AVAILABLE FOR THE find COMMAND

Type	Description
f	Regular or normal file
d	Directory
b	Block special device file
c	Character special device file (raw)
l	Symbolic link
p	Named pipe

find: -mtime, -atime, -ctime

The find -mtime option enables us to locate files that were last modified recently or have not been modified in a long time:

```
find / -mtime -5 -print
```

-mtime takes an integer argument that is measured in days. This find command locates files that were last modified fewer than five days ago. This is a useful option when you are sure you modified a file recently but can't remember its name or directory.

Following -mtime you must specify an integer value:

+n	Find only files last modified more than n days ago
n	Find only files last modified exactly n days ago
-n	Find only files last modified fewer than n days ago

To find files that have not been modified in the last *n* days, look for files that were last modified more than *n* days ago:

```
find / -mtime +90 -print
```

This shows all files that were last modified more than 90 days ago: that is, files that have not been modified in the last 90 days.

There are three forms of date checking and each takes +n, n, or -n as an argument:

-mtime	Finds files last modified more than, exactly, or fewer than *n* days ago
-atime	Finds files last accessed more than, exactly, or fewer than *n* days ago
-ctime	Finds files whose inode was last changed more than, exactly, or fewer than *n* days ago. An *inode* is an entry in a disk table that contains information about a file such as its owner, size, and last access date. The inode is changed when the file is first created and also later if the owner, group, or permissions are changed.

-atime IS OFTEN DEFEATED BY NIGHTLY BACKUPS

In theory, find's -atime option is useful if you are short of disk space and want to find files that have not been accessed in a long time so that you can archive them and delete them. However some backup programs, such as tar, prevent -atime from being useful because all files are accessed nightly during the system backup. cpio provides an -a option that remembers each file's last access date and time and restores it after the file has been backed up so that find's -atime option is still useful.

18

find: -size Option

The `find -size` option enables us to locate files based on the number of blocks in the file:

```
find / -size +2000 -print
```

This `find` command prints the names of all files that contain more than 2,000 blocks. It is useful when you want to find the largest files that are consuming disk space.

Following `-size`, you must specify an integer number:

+*n*	Finds only files that contain more than *n* blocks
n	Finds only files that contain exactly *n* blocks
-*n*	Finds only files that contain fewer than *n* blocks

> It is a very rare occasion when you need to search for files that contain an exact number of blocks. Usually you look for files that contain more than *n* blocks or fewer than *n* blocks. UNIX neophytes often forget the plus or minus sign for these types of `find` options and then wonder why `find` did not locate the expected files.

find: Combining Options

If you specify more than one option, the file must match all options to be displayed:

```
find / -name alpha -size +50 -mtime -3 -print
```

Here `find` displays files only when all the following are true:

- The name is *alpha*
- The size is greater than 50 blocks
- The file was last modified fewer than 3 days ago

You can specify a logical "or" condition using `-o`:

```
find / \( -size +50 -o -mtime -3 \) -print
```

Notice the use of the escaped parentheses to group the "either" and "or" options. This finds files that either have size greater than 50 blocks or were last modified fewer than 3 days ago.

find: Negating Options

You can use the ! sign to select files that do not match the given option:

```
find /dev ! \( -type b -o -type c -o type d \) -print
```

This locates all files in the /dev directory and its subdirectories that are not block special device files, character special device files, or directories. This is a useful command to locate device names that users have misspelled, which leaves a regular file in /dev that can waste a large amount of disk space.

find: -print Action

-print is an action that tells find to display the pathnames of all files that match the options given before -print. If you put the -print action before other options in the command line, those options are not used in the selection process:

```
find / -size -20 -print -mtime +30
```

This command prints all files that contain fewer than 20 blocks. The -mtime option is ignored because it comes after the -print action on the command line.

If no action is specified on the command line, -print is usually done by default. On older versions of UNIX, however, you must remember to include -print specifically, or no output is generated.

find: -exec Action

-exec is an action that lets you specify a UNIX command to run on each of the files that match the options given:

```
find / -name alpha -exec chmod a+r {} \;
```

Following -exec, you should specify a complete UNIX command and put {} where the filename will be inserted. Add \; at the end of the command to complete the required syntax. In the previous example, chmod runs on every file named alpha so that everyone can read the file.

```
find / -name core -exec rm -f {} \;
```

This example finds all files on the system named core and executes the rm command to delete them. The -f option to rm is specified so that rm does not ask for confirmation if you don't own the file and don't have write permission to the file. This is a useful command for root to run periodically because, if a process aborts, it might leave a debugging file named core in the current directory. After a while, these core files, which are not small, can collectively consume an unreasonable amount of disk space. This find command restores that disk space by finding and deleting those core files.

18

> If you have thousands of files to process, xargs (covered in the next section)
> is more efficient than -exec. For example,
>
> ```
> find / -name core -print ¦ xargs rm -f
> ```
>
> This command also deletes all core files much more quickly and with less
> overhead than the -exec option, which calls rm once for each file.

xargs

xargs is a command that accepts a list of words from standard input and provides those
words as arguments to a given command:

```
cat filelist ¦ xargs rm
```

You cannot pipe the output of cat directly to rm because rm does not look for filenames
on standard input. xargs reads the files being passed by cat and builds up a command
line beginning with rm and ending with the filenames. If there are a large number of files,
xargs runs the rm command multiple times, deleting some of the files each time. You can
specify how many arguments from standard input to build up on the command line with
the -n option:

```
cat filelist ¦ xargs -n 20 rm
```

-n 20 says to put only 20 arguments on each command line, so you delete only 20 files
at a time. Here is a different example to give you more insight into how xargs works:

```
$ ls
acme
report16
report3
report34
report527
$ ls ¦ xargs -n 2 echo ===
=== acme report16
=== report3 report34
=== report527
$
```

The first ls command shows us that there are only five files in the current directory.
(These five can be regular files or directories; it does not matter for this example.) Next
you pipe the output of ls to xargs, which composes and executes this command (the
first of several):

```
echo === acme report16
```

The command begins with echo === because these are the arguments given to the xargs command. The command then contains two filenames read from standard input. -n 2 tells xargs to add only two words from standard input to each echo command. I added === as the first echo argument so you can visually find the output from each separate echo command. You can see that xargs called echo three times to process all the standard input.

xargs can be used to solve this problem:

```
$ rm abc*
rm: arg list too long
```

The current directory contained too many filenames starting with *abc*, and the command buffer overflowed, so an error message was printed, and none of the files were deleted. xargs can solve this buffer overflow problem:

```
ls ¦ grep '^abc' ¦ xargs -n 20 rm
```
▷ *start of the line*

Here you use grep (covered in Chapter 15, "Text Filters") and regular expressions (covered in Chapter 16, "Filtering Text Using Regular Expressions") to filter the output of ls passing only filenames that begin with *abc*. xargs allows rm to operate on those files and delete them, no matter how many there are.

The expr Command

The expr command performs simple integer arithmetic:

```
$ expr 8 / 3
2
$
```

Notice that any fractional result is ignored. The general syntax is

```
expr integer1 operand integer2
```

Possible operands are given in Table 18.3.

TABLE 18.3 expr OPERANDS

Operand	Description
+	Addition
-	Subtraction
*	Multiplication
/	Integer division (any fraction in the result is dropped)
%	Remainder from a division operation (also called the modulus function)

Notice that the * sign must be quoted to prevent shell expansion (see Chapter 9), but the spaces around the * sign must not be quoted:

```
$ expr 3 \* 5
15
$
```

NEW TERM The *remainder* or *modulus* function is what remains after a division operation:

```
$ expr 19 % 7
5
$
```

In this operation, 7 goes into 19 two times with a remainder of 5. The modulus function is often called *mod* for short. You can say that 19 mod 7 equals 5.

expr requires separate arguments, each separated by a space, or you will not see the calculated result:

```
$ expr 3+2
3+2
$
```

expr is often used within backquotes in shell programming to increment a variable:

```
CNT=`expr $CNT + 1`
```

expr adds one to the current value in variable CNT, and the backquotes use command substitution to allow the new value to be assigned back to the variable CNT. (See the section "Command and Arithmetic Substitution" in Chapter 8.)

expr can also return the number of characters matched by a regular expression (see Chapter 16):

```
$ expr $ABC : '.*'        all char
7
$
```

.* is a regular expression pattern indicating all characters, so all characters of variable $ABC are counted. In this case, expr shows that it contains 7 characters.

```
$ expr $ABC : '[0-9]*'
4
$
```

[0-9]* is a regular expression pattern that matches any group of digits. In this example, expr counts the number of the digits that occur at the start of the string. Looking at the previous example, you know that there are four digits at the start of variable ABC.

Because you knew that there were seven characters total in ABC, you now know that the fifth character is not a digit.

If part of the regular expression pattern is grouped in escaped parentheses, expr returns the portion of the pattern indicated by the parentheses:

```
$ expr abcdef : '..\(..\)..'
cd
$
```

Each period is a regular expression wildcard that represents one character of the given string. The middle two periods are enclosed in escaped parentheses, so those two characters, cd, are output. This example also illustrates that the string following expr can be a literal string of characters, but it is more common in scripts for the string to be generated by variable or command substitution (see Chapter 8).

The bc Command

bc is an arithmetic utility not limited to integers:

```
$ bc
scale=4
8/3
2.6666
2.5 * 4.1/6.9
1.4855
quit
$
```

In this example, you invoke bc and set scale to 4, meaning that you want it to calculate any fraction to four decimal places. You ask it to calculate 8/3, which gives 2.6666 and then a more complex calculation. Note that spaces are optional. Finally you enter **quit** to return to the shell prompt. bc can handle addition (+), subtraction (-), multiplication (*), division (/), remainder or modulo (%), and integer exponentiation (^). bc can accurately compute numbers of any size:

```
9238472938742937 * 29384729347298472
271470026887302339647844620892264
```

bc can be used in shell variable assignment to assign calculated values to variables:

```
AVERAGE=`echo "scale=4; $PRICE/$UNITS" | bc`
```

The echo command is used here to print directives that are piped to bc. The first directive sets the scale to 4; the second directive is a division operation. These directives are piped to bc, which does the calculations and returns the result. The backquotes allow the result from bc to be stored in the variable AVERAGE.

18

bc allows conversion between different number bases:

```
$ bc
obase=16
ibase=8
400
100
77
3f
10*3
18
quit
$
```

obase=16 sets the output base to hexadecimal; ibase=8 sets the input base to octal. It is important to set the output base first. You enter **400**. It shows an octal 400 is a hex 100. You enter **77**. It shows an octal 77 is a hex 3f. Then you multiply 10 and 3, which equals 24 because 10 octal is 8 and 8*3 is 24. However, because the output base is hex, bc converts 24 to hex, which gives 18 as the reported result.

remsh/rsh/rcmd/remote (Remote Shell)

If you have several UNIX systems connected over a network, it is possible to invoke a remote shell to run a command on the remote system and return the output of that command to your screen:

```
remsh acron who
```

This shows us who is logged into the remote system called *acron*. The basic syntax is:

```
remsh remote-sys unix-command
```

remote-sys is the name of the remote system where the given *unix-command* runs. You can pipe text to remsh, which is passed to the *unix-command* being run on the remote system. Any standard output from *unix-command* on the remote system is passed to standard output on your system where it can be redirected if desired.

Different types of UNIX systems have different names for this command including: remsh, rsh, rcmd, or remote.

Check the man pages on your system to see which command is correct. Be careful to avoid confusion with the restricted shell command rsh, which is sometimes invoked as /usr/lib/rsh if rsh invokes the remote shell.

Using the remote shell requires setting up /etc/hosts.equiv, which indicates a trust relationship between the two systems. The simplest most trusting setup is to put each system name in the other system's host.equiv file. Usually the same user account is added to both systems. Then a remote command run by that user on one system runs with the same access permissions for that user on the other system. To use this facility for root, /.rhosts must be set up to contain the other system name.

Here is a more complex example that enables us to copy a whole directory tree to the remote system:

```
cd /sourcedir
find . -print ¦ cpio -ocva ¦
        remsh remote_sys \( cd /destdir \; cpio -icdum \)
```

The find command passes a list of files to cpio, which copies them to standard output. This is passed by the remote shell command to the remote system where the files are restored to the desired destination directory. Notice that many of the special characters must be escaped—that is, preceded by a backslash—so they are interpreted on the remote system and not on the local system.

Summary

In this chapter you have looked at several miscellaneous tools:

- eval
- :
- type
- sleep
- find
- xargs
- expr
- bc
- remsh/rsh/rcmd/remote

A large part of this chapter was spent on the basics of the find command. Peruse the man page on find, and you can see other useful find options for your scripts that I did not cover.

18

Questions

1. You are about to run a custom command called `process2`, but you would first like to determine where that command resides. Give a UNIX command to do this.

2. How can you determine all directories under `/data` that contain a file called `process2`, allowing any possible prefix or suffix to also be displayed (for example, you want to find names such as `process2-doc`).

3. How can you increase the numeric value in variable `PRICE` to be 3.5 times its current amount? Allow two digits to the right of the decimal point.

Terms

no-op   A command that does nothing and thus can be used as a dummy command or placeholder where syntax requires a command.

built-in   A command whose code is part of the shell as opposed to a utility which exists in a separate disk file which must be read into memory before it is executed.

reserved word   A nonquoted word that is used in grouping commands or selectively executing them, such as: `if`, `then`, `else`, `elif`, `fi`, `case`, `esac`, `for`, `while`, `until`, `do`, or `done`.

modulus function   See remainder function.

remainder function   The remainder of a division operation, which is the amount that is left over when the amounts are not evenly divisible.

inode   A table entry within a file system that contains file information such as the owner, group, permissions, last modification date or time, last access date or time, and the block list of the actual file data. There is one inode for each file. The inodes are numbered sequentially. The inode does not contain the filename. A directory is a table that maps filenames to inode numbers.

PART III
Advanced Topics

HOUR

HOUR 19

Dealing with Signals

NEW TERM   *Signals* are software interrupts sent to a program to indicate that an important event has occurred. The events can vary from user requests to illegal memory access errors. Some signals, such as the interrupt signal, indicate that a user has asked the program to do something that is not in the usual flow of control.

Because signals can arrive at any time during the execution of a script, they add an extra level of complexity to shell scripts. Scripts must account for this fact and include extra code that can determine how to respond appropriately to a signal regardless of what the script was doing when the signal was received.

In this chapter you will look at the following topics:

- The different types of signals encountered in shell programming
- How to deliver signals using the `kill` command
- Handling signals
- How to use signals within your script

How Are Signal Represented?

Each type of event is represented by a separate signal. Each signal is only a small positive integer. The signals most commonly encountered in shell script programming are given in Table 19.1. All the listed signals are available on all versions of UNIX.

TABLE 19.1 IMPORTANT SIGNALS FOR SHELL SCRIPTS

Name	Value	Description
SIGHUP	1	Hang up detected on controlling terminal or death of controlling process
SIGINT	2	Interrupt from keyboard
SIGQUIT	3	Quit from keyboard
SIGKILL	9	Kill signal
SIGALRM	14	Alarm Clock signal (used for timers)
SIGTERM	15	Termination signal

In addition to the signals listed in Table 19.1, you might occasionally see a reference to signal 0, which is more of a shell convention than a real signal. When a shell script exits either by using the exit command or by executing the last command in the script, the shell in which the script was running sends itself a signal 0 to indicate that it should terminate.

Getting a List of Signals

All the signals understood by your system are listed in the C language header file signal.h. The location of this file varies between UNIX flavors. Some common locations are

- Solaris and HPUX: /usr/include/sys/signal.h
- Linux: /usr/include/asm/signal.h

Some vendors provide a man page for this file which you can view with one of the following commands:

- In Linux: man 7 signal
- In Solaris: man -s 5 signal
- In HP-UX: man 5 signal

Another way that your system can understand a list of signals is to use the -l option of the kill command. For example on a Solaris system the output is:

```
$ kill -l
1) SIGHUP        2) SIGINT        3) SIGQUIT       4) SIGILL
 5) SIGTRAP       6) SIGABRT       7) SIGEMT        8) SIGFPE
 9) SIGKILL      10) SIGBUS       11) SIGSEGV      12) SIGSYS
13) SIGPIPE      14) SIGALRM      15) SIGTERM      16) SIGUSR1
17) SIGUSR2      18) SIGCHLD      19) SIGPWR       20) SIGWINCH
21) SIGURG       22) SIGIO        23) SIGSTOP      24) SIGTSTP
25) SIGCONT      26) SIGTTIN      27) SIGTTOU      28) SIGVTALRM
29) SIGPROF      30) SIGXCPU      31) SIGXFSZ      32) SIGWAITING
33) SIGLWP       34) SIGFREEZE    35) SIGTHAW      36) SIGCANCEL
37) SIGLOST
```

The actual list of signals varies between Solaris, HP-UX, and Linux.

Default Actions

Every signal, including those listed in Table 19.1, has a *default action* associated with it. The default action for a signal is the action that a script or program performs when it receives a signal.

Some of the possible default actions are

- Terminate the process.
- Ignore the signal.
- Dump core. This creates a file called core containing the memory image of the process when it received the signal.
- Stop the process.
- Continue a stopped process.

The default action for the signals that you should be concerned about is to terminate the process. Later in this chapter you will look at how you can change the default action performed by a script with a *signal handler*.

Delivering Signals

There are several methods of delivering signals to a program or script. One of the most common is for a user to type CONTROL-C or the INTERRUPT key while a script is executing. In this case a SIGINT is sent to the script and it terminates.

The other common method for delivering signals is to use the kill command as follows:

kill -*signal pid*

Here *signal* is either the number or name of the signal to deliver and *pid* is the process ID that the signal should be sent to.

TERM

In previous chapters you looked at the `kill` command without the signal argument. By default the `kill` command sends a TERM or terminates a signal to the program running with the specified pid. Recall from Chapter 6, "Processes," that a PID is the process ID given by UNIX to a program while it is executing. Thus the commands

```
kill pid
kill -s SIGTERM pid
```

are equivalent.

Now look at a few examples of using the `kill` command to deliver other signals.

HUP

The following command

```
$ kill -s SIGHUP 1001
```

sends the HUP or hang-up signal to the program that is running with process ID 1001. You can also use the numeric value of the signal as follows:

```
$ kill -1 1001
```

This command also sends the hang-up signal to the program that is running with process ID 1001. Although the default action for this signal calls for the process to terminate, many UNIX programs use the HUP signal as an indication that they should reinitialize themselves. For this reason, you should use a different signal if you are trying to terminate or kill a process.

QUIT and INT

If the default `kill` command cannot terminate a process, you can try to send the process either a QUIT or an INT (interrupt) signal as follows:

```
$ kill -s SIGQUIT 1001
```

or

```
$ kill -s SIGINT 1001
```

One of these signals should terminate a process, either by asking it to quit (the QUIT signal) or by asking it to interrupt its processing (the INT signal).

kill

NEW TERM Some programs and shell scripts have special functions called *signal handlers* that can ignore or discard these signals. To terminate such a program, use the kill signal:

```
$ kill -9 1001
```

Here you are sending the `kill` signal to the program running with process ID 1001. In this case you are using the numeric value of the signal, instead of the name of the signal. By convention, the numeric value of the `kill` signal, 9, is always used for it.

The `kill` signal has the special property that it cannot be caught, thus any process receiving this signal terminates immediately "with extreme prejudice." This means that a process cannot cleanly exit and might leave data it was using in a corrupted state. You should only use this signal to terminate a process when all the other signals fail to do so.

Dealing with Signals

A program or script can handle a signal in three different ways:

- Do nothing and let the default action occur. This is the simplest method for a script to deal with a signal.
- Ignore the signal and continue executing. This method is not the same as doing nothing, because ignoring a signal requires the script to have some code that explicitly ignores signals.
- Catch the signal and perform some signal-specific commands. In this method the script has a special routine that executes when a signal is received. This is the most complex and powerful method of dealing with signals.

The first method for dealing with a signal requires no additional code in your shell script. This is the default behavior for all shell scripts that do not explicitly handle signals. All the scripts that you have looked at so far handle signals using this method.

In this section you will look at the second and third methods of dealing with signals.

19

The `trap` Command

The `trap` command sets and unsets the actions taken when a signal is received. Its syntax is

```
trap name signals
```

Here *name* is a list of commands or the name of a shell function to execute when a signal in the list of specified *signals* is received. If *name* is not given, `trap` resets the action for the given signals to be the default action.

There are three common uses for `trap` in shell scripts:

- Clean up temporary files
- Always ignore signals
- Ignore signals only during critical operations

You will look at a fourth use, setting up a timer, later in this chapter.

Cleaning Up Temporary Files

Most shell scripts that create temporary files use a `trap` command similar to the following:

```
trap "rm -f $TMPF; exit 2" 1 2 3 15
```

Here you remove the file stored in `$TMPF` and then exit with a return code of 2 indicating that exit was abnormal, when either a `HUP`, `INT`, `QUIT`, or `TERM` signal is received. Usually when a script exits normally its exit code is `0`. If anything abnormal happens, the exit code should be nonzero.

Sometimes when more complicated clean up is required, a shell function can be used. In order to make the uu script (described in Chapter 12, "Parameters") signal safe, you would add something similar to the following at the beginning of the script:

```
CleanUp() {
    if [ -f "$OUTFILE" ] ; then
        printf "Cleaning Up… ";
        rm -f "$OUTFILE" 2> /dev/null ;
        echo "Done." ;
    fi
}
trap CleanUp 1 2 3 15
```

Here the function `CleanUp` is invoked whenever the script receives a `HUP`, `INT`, `QUIT`, or `TERM` signal. This function removes the output file of the script, if that file exists. By cleaning up when a signal is received, partially encoded files are not left around to confuse users.

> The main reason to use functions to handle signals is that it is nicer to have a shell function invoked when a signal is received rather than write in the appropriate code inline.
>
> Also, the commands that should be executed when a signal is received might be different depending on which point in the script the signal was received. In many cases it is difficult to capture that logic in a few commands, thus is it necessary to use a shell function as the signal handling routine.

In the previous examples, a single signal handler has been used for all signals. This is not required, and frequently different signals have different handlers. As an example, the following `trap` commands are completely valid:

```
trap CleanUp 2 15
trap Init 1
```

Here the script calls a clean up routine when an `INT` or `TERM` signal is received and calls its initialization routine when a `SIGHUP` is received. Declarations such as these are common in scripts that run as daemons.

For example, the following script, which is used to keep a process "alive," behaves differently depending on the signal that it receives:

```
#!/bin/sh

if [ $# -lt 1 ] ; then
    echo "USAGE: `basename $0` command."
    Exit 0
fi

Init() {
    printf "INFO: Initializing... "

    # check if the last backgrounded pid is valid, if it is
    # try an kill it.

    kill -0 $! 2> /dev/null;
    if [ $? -eq 0 ] ; then
        kill $! > /dev/null 2>&1
        if [ $? -ne 0 ] ; then
            echo "ERROR: Already running as pid $!. Exiting."
            exit 1
        fi
    fi

    # start a new program in the background

    $PROG &
    printf "Done.\n"
}

CleanUp() {
    kill -9 $! ; exit 2 ;
}

# main()
```

19

```
trap CleanUp 2 3 15
trap Init 1

PROG=$1
Init

while : ;
do
    wait $!
    $PROG &
done
```

Here you have two important functions, `Init` and `CleanUp`. The `Init` function is responsible for stopping any running instances of the program and then starting it again. The `CleanUp` function is responsible for killing the running program and then exiting.

All this script does is launch a program in the background and wait for it to finish. If the program finishes, it is launched again. The script exits when it receives an `INT`, `QUIT`, or `TERM` signal.

Ignoring Signals

Sometimes there is no intelligent or easy way to clean up if a signal is received. In these cases, it is better to ignore signals than to deal with them. There are two methods of ignoring signals:

```
trap '' signals
trap : signals
```

Here `signals` is a list of signals to ignore. The only difference between these two forms is that the first form passes a special argument, `''` or null, to the `trap` command and the second uses the `:` command. The form to use is largely based on programmer style because both forms produce the same result.

If you simply wanted the uu script from Chapter 12 to ignore all signals, instead of cleaning up when it received a signal, you could add the following to the beginning of the script:

```
trap '' 1 2 3 15
```

Ignoring Signals During Critical Operations

When this command is given in a script, the script ignores all signals until it exits. From a programmer's perspective, this might be a good idea, but from a user's perspective, it is not. A better idea is to have only the critical sections of a script ignore traps. This is achieved by unsetting the signal handler when a section of critical code has finished executing.

As an illustration, say you have a shell script with a shell function called DoImportantStuff(). This routine should not be interrupted. In order to ensure this, you can install the signal handler before the function is called and reset it after the call finishes:

```
trap '' 1 2 3 15
DoImportantStuff
trap 1 2 3 15
```

The second call to trap has only signal arguments. This causes trap to reset the handler for each of the signals to the default. By doing this, you enable the user to still terminate the script and ensure that critical operations are performed without interruption.

Setting Up a Timer

In many scripts, there are critical sections where commands that require a large amount of time to complete are executed. On rare occasions, these commands might not finish processing. In order to deal with this situation, you need to set up a timer within the script. When the timer expires, you should terminate the program and inform the user about the abnormal exit.

In this section you will walk through a simple script that demonstrates the major aspects of setting up a timer using the ALARM signal and a signal handler.

The main body of this script needs to perform the following actions:

1. Set a handler for the ALARM signal.
2. Set the timer.
3. Execute the program.
4. Wait for the program to finish executing.
5. Unset the timer.

If the timer expires before the program finishes executing, the handler for the ALARM signal needs to terminate the program.

The main body looks like the following:

```
# main()

trap AlarmHandler 14

SetTimer 15

$PROG &
CHPROCIDS="$CHPROCIDS $!"
wait $!
```

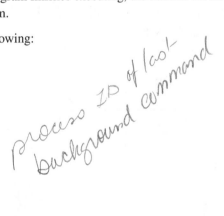

process ID of last
background command

19

```
UnsetTimer

echo "All Done."
exit 0
```

The only thing in the main body that was not explicitly mentioned previously is the
CHPROCIDS variable. This variable is required to maintain a list of all the child processes
of the script, because the possible child process are

- The timer

- The program

AlarmHandler

The first thing that you do is to install a handler for the ALARM signal. This handler is the
function AlarmHandler:

```
AlarmHandler() {
    echo "Got SIGALARM, cmd took too long."
    KillSubProcs
    exit 14
}
```

This is a simple function that prints a message to the screen, calls the function
KillSubProcs, and then exits with an exit code of 14 to indicate that the alarm was trig-
gered.

The KillSubProcs function is a simple function that kills all the child processes of the
script as stored in the variable CHPROCIDS:

```
KillSubProcs() {
    kill ${CHPROCIDS:-$!}        PID of last
    if [ $? -eq 0 ] ; then       background command
        echo "Sub-processes killed." ;
    fi
}
```

exit status of last command / *refer to exit status of last command*

SetTimer

The next task that you perform is to set the timer using the SetTimer function:

```
SetTimer() {
    DEF_TOUT=${1:-10};
    if [ $DEF_TOUT -ne 0 ] ; then        process ID
        sleep $DEF_TOUT && kill -s 14 $$ &
        CHPROCIDS="$CHPROCIDS $!"
        TIMERPROC=$!
    fi                                    signal 14
}
```

Child process ID

This function takes a single argument that indicates the number of sections that it should set a timer for. The default is 10 seconds.

As you can see, setting the timer is fairly trivial. All you do is issue a `sleep` command with a timeout and then use the `kill` command to send the shell's process ID (stored in $$) an ALARM signal. In order to continue processing, you place this timer command in the background.

Because the timer is a background process, you need to update the list of child processes with its ID. You also save the process ID of the timer in the variable TIMERPROC so that you can later unset the timer.

UnsetTimer

The last function is the UnsetTimer function that unsets the timer set by the SetTimer function. Unsetting the timer basically means killing its process:

```
UnsetTimer() {
    kill $TIMERPROC
}
```

The Complete Timer Script

The complete timer script follows:

```
#! /bin/sh

AlarmHandler() {
    echo "Got SIGALARM, cmd took too long."
    KillSubProcs
    exit 14
}

KillSubProcs() {
    kill ${CHPROCIDS:-$!}
    if [ $? -eq 0 ] ; then echo "Sub-processes killed." ; fi
}

SetTimer() {
    DEF_TOUT=${1:-10};
    if [ $DEF_TOUT -ne 0 ] ; then
        sleep $DEF_TOUT && kill -s 14 $$ &
        CHPROCIDS="$CHPROCIDS $!"
        TIMERPROC=$!
    fi
}

UnsetTimer() {
    kill $TIMERPROC
}
```

19

```
# main()

trap AlarmHandler 14

SetTimer 15
$PROG &
CHPROCIDS="$CHPROCIDS $!"
wait $!
UnsetTimer
echo "All Done."
exit 0
```

Conclusion

In this chapter, I introduced the concept of signals. Signals inform a program or script that an important event has occurred.

You learned about the most common signals encountered in shell programming. I also listed several methods of obtaining a complete list of all the signals understood by your system. In this section you also covered the concept of delivering signals and the default actions associated with a signal.

In the second section of this chapter I introduced the three main methods of handling a signal in a script. Now you know how to catch signals and handle them using signal handlers. You also know how to ignore signals. Finally I showed you how to use signals to set up a timer inside your scripts.

Questions

1. The following is the main body of the "alive" script presented earlier in this chapter. Please change it so that receiving a SIGQUIT causes it to exit when the wait command returns.

```
# main()

trap CleanUp 2 3 15
trap Init 1

PROG=$1
Init

while : ;
do
    wait $!
    $PROG &
done
```

2. Add a signal handler to the timer script to handle the INT signal.

HOUR 20

Debugging

In this book you have looked at scripts that are quite short. Thus, the issue of debugging them has boiled down to looking at their output and making sure it is correct.

For larger shell scripts, especially the kind that change system configurations, trying to deduce the source of a problem from a script's output is insufficient. Often, by the time you get the output, it is too late—the script will have made incorrect modifications or changes. Another common scenario is adding features to a large script that someone else developed. In such cases you need to make sure your changes don't affect the rest of the script. Fortunately, the shell provides several built-in commands for enabling different modes of debugging support.

In this chapter you learn how to enable debugging, and then you will look at how to use the following debugging modes:

- Syntax checking
- Shell tracing

Enabling Debugging

By now, you are quite familiar with the basic syntax for executing a shell script:

```
$ script arg1 arg2 ... argN
```

Here *script* is the name of the script, and *arg1* through *argN* are the arguments to the script. A frequently used alternative method to execute a shell script is

```
$ /bin/sh script arg1 arg2 ... argN
```

Here you explicitly specify the shell, in this case /bin/sh, that you used to execute the script. The advantage of this method is that you can enable a debugging mode by supplying arguments to the shell.

Using this method of script invocation, the basic syntax for enabling a debugging mode is

```
$ /bin/sh option script arg1 arg2 ... argN
```

Here *option* is one of the debugging options covered in Table 20.1.

A third way of enabling debugging is to change the first line of the *script*. Usually, the first line of a script is

```
#!/bin/sh
```

UNIX uses this line to determine the shell you can use to execute a script. This indicates that the shell /bin/sh should be used to execute the script. Modify this line to specify a debugging option as follows:

```
#!/bin/sh option
```

Here *option* is one of the debugging options listed in Table 20.1.

Because the previously mentioned methods for enabling debugging modes take effect when a script is invoked, they are sometimes referred to as *invocation activated* debugging modes.

TABLE 20.1   DEBUGGING OPTIONS FOR SHELL SCRIPTS

Option	Description
-n	Reads all commands, but does not execute them.
-v	Displays all lines as they are read.
-x	Displays all commands and their arguments as they execute. This option is often referred to as the *shell tracing* option.

Using the set command

In one of the invocation activated debugging modes, the default behavior is for that debugging mode to take effect at the first line of your script and remain in effect until the last line. Sometimes you just need to debug a particular function or section of your script. In these cases, enabling debugging for the entire script is overkill.

As you see later in this chapter, the debugging output is quite extensive, and it is often hard to sort out the real errors from the noise. Address this problem with the set command to enable the debugging modes.

By using the set command, you can enable and disable debugging at any point in your shell script.

Enabling Debugging Using set

The basic syntax follows:

set *option*

Here *option* is one of the options given in Table 20.1.

You can use the set command anywhere in your shell script, and many scripts use it to change the debugging flags as part of the normal execution of the script. Because these debugging modes are activated only when the shell script programmer uses the set command, they are sometimes referred to as "programmer activated" modes.

Consider the following excerpt from a shell script (the line numbers are provided for your reference):

```
1  #!/bin/sh
2  set -x
3  if [ -z "$1" ] ; then
4      echo "ERROR: Insufficient Args."
5      exit 1
6  fi
```

Here the shell programmer is requesting that shell tracing (the -x option) be activated with the command from line 2:

set -x

Because this command occurs before the if statement (lines 3 through 6), shell tracing will be active while the if statement executes. Unless it is explicitly disabled later in the script, shell tracing remains in effect until the script exits. You will learn about the effect that shell tracing has on the output of a script in the "Shell Tracing" section of this chapter.

20

Disabling Debugging Using set

In addition to enabling debugging modes, you can use the set command to disable debugging modes as follows:

```
set +option
```

Here *option* is the letter corresponding to one of the options given in Table 20.1. For example, the command

```
$ set +x
```

disables the shell tracing debugging mode.

All the debugging modes that are enabled for a script can be deactivated using the following command:

```
$ set -
```

Enabling Debugging for a Single Function

One of the most common uses of the set command is to enable a particular debugging mode before a function executes and then disable debugging when the function finishes.

For example, if you have a function called BuggyFunction() and you only want to enable the shell tracing debugging mode while that function executes, use the following command:

```
set -x ; BuggyFunction; set +x ;
```

Here the debugging mode is enabled just before the function is called and is disabled when the function completes. This method is favored over explicitly using the set command inside a function to enable debugging because it enables the implementation of the function to remain unchanged.

Syntax Checking

When dealing with any shell script, check the syntax of the script before trying to execute it. This enables you to fix most problems.

To enable syntax checking, use the -n option as follows:

```
/bin/sh -n script arg1 arg2 ... argN
```

Here *script* is the name of a script and *arg1* through *argN* are the arguments for that script. This command generates output only if errors occur in the specified *script*.

Check the syntax of the following script (the line numbers are included for your reference):

```
1   #!/bin/sh
2
3   YN=y
4   if [ $YN = "yes" ]
5       echo "yes"
6   fi
```

Can you spot the error?

If this script is stored in the file buggy1.sh, check its syntax as follows:

```
$ /bin/sh -n ./buggy1.sh
```

The output looks like the following:

```
./buggy1.sh: syntax error at line 7: 'fi' unexpected
```

This tells you that when the shell tried to read line 7, it found that the fi statement on line 6 was unexpected. By now you have probably figured out that the reason the shell was trying read line 7 is that the if statement on line 4

```
if [ $YN = "y" ]
```

is not terminated with a then statement. This line should read as follows:

```
if [ $YN = "y" ] ; then
```

Making this change, you find that the syntax of the script is okay because the command

```
$ /bin/sh -n buggy1.sh
```

produces no output.

Why You Should Use Syntax Checking

After looking at the shell script in the previous example, you might be wondering why you couldn't simply execute the shell script to determine the problem. After all, the command

```
$ /bin/sh ./buggy1.sh
```

produces the output

```
buggy1.sh: syntax error at line 7: 'fi' unexpected
```

This output is identical to the output of the following command:

```
$ /bin/sh -n ./buggy1.sh
```

For this script, it does not matter whether you use the syntax checking mode, but this is not always the case. As an example, consider the following script (the line numbers are included for your reference):

20

```
 1   #!/bin/sh
 2
 3   Failed() {
 4       if [ $1 -ne 0 ] ; then
 5           echo "Failed. Exiting." ; exit 1 ;
 6       fi
 7       echo "Done."
 8   }
 9
10   echo "Deleting old backups, please wait... \c"
11   rm -r backup > /dev/null 2>&1
12   Failed $?
13
14   echo "Make backup (y/n)? \c"
15   read RESPONSE
16   case $RESPONSE in
17       [yY]¦[Yy][Ee][Ss]¦*)
18           echo "Making backup, please wait... \c"
19           cp -r docs backup
20           Failed
21       [nN]¦[Nn][Oo])
22           echo "Backup Skipped." ;;
23   esac
```

There are at least three errors in this script. See if you can find them.

If this script is in a file called buggy2.sh, executing it produces the following output:

```
Deleting old backups, please wait... Done.
Make backup (y/n)?
```

Entering y at the prompt produces the following error:

```
./buggy3.sh: syntax error at line 21: ')' unexpected
```

Due to a bug in the script, you can't make a backup, and you have already lost your previous backup. As you can imagine, this is a very bad situation.

The reason the script gets that far before detecting an error is that the shell reads and executes each line of a shell script individually, just like it does on the command line. Here the shell reads and executes lines until it encounters a problem.

By using the -n option, the script does not execute. Instead, each line is checked to make sure that it has the correct syntax. This helps you avoid the situation encountered by running the buggy2.sh script because only the error is reported:

```
./buggy2.sh: syntax error at line 21: ')' unexpected
```

Using Verbose Mode

Now that you know why syntax checking should be employed, you can track down the source of the problem.

Looking at line 21 of buggy2.sh

```
21       [nN]¦[Nn][Oo])
```

it is hard to see why the shell thinks the parenthesis) is unexpected. Sometimes knowing where a syntax error occurs is not enough—you have to know the context in which the error occurs.

The shell provides you with the -v (*v* as in *verbose*) debugging mode in order to check the context in which a syntax error occurs. When this option is specified, the shell prints each line of a script as it is read.

If you issue the -v option by itself, every line in the script will execute. Because you want to check the syntax, you combine the -n and -v options as follows:

```
$ /bin/sh –nv script arg1 arg2 ... argN
```

If you execute buggy2.sh with the debugging options

```
$ /bin/sh –nv ./buggy2.sh
```

the output looks like the following (the line numbers are provided for your reference):

```
 1   #!/bin/sh
 2
 3   Failed() {
 4       if [ $1 -ne 0 ] ; then
 5           echo "Failed. Exiting." ; exit 1 ;
 6       fi
 7       echo "Done."
 8   }
 9
10   echo "Deleting old backups, please wait... \c"
11   rm -r backup > /dev/null 2>&1
12   Failed $?
13
14   echo "Make backup (y/n)? \c"
15   read RESPONSE
16   case $RESPONSE in
17       [yY]¦[Yy][Ee][Ss])
18           echo "Making backup, please wait... \c"
19           cp -r docs backup
20           Failed ;;
21       [nN]¦[Nn][Oo])
➥./buggy2.sh: syntax error at line 21: ')' unexpected
```

From this output, the reason that the shell issues an error is apparent. The problem is on line 20; the first pattern of the case statement is not terminated with the ;;. Make the change

```
Failed ;;
```

or

```
Failed
;;
```

to fix this script. After making this change, the command

```
$ /bin/sh -n buggy2.sh
```

does not produce an error message. As you will see in the next section, this does not necessarily mean that the script is free from bugs.

However, this is not to say that you should not use these modes. You should always make sure that these commands do not complain about syntax errors. It is much easier to concentrate on the real bugs, either in logic or program flow, when you know that major syntax errors are not present in your script.

For readers familiar with the C programming language, syntax checking your shell scripts using sh -n or sh -nv is equivalent to checking your source files with lint.

Shell Tracing

There are many instances when syntax checking gives your script a clean bill of health, but bugs are still lurking in your script. Running syntax checking on a shell script is similar to running a spelling checker on a text document—it might find most of the misspellings, but it can't fix problems like spelling *read* as *red*.

For text documents, you need to proofread them in order to find and fix all misspellings. To find and fix these types of problems in shell scripts, you need to use shell tracing.

In shell tracing mode the shell prints each command in the exact form in which it executes. For this reason, you sometimes see the shell tracing mode referred to as the *execution tracing mode*.

The shell tracing or execution tracing mode is enabled by using the -x option (*x* as in *execution*). For a complete script, it is enabled as follows:

```
$ /bin/sh -x script arg1 arg2 ... argN
```

As was mentioned before, it can also be enabled using the set command:

```
set -x
```

To get an idea of what the output of shell tracing looks like, try the following command:

```
$ set -x ; ls *.sh ; set +x
```

The output is similar to the following:

```
+ ls buggy.sh buggy1.sh buggy2.sh buggy3.sh buggy4.sh
buggy.sh    buggy1.sh  buggy2.sh  buggy3.sh  buggy4.sh
+ set +x
```

In the output, the lines preceded by the plus (+) character are the commands that the shell executes. The other lines are the output from those commands. As you can see from the output, the shell prints the exact `ls` command it executes. This is extremely useful in debugging because it enables you to determine whether all the substitutions were performed correctly.

Finding Syntax Bugs Using Shell Tracing

In the preceding example, you used the script `buggy2.sh`. One of the problems with this script is that it deleted the old backup before asking whether you wanted to make a new backup. To solve this problem, the script is rewritten as follows:

```
#!/bin/sh

Failed() {
    if [ $1 -ne 0 ] ; then
        echo "Failed. Exiting." ; exit 1 ;
    fi
    echo "Done."
}

YesNo() {
    echo "$1 (y/n)? \c"
    read RESPONSE
    case $RESPONSE in
        [yY]¦[Yy][Ee][Ss]) RESPONSE=y ;;
        [nN]¦[Nn][Oo]) RESPONSE=n ;;
    esac
}

YesNo "Make backup"
if [ $RESPONSE = "y" ] ; then

    echo "Deleting old backups, please wait... \c"
    rm -fr backup > /dev/null 2>&1
    Failed $?

    echo "Making new backups, please wait... \c"
    cp -r docs backup
    Failed

fi
```

20

There are at least three syntax bugs in this script and at least one logical oversight. See if you can find them.

Assuming that the script is called `buggy3.sh`, first check its syntax as follows:

```
$ /bin/sh -n ./buggy3.sh
```

Because there is no output, execute it:

```
$ /bin/sh ./buggy3.sh
```

The script first prompts you as follows:

```
Make backup (y/n)?
```

Answering y to this prompt produces output similar to the following:

```
Deleting old backups, please wait... Done.
Making new backups, please wait... buggy3.sh: test: argument expected
```

On Linux systems, the output might vary slightly. In any case, an error message is generated. Because this doesn't state which line of the script the error occurs on, you need to track it down manually.

From the output you know that the old backup was deleted successfully; therefore, the error is probably in the following part of the script:

```
echo "Making new backups, please wait... \c"
cp -r docs backup
Failed
```

Enable shell tracing for this section as follows:

```
set -x
echo "Making new backups, please wait... \c"
cp -r docs backup
Failed
set +x
```

The output changes as follows (assuming you answer y to the question):

```
Make backup (y/n)? y
Deleting old backups, please wait... Done.
+ echo Making new backups, please wait... \c
Making new backups, please wait... + cp -r docs backup
+ Failed
+ [ -ne 0 ]
buggy3.sh: test: argument expected
```

The execution trace varies slightly on Linux systems.

From this output you can see that the problem occurred in the following statement:

```
[ -ne 0 ]
```

From Chapter 10, "Flow Control", you know that the form of a numerical test command is

```
[ num1 operator num2 ]
```

Here it looks like *num1* does not exist. Also from the trace you can tell that this error occurred after executing the `Failed` function. Looking at the function

```
Failed() {
    if [ $1 -ne 0 ] ; then
        echo "Failed. Exiting." ; exit 1 ;
    fi
    echo "Done."
}
```

you find that there is only one numerical test. This test compares $1, the first argument to the function, to see whether it is equal to 0. Now the problem should be obvious. When you invoked the `Failed` function

```
echo "Making new backups, please wait... \c"
cp -r docs backup
Failed
```

you forgot to give it an argument, thus the numeric test failed. There are two possible fixes to this bug. The first is to fix the code that calls the function:

```
echo "Making new backups, please wait... \c"
cp -r docs backup
Failed $?    exit status
```

The second is to fix the function itself by quoting the first argument, `"$1"`:

```
Failed() {
    if [ "$1" -ne 0 ] ; then
        echo "Failed. Exiting." ; exit 1 ;
    fi
    echo "Done."
}
```

20

By quoting the first argument, `"$1"`, the shell uses the null or empty string when the function is called without any arguments. In this case the numeric test will not fail because both *num1* and *num2* have a value.

The best idea is to perform both fixes. After these fixes are applied, the shell tracing output is similar to the following:

```
Make backup (y/n)? y
Deleting old backups, please wait... Done.
```

```
+ echo Making new backups, please wait... \c
Making new backups, please wait... + cp -r docs backup
+ Failed
+ [   -ne 0 ]
+ echo Done.
Done.
+ set +x
```

Finding Logical Bugs Using Shell Tracing

As mentioned before, there is at least one logical bug in this script. With the help of shell tracing, you can locate and fix this bug.

Consider the prompt produced by this script:

```
Make backup (y/n)?
```

If you do not type a response and press Enter, the script reports an error similar to the following:

```
./buggy3.sh: [: =: unary operator expected
```

To determine where this error occurs, it is best to run the entire script in shell tracing mode:

```
$ /bin/sh -x ./buggy3.sh
```

The output is similar to the following:

```
+ YesNo Make backup
+ echo Make backup (y/n)? \c
+ /bin/echo Make backup (y/n)? \c
Make backup (y/n)? + read RESPONSE

+ [ = y ]
./buggy3.sh: [: =: unary operator expected
```

Here the blank line is the result of pressing Enter instead of typing a response to the prompt, as you can see from the next line that the shell executes:

```
[ = y ]
```

This is part of the if statement:

```
if [ $RESPONSE = "y" ] ; then
```

Although this can be fixed by changing the if statement

```
if [ "$RESPONSE" = "y" ] ; then
```

the correct fix for this problem is to track down the reason why the variable RESPONSE is not set. This variable is set by the function YesNo:

```
YesNo() {
    echo "$1 (y/n)? \c"
    read RESPONSE
    case $RESPONSE in
        [yY]¦[Yy][Ee][Ss]) RESPONSE=y ;;
        [nN]¦[Nn][Oo]) RESPONSE=n ;;
    esac
}
```

There are two problems with this script. The first is that the read command

```
read RESPONSE
```

does not set a value for RESPONSE if the user presses Enter without typing some input. Because you cannot change the read command, you need to look for some other method of solving this problem.

This leads you to a logical problem—the case statement is not validating the user input. A simple fix is the following:

```
YesNo() {
    echo "$1 (y/n)? \c"
    read RESPONSE
    case "$RESPONSE" in
        [yY]¦[Yy][Ee][Ss]) RESPONSE=y ;;
        *) RESPONSE=n ;;
    esac
}
```

(handwritten annotations: "End of pattern", "End of case statement", "OR")

Here you treat all responses other than "*yes*" responses as negative responses, including no response at all.

Using Debugging Hooks

In the previous examples, you were able to deduce the location of a bug by using shell tracing for either the entire script or for part of the script. In the case of enabling tracing for a part of a script, you had to edit the script to insert the debug command:

```
set -x
```

New Term   In larger scripts, a more common practice is to embed *debugging hooks*. Debugging hooks are functions that enable shell tracing during functions or critical code sections. They are activated in one of two ways:

- The script is run with a particular command line option (commonly -d or -x).
- The script is run with an environment variable set to true (commonly DEBUG=true or TRACE=true).

20

Here is a function that enables you to activate and deactivate debugging at will if the
variable DEBUG is set to true:

```
Debug() {
    if [ "$DEBUG" = "true" ] ; then
        if [ "$1" = "on"   -o "$1" = "ON" ] ; then
            set -x
        else
            set +x
        fi
    fi
}
```

To activate debugging, use the following:

```
Debug on
```

To deactivate debugging, use either of the following:

```
Debug
Debug off
```

Actually, any argument passed to this function other than on or ON deactivates debugging.

As an example of using this function, modify the functions in the script buggy3.sh to
have debugging automatically enabled if the variable DEBUG is set. The modifications are
as follows:

```
#!/bin/sh

Debug() {
    if [ "$DEBUG" = "true" ] ; then
        if [ "$1" = "on"   -o "$1" = "ON" ] ; then
            set -x
        else
            set +x
        fi
    fi
}

Failed() {
    Debug on
    if [ "$1" -ne 0 ] ; then
        echo "Failed. Exiting." ; exit 1 ;
    fi
    echo "Done."
    Debug off
}

YesNo() {
    Debug on
```

```
    echo "$1 (y/n)? \c"
    read RESPONSE
    case "$RESPONSE" in
        [yY]¦[Yy][Ee][Ss]) RESPONSE=y ;;
        *) RESPONSE=n ;;
    esac
    Debug off
}

YesNo "Make backup"
if [ "$RESPONSE" = "y" ] ; then

    echo "Deleting old backups, please wait... \c"
    rm -r backup > /dev/null 2>&1
    Failed $?

    echo "Making new backups, please wait... \c"
    cp -r docs backup
    Failed $?
fi
```

The output will be normal if the script executes in either of the following methods:

```
$ /bin/sh ./buggy3.sh
$ ./buggy3.sh
```

The output includes shell tracing if the same script executes in either of the following methods:

```
$ DEBUG=true /bin/sh ./buggy3.sh
$ DEBUG=true ./buggy3.sh
```

Summary

In the process of developing or maintaining large shell scripts, you need to find and fix bugs that occur in them. In this chapter you looked at the tools provided by the shell to ease the task of debugging shell scripts. Some of the topics you covered are

- Enabling debugging
- Syntax checking using sh -n and sh -nv
- Using shell tracing to find syntax and logic bugs
- Embedding debugging hooks in your shell scripts

By learning the techniques used in debugging shell scripts, you can fix your own scripts as well as maintain scripts written by other programmers.

20

Questions

1. What are the three main forms of enabling debugging in a shell script?

2. Enhance the Debug() function given in this chapter so that the programmer has to press Enter after deactivating the debugging mode.

   When you debug scripts that have several dozen functions, this feature enables you to study the debugging output of a particular function in detail before the script proceeds to the next function.

Hour 21

Problem Solving with Functions

In previous chapters you looked at writing short shell scripts that perform a specific task. In each shell script, you needed to perform a set of common tasks. Some examples of the required tasks are

- Displaying , ERROR, WARNING, and USAGE messages
- Prompting the user for input

In some cases you needed to repeat these tasks, so you used shell functions. You were able to tailor the output of these functions to suit your needs by using arguments. Many of your scripts reused functions developed for other shell scripts.

In this chapter, I will present a library of shell functions that you can use in your shell scripts to perform some common UNIX task. By using and improving on these implementations, you can avoid having to reinvent the wheel when faced with a particular problem.

Creating a Library of Functions

In previous chapters, when you wrote shell scripts that required the use of a function, you added that function to the shell scripts file. In that model, whenever you wanted to use a function in a script, you had to copy it from a different file.

When you have two or three scripts, this is fine, but as the number of scripts you write increases, so do the number of copies of the functions. Say you locate a bug in one of your functions. Imagine how hard it would be to fix every copy of that function if the function is used in ten or more shell scripts.

NEW TERM To reduce the complexity involved in maintaining shell functions, it would be ideal to create a central repository of functions that you could access from your shell script. In other programming languages, a central repository of functions is called a *library*.

Creating the Library

Creating a library of shell functions is exactly like creating a shell script. The main difference between the two is that a library contains only functions, whereas a script contains both functions and main code.

NEW TERM *Main code* consists of all the commands in a shell script that are not contained within a function. In the following shell script, lines 1, 2, and 4 are considered main code:

```
1   #!/bin/sh
2   MSG="hello"
3   echo_error() { echo "ERROR:" $@ >&2 ; }
4   echo_error $MSG
```

Line 3, which contains a function definition, is not considered main code.

In comparison, a library of shell functions does not contain any main code. It contains only functions. For example, the following would be considered a library:

```
#!/bin/sh
echo_error() { echo "ERROR:" $@ >&2 ; }
echo_warning() { echo "WARNING:" $@ >&2 ; }
```

Notice that this file contains only function definitions.

Strictly speaking, nothing is preventing a library from containing main code. The distinction between a script and a library is purely a conceptual one. To make it simpler for maintenance purposes, you should avoid having anything other than function definitions in a library script.

Including Functions from a Library

To use a set of functions defined in a library, you need to be able to include or require these functions in shell scripts. You can do this by using the . command. Its syntax is as follows:

```
. file
```

Here *file* is the name of a file that contains shell commands. If the shell functions given in the previous example were stored in a file called messages.sh, the command

```
. messages.sh
```

can be used to include the functions echo_error and echo_warning into a shell script. As an example, you can rewrite the script

```
1   #!/bin/sh
2   MSG="hello"
3   echo_error() { echo "ERROR:" $@ >&2 ; }
4   echo_error $MSG
```

to use messages.sh as follows:

```
1   #!/bin/sh
2   . $HOME/lib/sh/messages.sh
3   MSG="hello"
4   echo_error $MSG
```

Here you are assuming that the file messages.sh is stored in the directory $HOME/lib/sh. If this directory did not contain messages.sh, an error message similar to the following would be displayed:

```
sh: /home/ranga/lib/sh/messages.sh: No such file or directory
```

In most versions of the shell, the shell script exits at this point without executing any other commands. For this reason, most shell scripts include all their function libraries before executing any commands.

Naming Conventions

Unlike other languages, there are no widespread naming conventions for shell libraries or shell functions. Many programmers feel that descriptive names are best for both functions and libraries, whereas others feel that some structure such as that found in the C programming language should be used. In reality, both are good ideas.

21

Library Naming

For the purposes of this chapter, I assume that the shell functions that are covered are stored in the file

```
$HOME/lib/sh/libTYSP.sh
```

This naming scheme provides double redundancy and can be explained as follows:

- The `lib` in `libTYSP.sh` indicates that this file is a library. This is similar to the convention used in the C language.
- The `.sh` in `libTYSP.sh` indicates that this file contains Bourne shell code.
- The directory `$HOME/lib` indicates that this file is a library because it resides in the `lib` (*lib* as in *library*) directory.
- The directory `$HOME/lib/sh` indicates that this file is a Bourne Shell library because it resides in the `sh` directory under the `lib` directory.

To use this library in your scripts, you need to include it as follows:

```
. $HOME/lib/sh/libTYSP.sh
```

If you put the library in a different directory, say `/usr/local/lib/sh/libTYSP.sh`, your scripts need to access it as follows:

```
. /usr/local/lib/sh/libTYSP.sh
```

Function Naming

For functions, use the following naming scheme:

- `print`*String* for functions that display a message. Here *String* describes the type of message that is displayed.
- `prompt`*String* for functions that prompt the user for input. Here *String* is the name of a variable set by the function after reading input from the user.
- `get`*String* for functions that retrieve some type of data. Here *String* describes the information that is retrieved.

Useful Functions

Now that I have covered the background knowledge needed to create and use a library of shell functions, look at a shell library that provides you with the capability to perform common scripting tasks easily. A complete listing of the library is available at the end of this chapter.

Some of the functions you will look at are

- `printERROR`
- `printWARNING`
- `printUSAGE`
- `promptYESNO`
- `promptRESPONSE`
- `getSpaceFree`
- `getSpaceUsed`
- `getPID`
- `getUID`

In addition, you will be asked to develop four additional functions as part of the "Questions" section in this chapter:

- `toUpper`
- `toLower`
- `isSpaceAvailable`
- `isUserRoot`

By developing these functions, you can gain experience in working with a library of shell functions.

In the following sections, I will first present a brief description of each function or group of functions, followed by the implementation of the functions. At the end of each section is a discussion of the function's implementation along with caveats regarding its use.

Some of these functions need to be modified to work properly on all versions of UNIX. In this chapter, I will note the differences. In Chapter 23, "Scripting for Portability," I will show you how to modify these functions to account for the differences between different versions of UNIX.

Displaying Messages

Most of the messages that shell scripts display do not need special handling, such as prefixing the message with a description or having the output redirected to STDERR. The exceptions are error, warning, and usage messages. These messages require some extra handling. The following functions take care of this handling for you:

```
##################################################
# Name: printERROR
# Desc: prints an message to STDERR
```

21

```
# Args: $@ -> message to print
################################################

printERROR() {
    echo "ERROR:" $@ >&2
}


################################################
# Name: printWARNING
# Desc: prints an message to STDERR
# Args: $@ -> message to print
################################################

printWARNING() {
    echo "WARNING:" $@ >&2
}


################################################
# Name: printUSAGE
# Desc: prints a USAGE message and then exits
# Args: $@ -> message to print
################################################

printUSAGE() {
    echo "USAGE:" $@
    exit
}
```

All these commands work by calling the echo command and passing it two arguments:

- The message prefix, either ERROR, WARNING, or USAGE.
- The arguments are specified to these functions by the user. The arguments are stored in $@, as explained in Chapter 12, "Parameters."

The first two functions, printERROR and printWARNING, display error and warning messages. Both messages indicate to a user that something has gone wrong. Thus they redirect the output to STDERR, which is reserved for error reporting.

Usually an error indicates the occurrence of something unexpected that is difficult to recover from, such as a command failure. A warning message usually indicates that something unexpected occurred, but the script was able to recover from this.

The advantage of using these functions is that they provide a standard output format for errors and warning throughout you script. As an example, the following error message

```
echo "ERROR: File $MYFILE was not found." >&2
```

can be written

```
printERROR "File $MYFILE was not found."
```

Because the function printERROR always prefixes the message you want to display with the word ERROR and redirects the output to STDERR, you don't have to worry about forgetting these things when displaying an error message.

The third function, printUSAGE, displays a usage message and then exits. It informs the user that the script was invoked incorrectly. This type of message was discussed in depth in Chapter 12.

Asking a Question

In interactive shell scripts, you need to obtain input from the user. Sometimes this involves asking simple *yes* or *no* questions. In other instances, you need to ask the user a question that requires a more complicated response. For example, many scripts need to retrieve the name of a file on which to operate.

In this section, I present two functions that help you to prompt the user and get a response:

- promptYESNO
- promptRESPONSE

Asking a *Yes* or *No* Question

One of the most common types of questions asked by shell scripts is a *yes* or *no* question. For example, this shell script

```
Make backup (y/n)?
```

asks whether you want to make a backup.

The function, promptYESNO, provides you with a reusable method of asking a *yes* or *no* question and getting a response. The user's response, y indicating *yes* or n indicating *no*, is stored in the variable YESNO after the function completes.

```
################################################
# Name: promptYESNO
# Desc: ask a yes/no question
# Args: $1 -> The prompt
#       $2 -> The default answer (optional)
# Vars: YESNO -> set to the users response
#                y for yes, n for no
################################################

promptYESNO() {

    if [ $# -lt 1 ] ; then
        printERROR "Insufficient Arguments."
        return 1
```

21

no of postion parameters on command line

```
        fi

        DEF_ARG=""
        YESNO=""

        case "$2" in
            [yY]¦[yY][eE][sS])
                    DEF_ARG=y ;;
            [nN]¦[nN][oO])
                    DEF_ARG=n ;;
        esac

        while :
        do

            printf "$1 (y/n)? "

            if [ -n "$DEF_ARG" ] ; then
                printf "[$DEF_ARG] "
            fi

            read YESNO

            if [ -z "$YESNO" ] ; then
                YESNO="$DEF_ARG"
            fi

            case "$YESNO" in
                [yY]¦[yY][eE][sS])
                    YESNO=y ; break ;;
                [nN]¦[nN][oO])
                    YESNO=n ; break ;;
                *)
                    YESNO="" ;;
            esac

        done

        export YESNO
        unset DEF_ARG
        return 0
}
```

(Handwritten annotations: "Answer" pointing to YESNO line; "Prompt" pointing to printf "$1 (y/n)? "; "true if string has non zero size" pointing to if [-n "$DEF_ARG"]; "true if string empty" pointing to if [-z "$YESNO"].)

Before you look at an example of this function in use, examine how it works.

As indicated by the comments, this function can handle up to two arguments. It treats the first argument as the prompt and the second argument as the default answer to the prompt. First, this function checks that at least one argument is given. If no arguments are given, you return from the function with the error message

```
ERROR: Insufficient Arguments.
```

Next, set the variables DEF_ARG and YESNO to null, in order to avoid using the values stored in them from a previous call to this function. After this, try to set DEF_ARG, the default answer, by looking at the value of the second argument to the function, $2. If this argument is some form (regardless of case) of the words *YES* or *NO*, you set DEF_ARG; otherwise, you leave it as null.

At this point, you enter the body of an infinite while loop. You call the break command from inside the while loop after the user has entered a valid answer (some form of the words *YES* or *NO*).

The first thing the loop does is output a prompt using the printf command. You use the printf command to avoid problems with the echo command between different versions of UNIX. If a valid default answer was specified, you display it.

After the prompt is displayed, call the read command and read the user's response into the variable YESNO. If the user simply presses Enter, YESNO is set to null. In this case, you set it equal to the default answer stored in DEF_ARG. If the default argument was not given, this assignment is redundant.

The last step in the while loop is to check the value of YESNO and make sure that it contains some form of the words *YES* or *NO*. If it does, you call the break command to terminate the while loop.

If YESNO contains an invalid response, the loop repeats. This means that if the user simply types Enter in a case where no default was supplied, or if the user enters a response that the function does not understand, the same prompt is displayed again.

Before the function exits, it exports the variable YESNO to the environment to make sure that this variable is available to commands executed after the function exits.

Now that you know how this function works, look at an example of its use, as illustrated here:

```
promptYESNO "Make backup"
if [ "$YESNO" = "y" ] ; then
    cp -r docs backup
fi
```

This generates a prompt similar to the following:

```
Make Backup (y/n)?
```

If you enter some form of the words *YES* or *NO*, the function sets the variable YESNO to either y or n. The if statement in this example evaluates this response and performs the

21

appropriate action. Here you execute a `cp` command. If the user does not enter a valid response, the prompt repeats.

You can use a default argument as follows:

```
promptYESNO "Make backup" "y"
if [ "$YESNO" = "y" ] ; then
    cp -r docs backup
fi
```

[handwritten annotations: "Default"; "Recursive - use when destination is a directory"]

Now the prompt looks like the following:

```
Make Backup (y/n)? [y]
```

This lets the user simply press Enter and have the backup made. It also lets the user type a response.

Prompting for a Response

In many shell scripts, you need to gather more information from the user than a yes or no response. For example, installation scripts frequently have to ask for the name of a directory, the location of a file, or other system information.

The `promptYESNO` function cannot handle these types of questions. You need a different kind of prompting function, which you present as the `promptRESPONSE` function. This function displays a prompt, reads the user's response, and stores it in the variable `RESPONSE`. Validation of the user's response needs to be handled outside of the function.

```
###############################################
# Name: promptRESPONSE
# Desc: ask a question
# Args: $1 -> The prompt
#       $2 -> The default answer (optional)
# Vars: RESPONSE -> set to the users response
###############################################

promptRESPONSE() {

    if [ $# -lt 1 ] ; then
        printERROR "Insufficient Arguments."
        return 1
    fi

    RESPONSE=""
    DEF_ARG="$2"

    while :
    do
        printf "$1 ? "
        if [ -n "$DEF_ARG" ] ; then
```

```
        printf "[$DEF_ARG] "
    fi

    read RESPONSE

    if [ -n "$RESPONSE" ] ; then
        break
    elif [ -z "$RESPONSE" -a -n "$DEF_ARG" ] ; then
        RESPONSE="$DEF_ARG"
        break
    fi
done

export RESPONSE
unset DEF_ARG
return 0
}
```

Before you look at some examples of this function in use, examine how it works. This function is quite similar to the promptYESNO function.

As indicated by the comments, promptRESPONSE can handle up to two arguments. It treats the first argument as the prompt and the second argument as the default answer to the prompt. The first thing this function checks for is that at least one argument is given. If no arguments are given, you return from the function with the following error message:

ERROR: Insufficient Arguments.

Next you set the variable RESPONSE to null to avoid using a value stored in it from a previous call to this function. After this, you set DEF_ARG, the default answer, to the value of the second argument of the function, $2. If the second argument is not given, DEF_ARG is set to null, because of variable substitution.

At this point, you enter the body of an infinite while loop. You call the break command from inside the while loop after the user has entered a valid answer.

The first thing the loop does is display a prompt using the printf command. You use the printf command to avoid problems with the echo command between different versions of UNIX. If a valid default answer was specified, you display it out.

After the prompt is displayed, you call the read command and read the user's response into the variable RESPONSE. If the user entered a value, you call the break command to exit the while loop. If the user simply presses Enter, RESPONSE is set to null. In this case, you check to see whether DEF_ARG contains a default answer. If it does, you set RESPONSE

21

to this value and call the break command to exit the while loop. This behavior is similar to the promptYESNO function.

If the default argument was not given and the user presses Enter, the prompt is displayed again.

After a valid response is given, the while loop terminates. When this happens, the function exports the variable RESPONSE to the environment and returns by calling the return command.

Now that you know how this function works, look at an example of its use. The following set of commands could be used in an install script:

```
promptRESPONSE "In which directory do you want to install"
if [ ! -d "$RESPONSE" ] ; then
    echo "The directory $RESPONSE does not exist."
    promptYESNO "Create it" "y"
    if [ "$YESNO" = "y" ] ; then
        mkdir "$RESPONSE"
    else
        exit
    fi
fi
```

At first you are prompted as follows:

```
In which directory do you want to install ?
```

If you enter the name of a valid directory, no further prompts are generated; otherwise, you are asked whether the directory should be created:

```
The directory mydir does not exist.
Create it (y/n)? [y]
```

Here the default is to create the directory. You can modify the example slightly to provide a default directory as follows:

```
promptRESPONSE "In which directory do you want to install" "$HOME"
```

The prompt changes to look like the following:

```
In which directory do you want to install ? [/home/ranga]
```

Checking Disk Space

Shell scripts are commonly used to keep system administrators up to date about the amount of free space available in certain directories. For example, you don't want the incoming mail directory to fill up. An auxiliary task is to determine how much space a directory uses. For example, you don't want a single user to hog up all the disk space for extended periods.

The information about disk usage is also important to installation scripts because they need to warn a user when an installation is attempted in a directory that does not contain enough space.

In this section, I will present two functions that can help you determine disk space usage:

- getSpaceFree
- getSpaceUsed

Determining Free Space

To determine the free space in a directory, you use the df -k (k as in *KB*) command. Its output looks like the following:

```
$ df -k
Filesystem            1024-blocks  Used Available Capacity Mounted on
/dev/hda1               1190014   664661    463867     59%   /
/dev/hdd1               4128240  1578837   2335788     40%   /internal
/dev/hdb1               1521567   682186    760759     47%   /store
/dev/hda3                320086    72521    231034     24%   /tmp
```

When run on a single directory or file, the output looks like the following:

```
$ df -k /home/ranga
Filesystem            1024-blocks  Used Available Capacity Mounted on
/dev/hda1               1190014   664661    463867     59%   /
```

The output consists of a header line and information about the hard drive or hard drive partition that the directory or file you specified is located on. In this output, the amount of free space is stored in the fourth column. Your function uses awk to get at this value.

```
#################################################
# Name: getSpaceFree
# Desc: output the space avail for a directory
# Args: $1 -> The directory to check
#################################################

getSpaceFree() {

    if [ $# -lt 1 ] ; then
        printERROR "Insufficient Arguments."
        return 1
    fi

    df -k "$1" | awk 'NR != 1 { print $4 ; }'
}
```

[handwritten annotations: "skip first line" under the awk command, "4th column" pointing to print $4]

[handwritten annotation in right margin box: 21]

As you can see, the function is quite simple. It first checks to see whether it was given an argument. If no argument was given, it displays an error message and returns. Otherwise, it runs the df -k command and displays the number stored in the fourth column. You use the awk expression

```
NR != 1
```

to skip the first line that contains the header. For more information on awk, please look at Chapter 17, "Filtering Text with awk."

As an example of using this function, the command

```
getSpaceFree /usr/local
```

displays the following value on my system:

```
2335788
```

The number returned is in kilobytes, which means I have about 2.3GB free in the directory /usr/local.

Frequently you might want to compare the output of this function to some value. For example, the following if statement checks to see whether more than 20,000KB are available in the directory /usr/local:

```
if [ "`getSpaceFree /usr/local`" -gt 20000 ] ; then
    echo "Enough space"
fi
```

Determining Space Used

You have looked at determining the amount of disk space available in a directory, but sometimes you need to know how much disk space a directory uses. For example, you might have a public directory that needs to be cleaned out when it exceeds a certain size.

To perform this task, you need to use the du (*du* as in *disk usage*) command. Because you want the output for an entire directory and its contents, you need to specify the -s (*s* as in *sum*) option to du. You also need to specify the -k (*k* as in *kilobyte*) option for a consistent output on all versions of UNIX.

The output of the du -sk command looks like the following:

```
$ du -sk /home/ranga/pub
4922    /home/ranga/pub
```

The size of the directory in kilobytes is listed in the first column. Your function uses awk to obtain this number.

```
###############################################
# Name: getSpaceUsed
```

```
# Desc: output the space used for a directory
# Args: $1 -> The directory to check
##############################################

getSpaceUsed() {

    if [ $# -lt 1 ] ; then
        printERROR "Insufficient Arguments."
        return 1
    fi

    if [ ! -d "$1" ] ; then
        printERROR "$1 is not a directory."
        return 1
    fi

    du -sk "$1" | awk '{ print $1 ; }'
}
```

This function is almost as simple as getSpaceFree. It first checks whether it was given
an argument. If no argument was given, it displays an error message and returns.
Otherwise, it checks to see whether the first argument is a directory. If it is not, an error
message is displayed and the function returns.

Otherwise, the function executes the du -sk command and displays the number stored in
the first column.

As an example of using this function, the command

```
getSpaceUsed /usr/local
```

displays the following value on my system:

```
15164
```

The number returned is in kilobytes, which means that the directory /usr/local uses
about 15.1MB.

Frequently, you'll want to compare the output of this function to some value. For example, the following if statement checks to see whether more than 10,000KB are used by
the directory /home/ranga/pub:

```
if [ "`getSpaceSpace /home/ranga/pub`" -gt 10000 ] ; then
    printWARNING "You're using to much space!"
fi
```

21

Obtaining the Process ID by Name

One of the difficulties with the ps command is that it is hard to obtain the process ID of
a command by specifying only its name. In shell scripts that have to start and stop
processes, the capability to look through the output of ps and retrieve a list of process
IDs based on a command's name is essential.

In this section, I will present a function that displays a list of process IDs (pids) based on
a string supplied by the user.

```
##############################################
# Name: getPID
# Desc: outputs a list of process id matching $1
# Args: $1 -> the command name to look for
##############################################

getPID() {

    if [ $# -lt 1 ] ; then
        printERROR "Insufficient Arguments."
        return 1
    fi

    PSOPTS="-ef"

    /bin/ps $PSOPTS ¦ grep "$1" ¦ grep -v grep ¦ awk '{ print $2; }'
}
```

As you can see, this function is a set of filters on top of the command /bin/ps -ef. The
first grep command looks for all lines that match the first argument. As an example, executing this on the command line produces output similar to the following:

```
$ /bin/ps -ef ¦ grep sshd
```

Here you are looking for all the lines that contain the word *sshd*. The output should look
similar to the following:

```
root   1449     1  8 12:23:06 ?         0:02 /opt/bin/sshd
ranga  1451   944  5 12:23:08 pts/t0     0:00 grep sshd
```

As you can see, the output contains two lines. The first one contains the process ID of
the commands that you are looking for, but the second contains the process ID of the
grep command that just executed. In order to get rid of such lines, add the grep -v
grep to the pipeline.

Because the process ID is stored in the second column, use awk to extract it.

If more than one line matches, this function displays each process ID.

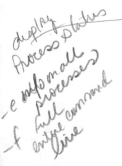

For example, the following command

```
getPID httpd
```

returns the following list of process IDs on my system:

```
330
331
332
333
334
335
336
323
```

Readers who are using Linux or FreeBSD-based systems have to change this function slightly for it to function properly. The value of the variable PSOPTS should be -auwx on these systems. In Chapter 23, I will show you how to incorporate these changes into the function so that it runs on all versions of UNIX.

Getting a User's Numeric User ID

Some shell scripts need to determine whether a user has sufficient permissions to execute commands. For example, an install script might need to run as root (UID 0) to modify system files correctly. In other instances, a script might need to detect whether a user has too many privileges.

To check the user's ID, you can use the id command, which can be run in two forms. The first form specifies a username whose ID should be returned. For example, the command

```
$ id vathsa
uid=501(vathsa) gid=100(users) groups=100(users)
```

returns the UID for the user vathsa. The second form omits the user ID. In this form, the current user's information is returned.

```
$ id
uid=500(ranga) gid=100(users) groups=100(users),101(ftpadmin)
```

Your function supports both.

```
#############################################
# Name: getUID
# Desc: outputs a numeric user id
# Args: $1 -> a user name (optional)
#############################################
```

21

```
getUID() {
    id $1 | sed -e 's/(.*$//' -e 's/^uid=//'
}
```

This function executes the `id` command and then uses a `sed` filter to delete all the unimportant information. When the function is called by itself

```
getUID
```

the output looks like the following:

```
500
```

When the function is called with a username

```
getUID vathsa
```

the output looks like the following:

```
500
```

Usually you need to compare this output to some known UID as follows:

```
if [ "`getUID`" -gt 100 ] ; then
    printERROR "You do not have sufficient privileges."
    exit 1
fi
```

Here the output of the `getUID` function is checked to see whether it is greater than 100.

The Complete Library

Listing 21.1 contains a complete listing of the shell library, `libTYSP.sh`, discussed in this chapter. The line numbers are present for your reference and should not be entered into a script library file that you plan to use.

LISTING 21.1—COMPLETE LISTING OF THE SHELL LIBRARY libTYSP.sh

```
1    #!/bin/sh
2
3    ###############################################
4    # Name: printERROR
5    # Desc: prints an message to STDERR
6    # Args: $@ -> message to print
7    ###############################################
8
9    printERROR() {
10       echo "ERROR:" $@ >&2
11   }
12
```

```
13      ###############################################
14      # Name: printWARNING
15      # Desc: prints an message to STDERR
16      # Args: $@ -> message to print
17      ###############################################
18
19      printWARNING() {
20          echo "WARNING:" $@ >&2
21      }
22
23      ###############################################
24      # Name: printUSAGE
25      # Desc: prints a USAGE message and then exits
26      # Args: $@ -> message to print
27      ###############################################
28
29      printUSAGE() {
30          echo "USAGE:" $@
31          exit
32      }
33
34      ###############################################
35      # Name: promptYESNO
36      # Desc: ask a yes/no question
37      # Args: $1 -> The prompt
38      #       $2 -> The default answer (optional)
39      # Vars: YESNO -> set to the users response
40      #                y for yes, n for no
41      ###############################################
42
43      promptYESNO() {
44
45          if [ $# -lt 1 ] ; then
46           printERROR "Insufficient Arguments."
47           return 1
48          fi
49
50          DEF_ARG=""
51          YESNO=""
52
53          case "$2" in
54          [yY]¦[yY][eE][sS])
55              DEF_ARG=y ;;
56          [nN]¦[nN][oO])
57              DEF_ARG=n ;;
58          esac
59
60          while :
61          do
62
```

continues

21

LISTING 21.1—CONTINUED

```
63          printf "$1 (y/n)? "
64
65          if [ -n "$DEF_ARG" ] ; then
66              printf "[$DEF_ARG] "
67          fi
68
69          read YESNO
70
71          if [ -z "$YESNO" ] ; then
72              YESNO="$DEF_ARG"
73          fi
74
75          case "$YESNO" in
76              [yY]|[yY][eE][sS])
77               YESNO=y ; break ;;
78              [nN]|[nN][oO])
79               YESNO=n ; break ;;
80              *)
81               YESNO="" ;;
82          esac
83
84      done
85
86      export YESNO
87      unset DEF_ARG
88      return 0
89  }
90
91  ###############################################
92  # Name: promptRESPONSE
93  # Desc: ask a question
94  # Args: $1 -> The prompt
95  #       $2 -> The default answer (optional)
96  # Vars: RESPONSE -> set to the users response
97  ###############################################
98
99  promptRESPONSE() {
100
101     if [ $# -lt 1 ] ; then
102      printERROR "Insufficient Arguments."
103      return 1
104     fi
105
106     RESPONSE=""
107     DEF_ARG="$2"
108
109     while :
110     do
111      printf "$1 ? "
```

```
112         if [ -n "$DEF_ARG" ] ; then
113             printf "[$DEF_ARG] "
114          fi
115
116        read RESPONSE
117
118        if [ -n "$RESPONSE" ] ; then
119            break
120        elif [ -z "$RESPONSE" -a -n "$DEF_ARG" ] ; then
121            RESPONSE="$DEF_ARG"
122            break
123         fi
124       done
125
126       export RESPONSE
127       unset DEF_ARG
128       return 0
129     }
130
131     ###############################################
132     # Name: getSpaceFree
133     # Desc: output the space avail for a directory
134     # Args: $1 -> The directory to check
135     ###############################################
136
137     getSpaceFree() {
138
139         if [ $# -lt 1 ] ; then
140          printERROR "Insufficient Arguments."
141          return 1
142         fi
143
144         df -k "$1" ¦ awk 'NR != 1 { print $4 ; }'
145     }
146
147     ###############################################
148     # Name: getSpaceUsed
149     # Desc: output the space used for a directory
150     # Args: $1 -> The directory to check
151     ###############################################
152
153     getSpaceUsed() {
154
155         if [ $# -lt 1 ] ; then
156          printERROR "Insufficient Arguments."
157          return 1
158         fi
159
160         if [ ! -d "$1" ] ; then
161          printERROR "$1 is not a directory."
162          return 1
```

21

continues

LISTING **21.1**—CONTINUED

```
163          fi
164
165          du -sk "$1" ¦ awk '{ print $1 ; }'
166      }
167
168      ###############################################
169      # Name: getPID
170      # Desc: outputs a list of process id matching $1
171      # Args: $1 -> the command name to look for
172      ###############################################
173
174      getPID() {
175
176          if [ $# -lt 1 ] ; then
177            printERROR "Insufficient Arguments."
178                return 1
179          fi
180
181          PSOPTS="-ef"
182
183          /bin/ps $PSOPTS ¦ grep "$1" ¦ grep -v grep ¦ awk
            ➥'{ print $2; }'
184      }
185
186      ###############################################
187      # Name: getUID
188      # Desc: outputs a numeric user id
189      # Args: $1 -> a user name (optional)
190      ###############################################
191
192      getUID() {
193          id $1 ¦ sed -e 's/(.*$//' -e 's/^uid=//'
194      }
195
```

Summary

In this chapter, I presented a library of shell functions that can be used in your shell scripts to handle many common tasks. By using and improving these implementations, you can avoid having to reinvent the wheel when faced with a particular problem.

Some of the problems that I addressed are

- Displaying standardized error, warning, and usage messages
- Prompting for a *yes* or *no* response

- Prompting for a general response
- Checking disk space
- Getting the process ID of a command using its name
- Getting the numeric user ID of a user

In addition to these tasks, I have covered many other useful functions throughout this book. By using these functions, you can concentrate on developing scripts to solve complicated problems without worrying about the basics.

Questions

1. Write a function called `toLower` that converts its arguments to all lowercase and displays the converted string to STDOUT. You don't have to worry about checking the number of arguments.

   (HINT: Use the `tr` command.)

2. Write a function called `toUpper` that converts its arguments to all uppercase and displays the converted string to STDOUT. You don't have to worry about checking the number of arguments.

   (HINT: Use the `tr` command.)

3. Write a function called `isSpaceAvailable` to check whether a directory contains a certain amount of disk space.

   Your function should accept two arguments. The first one indicates the directory to check, and the second one indicates the amount of space to check. An error should be reported if both arguments are not given. Your function should validate that the first argument is a directory.

   If sufficient space is present, your function should return 0; otherwise, it should return 1. This enables us to use it as follows:

   ```
   if isSpaceAvailable /usr/local 20000 ; then
       : # perform some action
   fi
   ```

   (HINT: Use the function `getSpaceFree`.)

4. Modify your `isSpaceAvailable` function to accept an optional third argument that specifies the units of the amount space to check.

   The default should remain in kilobytes, but you should support m or mb indicating megabytes and g or gb indicating gigabytes. If some other units are given, assume that the user meant kilobytes.

21

The following conversion factors apply to this problem: 1MB equals 1024KB, and 1GB equals to 1024MB.

(HINT: Use the bc command.)

5. Write a function called isUserRoot that checks to see whether the ID of a user is equal to 0. If no user is given, it should check to see whether the ID of the current user is root.

(HINT: Use the getUID function.)

Terms

Library—A file that contains only functions is called a library. Usually libraries contain no main code.

Main Code—Main code consists of all the commands in a shell script that are not contained within functions.

HOUR 22

Problem Solving with Shell Scripts

In Chapter 21, "Problem Solving with Functions," I showed you several useful functions that you can use in your shell scripts. In this chapter, I will present two shell scripts that demonstrate how you can use shell scripts to solve everyday problems.

These scripts illustrate using the tools I covered in previous chapters to create new tools that you can reuse. For each script I will first describe the motivations for its development, followed by some design issues. Then I will present the script in full. I will conclude the discussion of scripts by highlighting the script's flow and error checking.

The two tasks that I will look at are

- Moving directories
- Maintaining an Address Book

Moving Directories

NEW TERM In Chapter 4, "Working with Directories," I noted that the mv command could not be used to move directories across file systems. A *file system* can be thought of as a hard drive or hard drive partition.

The mv command works fine when you want to move a directory between different locations on the same file system (hard drive), but it doesn't work well when you want to move a file across file systems. Depending on your version of mv, an error message could be generated when you try to do this.

For example, consider this directory:

```
$ ls -F /tmp/ch22
ch22-01.doc ch22.doc@
```

If you use the mv command to move this directory in the directory /home/ranga on a different file system, an error message similar to the following is generated:

```
mv: cannot move 'ch22' across filesystems: Not a regular file
```

Some UNIX versions implement a workaround inside mv that executes the following commands:

```
$ rm -rf destination
$ cp -r source destination
$ rm -rf source
```

Here *source* and *destination* are directories.

The main problem with this strategy is that links in the source directory are not always copied correctly. Most of the time, the file that the link points to is copied instead of the link itself. In the case of the directory /tmp/ch22, you would end up with two copies of the file ch22-01.doc, which is not desirable.

In addition to this, there are two other minor problems with using cp:

- Some versions of the cp command do not copy a file's owner and group. With these versions of cp, the copied file has a different owner and group than the original.

- Some versions of cp do not copy a file's permissions correctly. With such a version of cp, the copied file might have different permissions than the original.

Using tar

NEW TERM The workaround for these problems is to use the tar (*tar* as in *tape archive*) command to copy directories. This command creates an archive or tar file that

22

contains files and directories. A *tar file* is similar to a zip file, except that its contents are not compressed. In addition, a tar file stores the file permission along with group and owner information for the files it contains. Thus by using `tar`, your copies automatically end up with the correct file attributes.

By using `tar` you can move directories using the following procedure:

1. Make a tar file of the source directory.
2. Change to the destination directory.
3. Extract the source directory in the destination directory.
4. Remove the source directory. Notice that your procedure does not include deleting the tar file of the source directory. Normally when you use the `tar` command, a tar file is created on your hard drive. If you use this behavior in your script, you need to worry about cleaning up the tar file whenever an error occurs. This adds a large amount of complexity to your script. To avoid all that unnecessary complexity, you can use a special feature of the `tar` command to avoid creating a tar file.

The `tar` command can create archives and write them to STDOUT instead of a file. It can also read archives from STDIN instead of from a file. By using a pipe character (¦), you can connect a `tar` command that creates a tar file with one that extracts a tar file, thus avoiding the creation of an intermediate tar file.

To create a tar file, use the following command:

```
tar -cpf - source
```

Here *source* is the pathname of a directory. The options specified to `tar` tell it to create a tar file, whereas the `-` indicates that the tar file it creates should be written to STDOUT.

To extract a tar file from STDIN, use the command:

```
tar -xpf -
```

Here the options specified to `tar` indicate that it should extract a tar file, whereas the `-` indicates that the tar file should be read from STDIN.

Because you need to extract the tar file in the correct directory, the final command you use is

```
tar -cpf - source ¦ ( cd destination ; tar -xpf - )
```

Here *source* and *destination* are directories. This single command takes care of the first three steps involved in moving a directory. The rest of your script performs error checking and ensures that sensible values for *source* and *destination* are used.

mvdir.sh

The script mvdir.sh is given in Listing 22.1 (the line numbers are provided for your reference).

LISTING 22.1 COMPLETE LISTING OF THE mvdir.sh SCRIPT

```
1   #!/bin/sh
2   # Name: mvdir
3   # Desc: Move directories across file systems
4   # Args: $1 -> src dir
5   #       $2 -> dest dir
6
7   PATH=/bin:/usr/bin ; export PATH
8
9   # function to print errors and exit
10
11  printERROR() { echo "ERROR: $@." >&2 ; exit 1; }
12
13  # function to print usage message and exit
14
15  printUSAGE() { echo "USAGE: `/bin/basename $0` $@." >&2 ;
    ➡exit 1; }
16
17  # check whether sufficient args are given
18
19  if [ $# -lt 2 ] ; then printUSAGE "[src] [dest]" ; fi
20
21  # check whether the source directory exists
22
23  if [ ! -d "$1" ] ; then
24      printERROR "The source $1 is not a directory, or does
        ➡not exist"
25  fi
26
27  # split up the source dir into its name and its parent's
28  # name for easier processing later on
29
30  SRCDIR_PARENT="`/usr/bin/dirname $1`"
31  SRCDIR_CHILD="`/bin/basename $1`"
32
33  # if dirname returns a relative dir we will be confused
34  # after cd'ing later on. So reset it to the full path.
35
36  SRCDIR_PARENT="`(cd $SRCDIR_PARENT ; pwd ; )`"
37
38  # check whether the destination exits
39
40  if [ -d "$2" ] ; then
```

```
41
42      DESTDIR=`( cd "$2" ; pwd ; )`
43
44  else
45
46      # if the destination doesn't exist then assume the
47      # destination is the new name for the directory
48
49      DESTDIR="`/usr/bin/dirname $2`"
50      NEWNAME="`/bin/basename $2`"
51
52      # if dirname returns a relative dir we will be confused
53      # after cd'ing later on. So reset it to the full path.
54
55      DESTDIR=`(cd $DESTDIR ; pwd ; )`
56
57      # if the parent of the destination doesn't exist,
58      # we're in trouble. Tell the user and exit.
59
60      if [ ! -d "$DESTDIR" ] ; then
61          printERROR "A parent of the destination directory
            ➥$2 does not exist"
62      fi
63
64  fi
65
66  # try and cd to the parent src directory
67
68  cd "$SRCDIR_PARENT" > /dev/null 2>&1
69  if [ $? -ne 0 ] ; then
70      printERROR "Could not cd to $SRCDIR_PARENT"
71  fi
72
73  # use tar to copy the source dir to the destination
74
75  /bin/tar -cpf - "$SRCDIR_CHILD" | ( cd "$DESTDIR" ;
    ➥/bin/tar -xpf - )
76
77  if [ $? -ne 0 ] ; then
78      printERROR "Unable to successfully move $1 to $2"
79  fi
80
81  # if a rename of the copy is requested
82
83  if [ -n "$NEWNAME" ] ; then
84
85      # try and change to the destination directory
86
87      cd "$DESTDIR" > /dev/null 2>&1
88      if [ $? -ne 0 ] ; then
```

continues

LISTING 22.1   CONTINUED

```
 89              printERROR "Could not cd to $DESTDIR"
 90          fi
 91
 92          # try and rename the copy
 93
 94          /bin/mv "$SRCDIR_CHILD" "$NEWNAME" > /dev/null 2>&1
 95          if [ $? -ne 0 ] ; then
 96              printERROR "Could not rename $1 to $2"
 97          fi
 98
 99          # return to the original directory
100
101          cd "$SRCDIR_PARENT" > /dev/null 2>&1
102          if [ $? -ne 0 ] ; then
103              printERROR "Could not cd to $SRCDIR_PARENT"
104          fi
105  fi
106
107  # try and remove the original
108
109  if [ -d "$SRCDIR_CHILD" ] ; then
110      /bin/rm -r "$SRCDIR_CHILD" > /dev/null 2>&1
111      if [ $? -ne 0 ] ; then
112          printERROR "Could not remove $1"
113      fi
114  fi
115
116  exit 0
```

A Walkthrough of `mvdir.sh`

I'll walk through the script and highlight some of the important points.

The first thing this script does is set the PATH variable (line 7). You do this to ensure that all the commands you use come from one of the two directories that you specified. When you write a script that can be run by many users, you have to take into account that some users might have modified their PATH such that the commands you are using are inaccessible or replaced by other versions. By setting the PATH variable explicitly, you avoid this problem.

Next the script defines a few utility functions (lines 11 and 15) used to print error usage messages. You can easily modify the script to replace these functions with the versions I gave you in Chapter 21.

After this the script validates its arguments as follows:

- It makes sure at least two arguments corresponding to *source* and `destination` directories are given (line 19).
- It makes sure the *source* is a directory (lines 23–25).

If at least two arguments are not given, you cannot be sure what the user wanted to move. Thus a usage message is printed and the script exits. If the *source* is not a directory or doesn't exist, there is nothing to move, thus the script prints an error message and exits.

The next two lines (lines 30 and 31) are used to access the different parts of the pathname for the *source*. If the user specifies a directory as follows

```
$ mvdir.sh /tmp/mydir /home/ranga
```

there are two pieces of information you need:

- The name of the directory that the user wants moved, in this case `mydir`. This value is stored in the variable `SRCDIR_CHILD` (line 31).
- The name of the directory that this directory is located in, in this case `/tmp`. This value is stored in the variable `SRCDIR_PARENT` (line 30).

When you issue the `mv` or `cp` command, each performs this separation internally. Because this is a shell script, you have to do it explicitly using the `dirname` and `basename` commands.

One problem you run into is when the user specifies a relative path. When a `cd` command is used, the relative path required to access the *source* and *destination* directories changes; thus you need to determine the absolute path to the `SRCDIR_PARENT`. By using a subshell, you can make this determination in one line (line 36).

After you have dealt with the *source* directory, you examine the *destination* directory, which requires special treatment because it can mean two different things:

- If the destination directory exists (line 40), the user wants the source directory moved into the *destination* directory.
- If the destination directory does not exist (line 44), the user wants the *source* directory moved and renamed in the parent directory of the specified *destination* directory.

In the first case you need to determine the absolute path to the destination directory (line 42). In the second case you need to obtain the following information:

- The name of the *destination* directory's parent directory. This value is stored in DESTDIR (line 49).

- The new name the user wants for the *source* directory. This value is stored in NEWNAME (line 50).

After you convert the value of DESTDIR to an absolute path, you check to make sure that it exists. If it doesn't, the script reports an error to the user and exits.

In the next few lines (lines 68–79), you try to move the files from the source to the destination using the values you determined for the *source* and *destination* directories. If something goes wrong during this process, you report an error and exit.

After a copy has been successfully made using tar, you check to see whether a rename has been requested (line 83). If it has been, you try to change the name of the copy from its original name to the new name (line 94). If this process fails, the script issues an error and exits.

Finally, if all the other operations are successful, you delete the original directory (line 110). Any error in this operation is reported.

Examples

Now look at two examples of using this script to move a directory between file systems.

In the first example, you want to move a source directory into a destination directory on a different file system:

```
$ ls /tmp
ch22            ps_data         sdtdbcache_:0
$ ./mvdir.sh /tmp/ch22 /home/ranga/docs/book
$ ls /tmp /home/ranga/docs/book
/tmp:
ps_data         sdtdbcache_:0

/home/ranga/docs/book
ch20      ch21      ch22      ch23
```

As you can see, the directory ch22 was moved from /tmp to the directory /home/ranga/docs/book.

In the second example, you move the same directory, but you also rename it:

```
$ ls /home/ranga/docs/book
ch20      ch21      ch22      ch23
$ ./mvdir /home/ranga/docs/book/ch22 /tmp/ch22-work
```

```
$ ls /home/ranga/docs/book /tmp
/home/ranga/docs/book:
ch20      ch21      ch23
/tmp:
ch22-work      ps_data      sdtdbcache_:0
```

Here the directory was moved and renamed.

Maintaining an Address Book

I often get business cards or email messages from people I need to keep in touch with. Sometimes I lose these email messages or business cards, leading to problems when I need to contact someone important.

A nice solution to this problem would be to store all the contact information on my computer so that I could access and manipulate it easily. In this section, I will look at developing a set of scripts that work together to maintain a simple address book.

The address book will store the following information:

- Name
- Email address
- Postal address
- Phone number

Each of these pieces of information can contain almost any character including spaces or other special characters such as the dash (-), period, (.), or single quote ('). Thus you need to hold the information in a format that allows for these characters. A commonly used format is to separate each piece of information using the colon (:) character. For example, the following information:

```
Sriranga Veeraraghavan
ranga@soda.berkeley.edu
1136 Wunderlich Dr. San Jose CA 95129
408-444-4444
```

can be stored as:

```
Sriranga Veeraraghavan:ranga@soda.berkeley.edu:1136 Wunderlich Dr.
➥San Jose CA 95129:408-444-4444
```

Here any special character, except the colon, can be used. Also this format enables you to make any field optional. For example,

```
:vathsa@kanchi.bosland.us::408-444-4444
```

could indicate that only the email address and phone number were known for a particular person.

To maintain your address book, you need a few scripts:

- `showperson` to show information about one or more people in the address book
- `addperson` to add a person to the address book
- `delperson` to delete a person from the address book

The following scripts assume that the address book is stored in the file `$HOME/address-book`.

Showing People

One of the main tasks any address book must perform is looking up a person. You will develop a script called `showperson` to accomplish this.

To find information about a person, you can use `grep` command. For example,

```
$ grep vathsa addressbook
```

lists all the lines that contain the word *vathsa* in the file `addressbook`. For your address book, the output might look like the following:

```
:vathsa@kanchi.bosland.us::408-444-4444
```

As you imagine, your `showperson` script should format the results of the `grep` command. A nice format would be to list the name, email address, postal address, and phone number on separate lines. You can do this using an `awk` command:

```
awk -F: '{ printf "Name: %s\nEmail: %s\nAddress: %s\nPhone:
➥%s\n\n",$1,$2,$3,$4 ; }'
```

By putting these commands together, you construct the `showperson` script given in Listing 22.2 (the line numbers are provided for your reference).

LISTING 22.2   LISTING OF THE `showperson` SCRIPT

```
 1  #!/bin/sh
 2  # Name: showperson
 3  # Desc: show matching records in addressbook
 4  # Args: $1 -> string to look for in addressbook
 5
 6  PATH=/bin:/usr/bin
 7
 8  # check that a string is given
 9
10  if [ $# -lt 1 ] ; then
11      echo "USAGE: `basename $0` name"
12      exit 1
13  fi
```

Flow Control and Loop Syntax

- The `if` statement:

  ```
  if list1 ; then list2 ; elif list3 ; then list4 else list5 fi
  ```

- The `case` statement:

  ```
  case expression in
      pattern1) list1 ;;
      ...
      patternN) listN ;;
  esac
  ```

- The `while` loop:

  ```
  while expression ; do list ; done
  ```

- The `for` loop:

  ```
  for var in word1 ... wordN ; do list ; done
  ```

- The `select` loop:

  ```
  select var in word1 ... wordN ; do list ; done
  ```

Variable Substitution

TABLE 2 VARIABLE SUBSTITUTION.

COMMAND	DESCRIPTION
${name}	Substitutes the value of *name*.
${name:-word}	Substitutes the value of *name*. If it is undefined, *word* is substituted.
${name:=word}	Substitutes the value of *name*. If it is undefined, *word* is assigned as the value of *name*.
${name:?msg}	Substitutes the value of *name*. If it is undefined, the error message *msg* is displayed.
${name:+word}	Substitutes *word* only if *name* is defined.

Redirection

The three main file descriptors and their corresponding numbers are standard input (STDIN - 0), standard output (STDOUT - 1), and standard error (STDERR – 2).

TABLE 3 INPUT/OUTPUT REDIRECTION.

REDIRECTION	DESCRIPTION
> file or 1> file	save STDOUT in *file*
>> file or 1>> file	append STDOUT to *file*
2> file	save STDERR in *file*
2>> file	append STDERR in *file*
< file or 0< file	read STDIN from *file* instead of keyboard
cmd1 | cmd2	pipe STDOUT of *file* to STDIN of *file*
2>&1	redirect STDERR into STDOUT
>&2 or 1>&2	redirect STDOUT to STDERR

Teach Yourself in 24 Hours

Sams Teach Yourself in 24 Hours books provide quick and easy answers in a proven step-by-step approach that works for you. In just 24 sessions of one hour or less, you will tackle every task you need to get the results you want. Let our experienced authors present the most accurate information to get you reliable answers—fast!

Shell Programming

This tear-out card is a quick reference for you. It covers the major commands and the syntax of the programming constructs available in the shell.

Here is a brief description some of the built-in commands and their availability in the different shells, sh, ksh, and bash.

TABLE 1 BUILT-IN COMMANDS AND THEIR AVAILABILITY.

COMMAND	SHELLS	DESCRIPTION	COMMAND	SHELLS	DESCRIPTION
alias	ksh & bash	creates a shorthand for a command	pwd	all	prints the current directory
bg	ksh & bash	backgrounds a job	return	all	returns from a function
cd	all	changes the directory	set	all	changes shell options
exec	all	replaces the current process with a new process	shift	all	removes the first argument and shifts up the others
exit n	all	exits from the shell with status n	trap	all	used to specify the code needed to deal with a signal
export	all	puts variables into the environment			
fg	ksh & bash	puts a job in the foreground	type	all	displays the path to a command
jobs	ksh & bash	lists the background and suspended jobs	unalias	ksh & bash	removes an alias
kill	all	used to send a signal to a process	unset	all	undefines variables

```
14
15   # check that the address book exists
16
17   MYADDRESSBOOK="$HOME/addressbook"
18   if [ ! -f "$MYADDRESSBOOK" ] ; then
19       echo "ERROR: $MYADDESSBOOK does not exist, or is not a
         ➥file." >&2
20       exit 1
21   fi
22
23   # get all matches and format them
24
25   grep "$1" "$MYADDRESSBOOK" |
26       awk -F: '{
27           printf "%-10s %s\n%-10s %s\n%-10s %s\n%-10s %s\n\n",\
28               "Name:",$1,"Email:",$2,"Address:",$3,
               ➥"Phone:",$4 ;
29       }'
30
31   exit $?
```

[handwritten annotation: "status code" pointing to line 20; "status code of last command" pointing to line 31]

There are three main parts to the script:

1. Verify the number of arguments.
2. Check to see whether the address book exists.
3. Find all matches and print them.

In the first part (lines 10–13) you check to see whether at least one argument is given. If so, the script continues; otherwise, it prints a usage message and exits.

In the second part, you check to see whether the address book exits. If it does not, the script prints an error and then exits; otherwise, it continues.

In the last part of the script, you use `grep` to obtain a list of matches and `awk` to format this list. To ensure even spacing of the output, the `awk` command uses formatting for both the information and its description. As an example,

```
$ ./showperson ranga
```

produces output similar to the following:

```
Name:      Sriranga Veeraraghavan
Email:     ranga@soda.berkeley.edu
Address:   1136 Wunderlich Dr. San Jose CA
Phone:     408-444-4444
```

Notice how all the information in the second column is correctly aligned.

You can also use showperson to look for matches of a particular string. For example,

```
$ ./showperson va
```

produces two matches:

```
Name:      Sriranga Veeraraghavan
Email:     ranga@soda.berkeley.edu
Address:   1136 Wunderlich Dr. San Jose CA
Phone:     408-444-4444

Name:      N/A
Email:     vathsa@bosland.us
Address:   N/A
Phone:     408-444-4444
```

Adding a Person

One of the most important things about any address book is the capability to add information to it easily. If you need to edit the address book manually to add information, you're bound to make errors such as forgetting to add a colon to separate fields. By using a script, you can avoid such errors.

In this section I will look at a script, addperson, that enables you to add entries into the address book in two ways:

- Interactively
- Using command line options

The script enters interactive mode when no options are given. If the noninteractive mode is being used, it tries to obtain information from the command line options.

In both modes you put the user-provided information into the following variables:

- NAME, stores the name given by the user
- EMAIL, stores the email address given by the user
- ADDR, stores the postal address given by the user
- PHONE, stores the phone number given by the user

In interactive mode, you can prompt for the information in each record as follows:

```
printf "%-10s " "Name:"    ; read NAME
printf "%-10s " "Email:"   ; read EMAIL
printf "%-10s " "Address:" ; read ADDR
printf "%-10s " "Phone:"   ; read PHONE
```

After each prompt, you read and store the user's input, including spaces and special characters inside the appropriate variable.

In noninteractive mode, you can use getopts to scan the options:

```
while getopts n:e:a:p: OPTION
do
        case $OPTION in
            n) NAME="$OPTARG" ;;
            e) EMAIL="$OPTARG" ;;
            a) ADDR="$OPTARG" ;;
            p) PHONE="$OPTARG" ;;
            \?) echo "USAGE: $USAGE" >&2 ; exit 1 ;;
        esac
done
```

As you can see, the options understood by the script in noninteractive mode are

- -n for the name (sets NAME)

- -e for the email address (sets EMAIL)

- -a for the postal address (sets ADDR)

- -p for the phone number (sets PHONE)

After you have obtained the required information, you can update the file by appending a formatted record to the end of the addressbook file as follows:

```
echo "$NAME:$EMAIL:$ADDR:$PHONE" >> "$MYADDRESSBOOK"
```

Here you are assuming that the variable MYADDRESSBOOK contains the pathname to the address book file.

The complete addperson script is given in Listing 22.3 (the line numbers are provided for your reference).

LISTING 22.3   COMPLETE LISTING OF THE addperson SCRIPT

```
 1  #!/bin/sh
 2  # Name: addperson
 3  # Desc: add a person addressbook
 4  # Args: -n <name>
 5  #       -e <email>
 6  #       -a <postal address>
 7  #       -p <phone number>
 8
 9  # initialize the variables
10
11  PATH=/bin:/usr/bin
12  MYADDRESSBOOK=$HOME/addressbook
13  NAME=""
14  EMAIL=""
```

continues

LISTING 22.3   CONTINUED

```
15   ADDR=""
16   PHONE=""
17
18   # create a function to remove the : from user input
19
20   remove_colon() { echo "$@" | tr ':' ' ' ; }
21
22   if [ $# -lt 1 ] ; then
23
24       # this is interactive mode
25
26       # enable erasing input
27
28       stty erase '^?'
29
30       # prompt for the info
31
32       printf "%-10s " "Name:"    ; read NAME
33       printf "%-10s " "Email:"   ; read EMAIL
34       printf "%-10s " "Address:" ; read ADDR
35       printf "%-10s " "Phone:"   ; read PHONE
36
37   else
38
39       # this is noninteractive mode
40
41       # initialize a variable for the usage statement
42
43       USAGE="`basename $0` [-n name] [-e email] [-a address]
     ➥[-p phone]"
44
45       # scan the arguments to get the info
46
47       while getopts n:e:a:p:h OPTION
48       do
49           case $OPTION in
50               n) NAME="$OPTARG" ;;
51               e) EMAIL="$OPTARG" ;;
52               a) ADDR="$OPTARG" ;;
53               p) PHONE="$OPTARG" ;;
54               \?|h) echo "USAGE: $USAGE" >&2 ; exit 1 ;;
55           esac
56       done
57   fi
58
```

(Handwritten annotations:)
- Change colon to space
- Set display on terminal parameters
- Delete Key
- 10 char string
- what error?
- matches 0 or 1 of previous elements

```
59  NAME="`remove_colon $NAME`"
60  EMAIL="`remove_colon $EMAIL`"
61  ADDR="`remove_colon $ADDR`"
62  PHONE="`remove_colon $PHONE`"
63
64  echo "$NAME:$EMAIL:$ADDR:$PHONE" >> "$MYADDRESSBOOK"
65
66  exit $?   > last status code
```

This script first initializes its variables (lines 11–16). You set the internal variables that store the user information to null in order to avoid conflicts with exported variables in the user's environment.

The next step is to create the following function (line 20):

```
remove_colon() { echo "$@" | tr ':' ' ' ; }
```

You use this function to make sure that the user's input doesn't contain any colons.

You then check to see whether any arguments are given (line 22). If this is so, you enter interactive mode (lines 23–36); otherwise, you enter noninteractive mode (lines 38–56).

In interactive mode, you prompt for each piece of information and read it in. Before you produce the first prompt, you issue a stty command (line 28) to make sure the user can erase any mistakes made during input.

In noninteractive mode, you use getopts to obtain the information provided on the command line. In this section you also initialize the variable USAGE to contain the usage statement for this command.

After the information has been obtained, you call the remove_colon function for each variable (lines 59–62). Because the user can potentially specify information that contains colons, skipping this step could corrupt the address book and confuse the showperson script.

Finally you update the address book and exit.

An example of using the script in interactive mode is

```
$ ./addperson
Name:      James Kirk
Email:     jim@enterprise-a.starfleet.mil
Address:   1701 Main Street James Town Iowa UFP
Phone:
```

Here you provided only the name, email address, and postal address for *Jim Kirk*. When you look up *James Kirk* in the address book, you find that this field is empty:

```
$ ./showperson
Name:      James Kirk
Email:     jim@enterprise-a.starfleet.mil
Address:   1701 Main Street James Town Iowa UFP
Phone:
```

You can do the same addition using the noninteractive form:

```
$ ./addperson -n "James Kirk" -e jim@enterprise-a.starfleet.mil \
-a "1701 Main Street James Town Iowa UPF"
```

Notice that on the command line you need to quote the entries that contain spaces.

Deleting a Person

Occasionally, you need to delete a person from the address book. In this section, I will look at a script called `delperson` that deletes people from the address book.

Deleting a person from the address book is a harder task because you have to make sure that those people you really want to delete are deleted. The two main tasks you need to perform are

1. Make a list of the lines in the address book that match the specified name.
2. Based on user feedback, delete the appropriate entries from the address book.

Because the delete operation can potentially remove information from the address book, you have to be extra careful about making backups and working on copies of the original address book.

To simplify prompting and printing error messages, this script uses the shell function library `libTYSP.sh` that was introduced in Chapter 21.

The basic flow of the script is

1. Make a copy of the address book and use the copy for all modifications.
2. Get a list of all matching lines from this copy and store them in a deletion file.
3. For each line in the deletion file, print it out formatted and ask the user whether the line should be deleted.
4. If the user wants the line deleted, remove the line from the copy of the address book.
5. After all the deletions are performed, make a backup of the original address book.
6. Make the edited copy the address book.
7. Clean up temporary files and exit.

22

For each of these steps, you use a function to make sure that the operations performed succeeded.

The complete delperson script is given in Listing 22.4 (the line numbers are provided for your reference).

LISTING 22.4   COMPLETE LISTING OF THE delperson SCRIPT

```
 1  #!/bin/sh
 2  # Name: delperson
 3  # Desc: del a person addressbook
 4  # Args: $1 -> name of person to delete
 5
 6  # get the helper functions
 7
 8  . $HOME/lib/sh/libTYSP.sh
 9
10  PATH=/bin:/usr/bin
11
12  # check that a name is given
13
14  if [ $# -lt 1 ] ; then
15      printUSAGE "`basename $0` name"
16      exit 1
17  fi
18
19  # check that the address book exists
20
21  MYADDRESSBOOK="$HOME/addressbook"
22  if [ ! -f "$MYADDRESSBOOK" ] ; then
23      printERROR "$MYADDESSBOOK does not exists, or is
        ➥not a file."
24      exit 1
25  fi
26
27  # initialize the variables holding the location of the
28  # temporary files
29  TMPF1=/tmp/apupdate.$$          Process ID
30  TMPF2=/tmp/abdelets.$$    /
31
32  # function to clean up temporary files
33
34  doCleanUp() { rm "$TMPF1" "$TMPF1.new" "$TMPF2" 2>
    ➥/dev/null ; }
35
36  # function to exit if update failed
37  Failed() {
38      if [ "$1" -ne 0 ] ; then
39          shift
```

continues

LISTING 22.4   CONTINUED

```
40              printERROR $@
41              doCleanUp
42              exit 1
43      fi
44  }
45
46  # make a copy of the address book for updating,
47  # proceed only if sucessful
48
49  cp "$MYADDRESSBOOK" "$TMPF1" 2> /dev/null
50  Failed $? "Could not make a backup of the address book."
51
52  # get a list of all matching lines from the address book copy
53  # continue if one or more matches were found
54
55  grep "$1" "$TMPF1" > "$TMPF2" 2> /dev/null
56  Failed $? "No matches found."
57
58  # prompt the user for each entry that was found
59
60  exec 5< "$TMPF2"
61  while read LINE <&5
62  do
63
64      # display each line formatted
65
66      echo "$LINE" ¦ awk -F: '{
67          printf "%-10s %s\n%-10s %s\n%-10s %s\n%-10s %s\n\n",\
68                  "Name:",$1,"Email:",$2,"Address:",$3,
                    ➥"Phone:",$4 ;
69      }'
70
71      # prompt for each line, if yes try to remove the line
72
73      promptYESNO "Delete this entry" "n"
74      if [ "$YESNO" = "y" ] ; then
75
76          # try to remove the line, store the updated version
77          # in a new file
78
79          grep -v "$LINE" "$TMPF1" > "$TMPF1.new" 2> /dev/null
80          Failed $? "Unable to update the address book"
81
82          # replace the old version with the updated version
83
84          mv "$TMPF1.new" "$TMPF1" 2> /dev/null
85          Failed $? "Unable to update the address book"
86
```

```
 87      fi
 88  done
 89  exec 5<&-
 90
 91  # save the original version
 92
 93  mv "$MYADDRESSBOOK" "$MYADDRESSBOOK".bak 2> /dev/null
 94  Failed $? "Unable to update the address book"
 95
 96  # replace the original with the edited version
 97
 98  mv "$TMPF1" "$MYADDRESSBOOK" 2> /dev/null
 99  Failed $? "Unable to update the address book"
100
101  # clean up
102
103  doCleanUp
104
105  exit $?
```

In the first part of the script (lines 8–30), you perform some initialization. Specifically, you perform the following actions:

1. Retrieve the helper functions from libTYSP.sh (line 8).

2. Check to make sure a name to delete is given (lines 14–17).

3. Check to make sure that the address book exits (lines 21–25).

4. Initialize the variables for the temporary files (lines 29 and 30) and the PATH (line 10).

After initialization, you create a few additional helper functions:

- doCleanUp, to remove the temporary files (line 34)

- Failed, to issue an error message, remove the temporary files and exit if a critical command fails (lines 37–44)

The first main step in the script is to make a copy of the address book (line 49). If this step fails, you exit (line 50). If this step is successful, you make a list of all the lines in the address book that match the name specified by the user (line 55). If you cannot successfully make this file, you exit (line 56).

Next you enter the delete loop (lines 60–89). For each line that matches the name provided by the user you print a formatted version of the line (lines 66–69). Notice that you are using the same awk statement from the showperson script.

For each matching line, you ask the user whether the entry should be deleted (line 73). If the user agrees (line 74), you do the following:

1. Try to delete the line from the copy of the address book. Store the modified version in a different file (line 79).

2. Replace the copy of the address book with the modified copy (line 84).

If either of these operations fail, you exit (lines 80 and 85).

After the deletes are finished, you make a backup of the original address book (line 93). Then you replace the address book with the fully edited version (line 98). Again you exit if either operation fails (lines 94 and 99).

Finally you clean up and exit.

Here is an example of this script in action:

```
$ ./delperson Sriranga
Name:      Sriranga Veeraraghavan
Email:     ranga@soda.berkeley.edu
Address:   1136 Wunderlich Dr. San Jose CA
Phone:     408-444-4444

Delete this entry (y/n)? [n] y
```

Here I replied *yes* to the question. You can confirm that the delete worked as follows:

```
$ ./showperson Sriranga
$
```

Because there is no output from showperson, this entry has been deleted.

Summary

In this chapter I covered using shell scripts to solve two problems:

- Moving directories
- Maintaining an address book

In the first example, I showed you how to move a directory between file systems using the tar command. This example also showed you how to use the basename and dirname commands to extract parts of a path for your use.

In the second example, you developed three scripts that you used to modify and view the contents of an address book. Some of the highlights of these scripts are:

- The showperson script showed you how the grep and awk commands can be used to format input.
- The addperson script showed you how a single script can be used in both interactive and noninteractive modes.
- The delperson script showed you how to use the grep command and file descriptors to update a file accurately.

The examples in this chapter demonstrate how you can apply the tools that you have covered in previous chapters to solve real problems. Using these scripts as examples, you can see some of the techniques used to solve everyday problems.

In the next chapter I will show you how to make sure the scripts you write are portable between different versions of UNIX.

Questions

1. How might you simplify the following portion of the mvdir script? Specifically, how could you rewrite the main if statement, such that the else clause was unnecessary?

```
40  if [ -d "$2" ] ; then
41
42      DESTDIR=`( cd "$2" ; pwd ; )`
43
44  else
45
46      # if the destination doesn't exist then
47      # assume the destination is the new name
48      # for the directory
49      DESTDIR="`/usr/bin/dirname $2`"
50      NEWNAME="`/bin/basename $2`"
51
52      # if dirname returns a relative dir we will
53      # be confused after cd'ing later on. So
54      # reset it to the full path.
55      DESTDIR=`(cd $DESTDIR ; pwd ; )`
56
57      # if the parent of the destination doesn't
58      # exist, we're in trouble. Tell the user
59      # and exit.
```

```
60        if [ ! -d "$DESTDIR" ] ; then
61            printERROR "A parent of the destination
             ➥directory $2 does not exist"
62        fi
63
64    fi
65
```

2. The showperson script lists all matching entries in the address book based on a
   name provided by the user. The matches produced are case sensitive. How can you
   change the matches so they aren't case sensitive?

3. Both the showperson and delperson scripts reproduce exactly the following pieces
   of code

```
PATH=/bin:/usr/bin

# check that a name is given

if [ $# -lt 1 ] ; then
    printUSAGE "`basename $0` name"
    exit 1
fi

# check that the address book exists

MYADDRESSBOOK="$HOME/addressbook"
if [ ! -f "$MYADDRESSBOOK" ] ; then
    printERROR "$MYADDESSBOOK does not exists, or is
    ➥not a file."
    exit 1
fi
```

and

```
awk -F: '{
        printf "%-10s %s\n%-10s %s\n%-10s %s\n%-10s
        ➥%s\n\n",\
                "Name:",$1,"Email:",$2,"Address:",$3,
                ➥"Phone:",$4 ;
    }'
```

How might you rewrite these script fragments so that they can be shared between
these scripts instead of being replicated in both?

4. The delperson script uses the grep command to generate a list of matching entries. This might confuse the user in the following instance:

```
$ ./delperson.01 to
Name:      James T. Kirk
Email:     jim@enterprise.mil
Address:   1701 Main Street Anytown Iowa
Phone:     555-555-5555

Delete this entry (y/n)? [n]
```

Here the to in Anytown was matched.

What changes should be made to the delperson script so that only those entries whose names match the user-specified name are selected for deletion?

(HINT: Use the sed command instead of grep).

5. If the delperson script gets a signal while it is processing deletes, all the intermediate files are left behind. What can be done to prevent this?

Terms

File System   A file system is used by UNIX to store files and directories. Usually a file system corresponds to a hard drive or hard drive partition.

Tar File   A tape archive file created by the tar command. A tar file can contain both files and directories, making it similar to a zip file.

HOUR 23

Scripting for Portability

Shell programming is an important part of UNIX because shell scripts are portable between different versions of UNIX. In many cases, no changes are required for a shell script to function correctly on multiple systems.

The easiest way to ensure that your shell scripts are completely portable is to restrict yourself to using only those commands and features that are available on all versions of UNIX. Sometimes, you have to implement workarounds to deal with the limitations of a particular version of UNIX.

In this chapter, you will first learn how to determine which version of UNIX is running. Then you will learn how to adapt your shell scripts to different versions of UNIX by examining some of the problems encountered when porting scripts between the versions.

Determining UNIX Versions

Before you can begin adjusting shell scripts to be portable, you need to know what the different types of UNIX are and how to tell them apart.

The two major types of UNIX are

- BSD (Berkeley Software Distribution)
- System V

The locations of commands and the options supported by certain commands are different between these two types of UNIX. This chapter highlights the major differences and commands in particular.

BSD Versus System V

BSD UNIX was developed by the Computer Systems Research Group at the University of California at Berkeley. In the early 1980s, the University of California acquired the source code to UNIX from AT&T Bell Labs and significantly modified it to produce BSD UNIX.

Although the University of California has stopped distributing BSD UNIX, current versions of it are available from many sources. The most common versions of BSD are OpenBSD, NetBSD, and FreeBSD. Some older machines from Sun Microsystems run a modified version of BSD called SunOS.

System V (sometimes abbreviated as SysV) is the latest version of UNIX released by AT&T Bell Labs. It is based on the original version of UNIX developed in the early 1970s. System V UNIX is the standard for commercial versions of UNIX. Both Solaris (the newest version of SunOS) and HP-UX are based on System V UNIX.

The main difference between BSD UNIX and System V UNIX is in system administration and networking. System V UNIX is newer than BSD UNIX and provides many standardized tools for configuring a system, installing prepackaged software, and network programming.

Also, the layout of the file system in System V UNIX has changed to some extent. Table 23.1 lists the BSD directories and their System V equivalents.

TABLE 23.1   SYSTEM V EQUIVALENTS OF BSD DIRECTORIES

BSD	System V
/bin	/usr/bin
/sbin	/usr/sbin
/usr/adm	/var/adm
/usr/mail	/var/mail or /var/spool/mail
/usr/tmp	/var/tmp

The directories /bin and /sbin still exist on some System V–based UNIX versions. On Solaris, these directories are links to /usr/bin and /usr/sbin, respectively. On HP-UX, these directories still contain some commands essential at boot time. The commands stored in these directories are not the same commands as in BSD. Most vendors who have switched from BSD to System V still provide BSD versions in the directory /usr/ucb.

In addition to these changes, many System V–based UNIX versions have introduced the directory /opt in an attempt to standardize the installation locations of prepackaged software products. On older systems, many different locations, including /usr, /usr/contrib, and /usr/local, were used to install optional software packages.

23

Linux is hard to classify because it is not based on either BSD or System V source code. It was written from scratch by Linus Torvalds at the University of Helsinki in Finland and is considered by some to be a third type of UNIX that incorporates the best features found in both System V and BSD. The commands and the networking layer in Linux are both based on BSD, whereas the standardized tools for system configuration and installation of prepackaged software are similar to System V. Some of the major vendors of Linux are Caldera and Red Hat.

Using uname

The first step in writing portable shell scripts is to determine which version of UNIX is executing your shell script. You can determine this using the uname command:

uname *options*

Here, *options* is one or more of the options given in Table 23.2.

TABLE 23.2 OPTIONS FOR THE uname COMMAND

Option	Description
-a	Prints all information
-m	Prints the current hardware type
-n	Prints the hostname of the system
-r	Prints the operating system release level
-s	Prints the name of the operating system (default)

By default, the uname command prints the name of the operating system. The output looks like the following:

```
$ uname
Linux
```

Here, the output indicates that the operating system name of the machine is Linux. Usually, this is enough to determine the UNIX version. For example, on FreeBSD systems, the output is FreeBSD and on HP-UX systems the output is HP-UX. The major exception to this is SunOS.

Using the Operating System Release Level

As previously mentioned, SunOS is the name of the UNIX operating system developed by Sun Microsystems. SunOS was originally based on BSD UNIX but has since changed to be based on System V UNIX. Although Sun Microsystems changed the marketing name of the new version to Solaris, both versions produce the output SunOS when uname is run.

To use the correct versions of commands, shell scripts that have to run on both Solaris and the old SunOS must be able to detect the difference between these two versions.

To determine whether a system is running Solaris or SunOS, you need to determine the version of the operating system. SunOS versions 5 and higher are Solaris (System V–based); SunOS versions 4 and lower are SunOS (BSD-based).

To determine the version of the operating system, use the -r option of uname:

```
$ uname -r
5.5.1
```

This indicates that the version of the operating system is 5.5.1. If you want to add the operating system's name to this output, use the -r and the -s options:

```
$ uname -rs
SunOS 5.5.1
```

This indicates the machine is running Solaris. A machine running the BSD-based SunOS displays the following output:

```
SunOS 4.1.3
```

Determining the Hardware Type

Sometimes a shell script is written as a wrapper around a hardware-specific program. For example, install scripts are usually the same for different hardware platforms supported by a particular operating system. Although the install script might be the same for every hardware platform, the files that are installed are usually different.

To determine the hardware type, use the -m option of the uname command:

```
$ uname -m
sun4m
```

Some common return values and their hardware types are given in Table 23.3.

TABLE 23.3   HARDWARE TYPES RETURNED BY THE uname COMMAND

Hardware	Description
9000/xxx	Hewlett-Packard 9000 series workstation. Some common values of *xxx* are 700, 712, 715, and 750.
i386	Intel 386-, 486-, Pentium-, or Pentium II–based workstation.
sun4x	A Sun Microsystems workstation. Some common values of *x* are c (SparcStation 1 and 2), m (SparcStation 10 and 20), and u (UltraSparc).
alpha	A workstation based on the Digital Electronics Corporation ALPHA micro-processor.

Determining the hostname of a System

Many shell scripts need to check the hostname of a system. The traditional method of doing this on BSD systems is to use the hostname command, as in the following example:

```
$ hostname
soda.CSUA.Berkeley.EDU
```

In System V, the hostname command is not always available. The uname -n command is used instead:

```
$ uname -n
kashi
```

Because the uname -n command is available on both System V and BSD UNIX, it is preferred for use in portable shell scripts.

Determining the UNIX Version Using a Function

Now that you have looked at using the uname command to gather information about the version of UNIX that is being used, you need a method for using this information in a shell script. As you saw in Chapter 21, "Problem Solving With Functions," creating a shell function that determines the version of UNIX gives the greatest flexibility.

A shell function that returns the operating system type is as follows:

```
getOSName() {
    case `uname -s` in
        *BSD)
            echo bsd ;;
        SunOS)
            case `uname -r` in
                5.*) echo solaris ;;
                  *) echo sunos ;;
            esac
```

```
             ;;
         Linux)
             echo linux ;;
         HP-UX)
             echo hpux ;;
         AIX)
             echo aix ;;
         *) echo unknown ;;
     esac
}
```

As you can see, this function is not very complicated. It checks the output of uname -s and looks for a match. In the case of SunOS, it also checks the output of uname -r to determine whether the operating system is Solaris or SunOS.

In many cases, you need to tailor the options of a command, such as ps or df, so that the command can generate the desired output. In such cases, you need the capability to "ask" whether the operating system is of a certain type. A shell function that performs this task follows:

```
isOS() {
    if [ $# -lt 1 ] ; then
        echo "ERROR: Insufficient Aruments." >&2
        return 1
    fi

    REQ=`echo $1 ¦ tr '[A-Z]' '[a-z]'`
    if [ "$REQ" = "`getOSName`" ] ; then return 0 ; fi
    return 1
}
```

This function compares its first argument to the output of the function getOSName and returns 0 (true) if they are the same; otherwise, it returns 1 (false). Using this function, you write if statements of the following type:

```
if isOS hpux ; then
    : # HP-UX specific commands here
elif isOS solaris ; then
    : # Solaris specific comands here
else
    : # generic unix commands here
fi
```

The reason that you do not directly check the value of $1 but instead use the variable REQ, is that this enables a greater flexibility on the part of the function's user. For example, you can use either of the following to check whether a system is Linux:

```
isOS LINUX
isOS linux
```

Techniques for Increasing Portability

Shell scripts that run on multiple versions of UNIX often include code that is version-specific. For example, you might need to use a different command on Linux than Solaris to obtain some system information.

There are two common techniques to increase the portability of a shell script between different versions of UNIX:

- Conditional execution
- Abstraction

Conditional execution alters the execution of a script based on the system type, whereas abstraction retains the same basic flow of the script by placing the conditional statements within functions.

Conditional Execution

A script that uses conditional execution for portability contains an `if` statement at the beginning. The `if` statement sets several variables indicating the set of commands to use on a particular platform.

In this section, you look at two common cases of conditional execution:

- Determining the remote shell command
- Determining the proper method of using the `echo` command in prompts

The first case illustrates setting a variable based on the operating system type. The second case illustrates setting variables based on the behavior of a command (`echo`) on a particular system.

Executing Remote Commands

A common use of conditional execution is in scripts that need to execute commands on remote systems. On most versions of UNIX, you can use the `rsh` (remote shell) command to execute commands on a remote system. Unfortunately, you cannot use this command on all versions of UNIX.

On HP-UX, `rsh` is available, but it is not the remote shell program—it is the restricted shell program. On HP-UX, you need to use the command `remsh` to execute commands on a remote system.

A script that needs to execute commands on a remote system might have an `if` statement of the following form at its beginning:

```
if SystemIS HPUX ; then
    RCMD=remsh
else
    RCMD=rsh
fi
```

After the variable $RCMD is set, remote commands can execute as follows:

```
"$RCMD" host command
```

Here, *host* is the hostname of the remote system, and *command* is the command to execute.

Problems with the echo Command in Prompts

Most programs that need to prompt the user need to be able to print a prompt that is not terminated by a newline. In Chapter 13, "Input/Output," there were several problems with using the \c escape sequence of the echo command to do this. The workaround was to use the /bin/echo command.

Although this works for UNIX versions based on System V, on some BSD-based systems this does not work. You need to specify the -n option to echo instead. By using the following shell script, you can create a shell function, echo_prompt, to display a prompt reliably across all versions of echo:

```
_ECHO=/bin/echo
_N=
_C="\c"
ECHOOUT=`$_ECHO "hello $_C"`
if [ "$ECHOOUT" = "hello \c" ] ; then
     _N="-n"
     _C=
fi
export _ECHO _N _C

echo_prompt() {  $_ECHO $_N $@ $_C ; }
```

This script fragment implements the /bin/echo workaround by using it as the base from which to construct the correct echo command. It then checks the output of an echo command to see whether the \c sequence is treated correctly. If it is not, you need to use the -n option.

After this has been determined, the function echo_prompt is created using the correct variables. This function enables us to reliably output prompts, as in the following example:

```
$ echo_prompt "Do you want to play a game?" ; read response
Do you want to play a game?
```

Abstraction

NEW TERM   *Abstraction* is a technique used to hide the differences between the versions of UNIX inside shell functions. By doing this, the overall flow of a shell script is not affected. When a function is called, it makes a decision as to what commands to execute.

In this section you look at two different examples of abstraction:

- Adapting the getFreeSpace function to run on HP-UX
- Adapting the getPID function to run on BSD and System V

You make use of the functions getOSName and isOS given earlier in this chapter in order to adapt these functions.

Adapting getFreeSpace for HP-UX

Recall the getFreeSpace function introduced in Chapter 21:

```
getFreeSpace() {
    if [ $# -lt 1 ] ; then
        echo "ERROR: Insufficient Arguments." >&2
        return 1
    fi

    DIR="$1"
    if [ ! -d "$DIR" ] ; then
        DIR=`/usr/bin/dirname $DIR`
    fi

    df -k "$DIR" | awk 'NR != 1 { print $4 ; }'
}
```

This function prints the amount of free space in a directory in kilobytes. You use this function's output in the isSpaceAvailable function to determine whether there is enough space in a particular directory.

Although this works for most systems (Solaris, Linux, BSD), the output of df -k on HP-UX is much different. For example,

```
$ df -k /usr/sbin
/usr            (/dev/vg00/lvol8       ) :   737344 total allocated Kb
                                             368296 free allocated Kb
                                             369048 used allocated Kb
                                                 50 % allocation used
```

To get a single output line, you need to use the command df -b instead:

```
$ df -b /usr/sbin
/usr            (/dev/vg00/lvol8       ) :   392808 Kbytes free
```

In order to use isSpaceAvailable on all systems, including HP-UX, you need to change the function getFreeSpace to take these factors into account. The modified version looks like the following:

```
getFreeSpace() {
    if [ $# -lt 1 ] ; then
        echo "ERROR: Insufficient Arguments." >&2
        return 1
    fi

    DIR="$1"
    if [ ! -d "$DIR" ] ; then
        DIR=`/usr/bin/dirname $DIR`
    fi

    if isOS HPUX ; then
        df -b "$DIR" | awk '{ print $5 ; }'
    else
        df -k "$DIR" | awk 'NR != 1 { print $4 ; }'
    fi
}
```

Here, you are calling the isOS function given earlier in this chapter to determine which commands to execute.

Adapting getPID for BSD UNIX

Recall the getPID function introduced in Chapter 21:

```
getPID() {

    if [ $# -lt 1 ] ; then
        echo "ERROR: Insufficient Arguments." >&2
        return 1
    fi

    PSOPTS="-ef"

    /bin/ps $PSOPTS | grep "$1" | grep -v grep | awk '{ print $2; }'
}
```

Remember that it works correctly only on systems where the command

```
ps -ef
```

produces a listing of all running processes. This is not the case on Linux and BSD systems. On BSD systems, we need to use the command

```
ps -auwx
```

to get the correct output. This works on older Linux systems, but on newer Linux systems an error message similar to the following is generated:

```
warning: '-' deprecated; use 'ps auwx', not 'ps -auwx'
```

By using the getOSName function given earlier in this chapter, we can adapt the getPID function to work with both the BSD and System V versions of ps. The modified version of getPID is as follows:

```
getPID() {

    if [ $# -lt 1 ] ; then
        echo "ERROR: Insufficient Arguments." >&2
        return 1
    fi

    case `getOSName` in
        bsd|sunos|linux)
            PSOPTS="-auwx" ;;
        *)
            PSOPTS="-ef" ;;
    esac

    /bin/ps $PSOPTS 2> /dev/null ¦ grep "$1" ¦ grep -v grep ¦ awk '{
    ➥print $2; }'
}
```

The two main changes are

- A case statement sets the variable PSOPTS based on the operating system name.
- The STDERR of ps is redirected to /dev/null in order to discard the warning message generated on newer versions of Linux.

Summary

In this chapter, you learned how to determine which version of UNIX you are running by using the uname command. In addition, you developed the getOSName and isOS functions to help you adapt your shell scripts to multiple versions of UNIX.

You also looked at the following techniques for improving the portability of shell scripts:

- Conditional execution
- Abstraction

In conditional execution, you modify the flow of your script depending on the version of UNIX being used. In abstraction, you change the implementation of your functions to account for the differences between the versions of UNIX. Here, the flow of your script remains the same.

Using the techniques and tips in this chapter, you can port your shell script across different versions of UNIX.

Questions

1. Write a function called getCharCount that prints the number of characters in a file. Use wc to obtain the character count.

   On Linux, FreeBSD, and SunOS (not Solaris), use the -c option for wc,. On other versions of UNIX, use the -m option instead. You can use the function getOSName to get the name of the operating system.

Terms

Conditional Execution   Conditional execution alters the execution of a script based on the system type. A script that uses conditional execution usually contains an if statement at the beginning that sets variables to indicate the commands to use on a particular platform.

Abstraction   Scripts that use abstraction retain the same basic flow by placing the conditional execution statements within functions. When a function is called, it makes a decision as to what commands execute for a given platform.

HOUR 24

Shell Programming FAQs

Each of the previous chapters has focused on an individual topic in shell programming, such as variables, loops, or debugging. As you progressed through the book, you worked on problems that required knowledge from previous chapters. In this chapter, I'm taking a slightly different approach. I will try to answer some common shell programming questions that frequently arise. Specifically I will cover questions from three main areas of shell programming:

- The shell and commands
- Variables and arguments
- Files and directories

Each section includes several common questions (along with answers) that occur in shell programming. These questions are designed to help you solve or avoid problems while programming using the shell.

Some of the questions provide deeper background information about UNIX, whereas others illustrate concepts covered in previous chapters.

Shell and Command Questions

In this section I will cover some of the common questions that arise in regard to the shell itself. Also included are a few questions regarding the execution of commands.

Why does `#!/bin/sh` have to be the first line of my scripts?

In Chapter 2, "Script Basics," I stated that `#!/bin/sh` must be the first line in your script to ensure that the correct shell is used to execute your script. This line must be the first line in your shell script because of the underlying mechanism used by a shell to execute commands.

NEW TERM When you ask a shell to execute the command `$ date`, the shell uses the system call `exec` to ask the UNIX kernel to execute the command you requested. For those readers who are not familiar with the term *system call*, a system call is a C language function built in to the UNIX kernel that enables you to access features of the kernel.

The shell passes the name of the command that should be executed to the `exec` system call. This system call reads the first two characters in a file to determine how to execute the command. In the case of shell scripts, the first two characters are `#!`, indicating that the script needs to be interpreted by another program instead of executed directly. The rest of the line is treated as the name of the interpreter to use.

Usually the interpreter is `/bin/sh`, but you can also specify options to the shell on this line. Sometimes options such as `-x` or `-nv` are specified to enable debugging. This also enables you to write scripts tuned for a particular shell such as `ksh` or `bash` by using `/bin/ksh` or `/bin/bash` instead of `/bin/sh`.

How can I access the name of the current shell in my initialization scripts?

In your shell initialization scripts, the name of the current shell is stored in the variable `$0`.

Users who have a single `.profile` that is shared by `sh`, `ksh`, and `bash` use this variable in conjunction with a `case` statement near the end of this file to execute additional shell specific startup.

For example, I use the following `case` statement near the end of my `.profile` to set up the prompt, `PS1`, differently depending on the shell I am using:

```
case "$0" in
    *bash) PS1="\t \h \#$ " ;;
    *ksh) PS1="`uname -n` !$ " ;;
    *sh) PS1="`uname -n`$ " ;;
```

```
esac
export PS1
```

I have specified the shells as `*bash`, `*ksh`, and `*sh`, because some versions of UNIX place the - character in front of login shells, but not in front of other shells.

How do I tell whether the current shell is interactive or noninteractive?

Some scripts will need the capability to determine whether they are running in an interactive shell or noninteractive shell.

Usually this is restricted to your shell initialization scripts because you don't want to perform a full-blown initialization every time these scripts execute. Some other examples include scripts that can run from the `at` or `cron` commands.

Two common methods can determine whether a shell is interactive:

- `test -t` or `[ -t ]`
- `tty -s`

Both commands exit with zero status if STDIN is connected to a terminal. For example, the commands

```
$ if [ -t ] ; then echo interactive ; fi
```

and

```
$ if tty -s ; then echo interactive ; fi
```

produce the same result if the current shell is interactive:

```
interactive
```

On modern versions of UNIX both forms work equally well. On some older versions of UNIX the `test -t` command was not available, so the `tty -s` command had to be used.

How do I discard the output of a command?

Sometimes you will need to execute a command, but you don't want the output displayed to the screen. In these cases you can discard the output by redirecting it to the file `/dev/null`:

```
command > /dev/null
```

Here *command* is the name of the command you want to execute. The file is a special file (called the bit bucket) that automatically discards all its input.

24

To discard both output of a command and its error output, use standard redirection to redirect STDERR to STDOUT:

```
command > /dev/null 2>&1
```

How can I display messages on STDERR?

You can display a message on to STDERR by redirecting STDIN into STDERR as follows:

```
echo message 1>&2
```

Here message is the message you want to display.

If you are interested in shell functions that perform additional formatting please consult Chapter 21, "Problem Solving with Functions," which covers several shell functions that display messages on to STDERR.

How can I check whether a command was successful?

A command is successful if it exits with a status of zero. A nonzero exit code indicates that an error has occurred.

To check the exit code of the most recent command you executed, use the variable $?. For example:

```
grep root /etc/passwd > /dev/null 2>&1
if [ $? -ne 0 ] ; then echo "No one is in charge!" ; fi
```

Here you execute a grep command and then check the exit status of this command using the value stored in $?.

How do I determine whether the shell can find a particular command?

You can check to make sure that the shell can find a command or shell function by using the type command covered in Chapter 18, "Miscellaneous Tools":

```
type name > /dev/null 2>&1 ; if [ $? -ne 0 ] ; then list ; fi
```

Here name is the name of the command you want check for, and list is the list of commands to execute if the shell does not know about name. Usually list is used to determine a fallback command.

The type command is a builtin in sh and bash. In ksh, it is usually an alias, whence -v.

How do I determine whether job control is available in the shell?

Job control, covered in Chapter 6, "Processes," is the shell feature that enables you to control background processes based on a job ID. This feature is not available in the Bourne shell, sh. It is available in ksh and bash.

A common method used to check whether job control is enabled is to check whether the jobs command is defined:

```
if type jobs > /dev/null 2>&1 ; then
    echo "We have job control"
fi
```

This check is effective in most cases because the jobs command is not available in most versions of the Bourne shell.

Unfortunately, some versions of UNIX such as Sun Solaris, include a version of the Bourne shell that has a built-in command called jobs. On these systems when the shell is invoked as /bin/sh, the jobs command exists but does nothing. If the shell is invoked as /bin/jsh (as in job control shell), the jobs command behaves normally.

Variable and Argument Questions

In this section I will examine some questions related to variables and their use in shell scripts. I will also cover some questions related to command line arguments.

How can I include functions and variable definitions from one file into another file?

To include functions and variable definitions defined in one file into another file you need to use the . command as follows:

```
. file
```

Here *file* is the name of the file you want to include. I covered this topic in Chapter 22, "Problem Solving with Shell Scripts."

Is it possible to consider each argument to a shell script one at a time?

You can do this using a for loop:

```
for arg in "$@"
do
    list
done
```

Here the variable arg will be set to each argument in turn. The specified list of commands, *list*, will be executed for each argument.

You use $@ in this example for the arguments instead of $*, because $@ preserves the quoting used when the command was issued. The difference between $@ and $* was discussed in Chapter 12, "Parameters."

How can I forward all the arguments given to my script to another command?

A common task for shell programmers is writing a wrapper script for command. A wrapper script might need to define a set of variables or change the environment in some way before a particular command starts executing.

When writing wrapper scripts, you will need to forward all the arguments given to your script to a command. Usually the following is sufficient:

```
command "$@"
```

Here *command* is the name of the command you want to execute.

The one problem with this is that if no arguments were specified to your script, some versions of the shell will expand "$@" to "". If no arguments were specified, you want to execute *command*, not *command* "".To avoid this problem, use the form:

```
command ${@:+"$@"}
```

Here you are using one of the forms of variable substitution discussed in Chapter 8, "Substitution." In this case you check to see whether the variable $@ has a value. If it does, you substitute the value "$@" for it. If your script was not given any command line arguments, $@ will be null; thus no value will be substituted.

How do I use the value of a shell variable in a sed command?

The simplest method to use variables in a sed command is to enclose your sed command in double quotes (") instead of single quotes ('). Because the shell performs variable substitution on double-quoted strings, the shell will substitute the value of any variables you specify before sed executes.

For example, the command

```
sed "/$DEL/d" file1 > file2
```

deletes all the lines in *file1* that contain the value stored in the variable $DEL.

How do I check to see whether a variable has a value?

There are several methods for determining this. The simplest is the if statement:

```
if [ -z "$VAR" ] ; then list ; fi
```

Here VAR is the name of the variable, and list is the command to execute if VAR does not contain a value. Usually list initializes VAR to some default value.

You can initialize variables more succinctly using variable substitution. For example, the previous if statement can be written as

```
: ${VAR:=default}
```

Here default is the default that should be assigned to VAR, if VAR does not have a value.

If you need execute a set of commands to obtain a default value, use command substitution with the backquote (`) operator to obtain the value that should be substituted:

```
: ${VAR:=`default`}
```

Here default is a list of commands to execute. If VAR does not have a value, the output of these commands will be assigned to it.

File and Directory Questions

In this section, I will look at some questions about files and directories. These questions include issues with specific commands and examples that illustrate the usage of commands to solve particular problems.

How do I determine the full pathname of a directory?

Shell scripts that work with directories often need to determine the full pathname of a directory to perform the correct operations on these directories.

You can determine the full pathname of a directory by using the cd and pwd commands:

```
FULLPATH=`(cd dir ; pwd)`
```

Here dir is the name of a directory. This command changes directories to the specified directory, dir, and then displays the full pathname of the directory using the pwd command. Because command substitution is used, the full pathname is assigned to the variable FULLPATH.

Because the cd command changes the working directory of the current shell, you execute it in a subshell. Thus the working directory of the shell script is unchanged.

24

How do I determine the full pathname of a file?

Determining the full pathname of a file is slightly harder than determining the full path-name of a directory. You need to use the `dirname` and `basename` commands in conjunction with the `cd` and `pwd` commands to determine the full pathname of a file:

```
CURDIR=`pwd`
cd `dirname file`
FULLPATH="`pwd`/`basename file`"
cd $CURDIR
```

Here `file` is the name of a file whose full pathname you want to determine. First you save the current path of the current directory in the variable `CURDIR`. Next you change to the directory containing the specified file, `file`.

Then you join the output of the `pwd` command and the name of the `file` determined using the `basename` command to get the full pathname. This value gets stored in the variable `FULLPATH`. Finally you change back to the original directory.

How can locate a particular file?

The structure of the UNIX directory tree sometimes makes locating files and commands difficult. To locate a file, often you need to search through a directory and all its subdirectories. The easiest way to do this is to use the `find` command:

```
find dir -name file -print
```

Here `dir` is the name of a directory where `find` should start its search, and `file` is the name of the file it should look for.

The `name` option of the `find` command also works with the standard filename substitution operators covered in Chapter 8. For example, the command

```
find dir -name "*txt" -print
```

displays a list of all the files in the directory `dir` and all its subdirectories that end with the string `txt`.

How can I `grep` for a string in every file in a directory?

When you work on a large project involving many files, remembering the contents of the individual files becomes difficult. It is much easier to look through all the files for a particular piece of information.

You can use the `find` command in conjunction with the `xargs` command to look for a particular string in every file contained within a directory and all its subdirectories:

```
find dir -type f -print ¦ xargs grep "string"
```

Here *dir* is the name of a directory in which to start searching, and *string* is the string to look for. Here you specify the -type option to the find command so that only regular files are searched for the *string*.

How do I remove all the files in a directory matching a particular name?

Some editors and programs create large numbers of temporary files. Often you need to clean up after these programs, to prevent your hard drive from filling up.

To generate the list of files to delete, you can use the find command. Most of the time you can combine the find command with the xargs command, but in this case the file-names can contain one or more spaces. Spaces can confuse the xargs command, so you need to use a for loop instead:

```
OLDIFS="$IFS"
IFS='
'
for FILE in `find . -type f -name "*string*" -print`
do
     rm "$FILE"
done
IFS="$OLDIFS"
```

24

Here *string* is a string that should be part of the name of each file you want to delete. So that the for loop is set to the correct value of FILE in each iteration, IFS needs to be set to the newline character.

If you do not change IFS, filenames that contain spaces will be interpreted as multiple files instead of as a single file.

What command can I use to rename all the *.aaa files to *.bbb files?

In DOS and Windows, you can rename all the *.aaa files in a directory to *.bbb by using the rename command as follows:

```
rename *.aaa *.bbb
```

In UNIX you can use the mv command to rename files, but you cannot use it to rename more than one file at the same time. To do this, you need to use a for loop:

```
OLDSUFFIX=aaa
NEWSUFFIX=bbb
for FILE in *."$OLDSUFFIX"
do
     NEWNAME=`echo "$FILE" | sed -e "s/${OLDSUFFIX}\$/$NEWSUFFIX/"`
     mv "$FILE" "$NEWNAME"
done
```

Here you generate a list of all the files in the current directory that end with the value of the variable OLDSUFFIX. Then you use sed to modify the name of each file by removing the value of OLDSUFFIX from the filename and replacing it with the value of NEWSUFFIX. You use the $ character in your sed expression to anchor the suffix in OLDSUFFIX to the end of the line. You do this to make sure the pattern that is replaced is really a filename suffix.

After you have a new name, you rename the file from its original name, stored in FILE, to the new name stored, stored in NEWNAME.

To prevent a potential loss of data, you might need to modify this loop to specify the -i option to the mv command. For example, if the files 1.aaa and 1.bbb exist prior to executing this loop, after the loops exits, the original version of 1.aaa will be overwritten when 1.bbb is renamed as 1.aaa. If mv -i is used, you will be prompted before 1.bbb is renamed:

```
mv: overwrite 1.aaa (yes/no)?
```

You can answer *no* to avoid losing the information in this file. The actual prompt produced by mv might be different on your version of UNIX.

What command can I use to rename all the aaa* files to bbb* files?

The technique used in the last question can be used to solve this problem as well. In this case you will use the variables OLDPREFIX to hold the prefix a file currently has and NEWPREFIX to hold the prefix you want the file to have.

As an example, you can use the following for loop to rename all files that start with *aaa* to start with *bbb* instead:

```
OLDPREFIX=aaa
NEWPREFIX=bbb
for FILE in "$OLDPREFIX"*
do
    NEWNAME=`echo "$FILE" ¦ sed -e "s/^${OLDPREFIX}/$NEWPREFIX/"`
    mv "$FILE" "$NEWNAME"
done
```

How can I set my filenames to lowercase?

When you transfer a file from a Windows or DOS system to a UNIX system, the filename ends up in all capital letters. You can rename these files to lowercase using the following command:

```
for FILE in *
do
    mv -i "$FILE" `echo "$FILE" ¦ tr '[A-Z]' '[a-z]'` 2> /dev/null
done
```

You are using the `mv -i` command here in order to avoid overwriting files. For example, if the files APPLE and apple both exist in a directory you do not want to rename the file APPLE.

How do I eliminate carriage returns (^M) in my files?

If you transfer text files from a DOS machine to a UNIX machine, you might see a ^M before the end of each line. This character corresponds to a carriage return.

In DOS a newline is represented by the character sequence \r\n, where \r is the carriage return and \n is newline. In UNIX a newline is represented by \n. When text files created on a DOS system are viewed on UNIX, the \r is displayed as ^M.

You can strip these carriage returns out by using the `tr` command as follows:

```
tr -d '\015' < file > newfile
```

Here *file* is the name of the file that contains the carriage returns, and *newfile* is the name you want to give the file after the carriage returns have been deleted.

Here you are using the octal representation \015 for carriage return, because the escape sequence \r will not be correctly interpreted by all versions of `tr`.

24

Summary

In this chapter I have looked at some common questions encountered in shell programming. These questions and their answers will help you write bigger and better scripts.

Now that you have finished all 24 chapters, you have learned about using both the basics of the shell and its advanced features. As you continue to program, use this book as a reference to help you remember the intricacies of shell programming.

I hope that you learned not only to program efficiently using the shell but also to enjoy shell programming.

PART IV
Appendixes

APPENDIX A

Command Quick Reference

by Frank Watson

This appendix summarizes and reviews the script elements you have covered:

- Reserved words and built-in shell commands
- Conditional expressions
- Arithmetic expressions (available Korn/Bash only)
- Parameters and variables
- Parameter substitution
- Pattern matching
- I/O

- Miscellaneous command summaries
- Regular expression wildcards

You can also find details not discussed earlier that are included here for completeness.

Reserved Words and Built-in Shell Commands

. (period) executes the following command in the current shell instead of as a child process.

: (colon) no-op command. Its arguments are processed for variable substitution.

!! (Bash) re-executes the previous command.

alias (only Korn/Bash) creates a short name for the command.

bg (Korn/Bash) starts a suspended job running in background.

break exits from current `for`, `while`, or `until` loop.

case executes commands given for first pattern that match `expr`. Patterns can contain filename expansion wildcards.

```
case expr in
    pattern1) commands ;;
    pattern2) commands ;;
esac
```

cd changes the directory.

continue skips the rest of the commands in a loop and starts the next iteration of a loop.

do indicates the start of a block of code, for example, in a `for`, `while`, or `until` loop.

done indicates the end of a block of code, for example, in a `for`, `while`, or `until` loop.

echo displays its arguments to standard output. Sometimes this is a built-in shell command replacing the external `echo` command.

esac denotes the end of a case statement.

eval causes the shell to reinterpret the command that follows.

exec executes the following command which replaces the current process instead of running it as a child process.

exit n ends the shell script with status code n.

export marks the following variables, flagging them to be passed to any child processes and called programs. Korn/Bash enable assignment within the export command:

```
export VAR1=value VAR2=value
```

false (Korn/Bash builtin) command that always returns an unsuccessful or logical false result.

fc (Korn/Bash) displays or edits a command in history list.

fg (Korn/Bash) brings a background or suspended job to the foreground.

fi denotes the end of an if statement.

for executes a block of code multiple times.

```
for variable [in list]
do
      commands
done
```

function (Korn/Bash) keyword to define a function enabling local variables.

getopts a function called repeatedly in a loop to process the command line arguments.

history (Korn/Bash) shows the most recent commands run by this user.

if allows conditional execution.

```
if test-command
then commands
[elif commands]
[else commands]
fi
```

integer (Korn/Bash) specifies an integer variable.

jobs (Korn/Bash) lists the background and suspended jobs.

kill sends a signal to a process; often used to terminate a process or to reinitialize a daemon background process.

let (Korn/Bash) performs integer arithmetic.

newgrp (Korn) changes your primary group, affecting the group of all new files and directories that you create.

print (Korn) an alternative to echo.

pwd prints the present working or current directory.

r (Korn) re-executes the previous command.

A

read waits for one line of standard input and saves each word in the following variables. If there are more words than variables, it saves the remaining words in the last variable.

readonly marks the following variables to give error if an attempt to assign a new value is made.

return returns from a function.

select (Korn/Bash) presents a menu and enables user selection.

set displays or changes shell options.

shift discards $1 and shifts all the positional parameters up one to take its place.

test (Korn/Bash builtin) provides many options to check files, strings, and numeric values. Often denoted by [(left bracket).

trap designates code to execute if a specific signal is received, such as:

```
0       exit from script
1       hangup/disconnect
2       intr key pressed (Ctrl-C or DEL)
3       quit key pressed
15      request to terminate process
```

type displays the pathname of the following command or indicates whether it is built-in or an alias.

typeset (Korn/Bash) sets the type of variable and optionally its initial value.

ulimit displays or sets the largest file or resource limit.

umask displays or sets a mask to affect permissions of any new file or directory you create.

unalias (Korn/Bash) removes an alias.

unset undefines the variables that follow.

until (Korn/Bash) loops until the test command is true (successful).

```
until test-command
do
     commands
done
```

wait pauses until all background jobs are complete.

whence (Korn) similar to the type command.

while loops while a test command is true (successful).

```
while test-command
do
      commands
done
```

Conditional Expressions

These can be used with

```
if [ test-expression ]
while [ test-expression ]
until [ test-expression ]
```

File Tests

-a *file*	true if the file exists (Korn/Bash)
-b *file*	true if the file is a block special device
-c *file*	true if the file is a character special device
-d *file*	true if the file is a directory
-f *file*	true if the file is a regular file
-g *file*	true if the file has the SGID permission bit set
-G *file*	true if the file's group matches the user's group
-k *file*	true if the file has the sticky bit set
-L *file*	true if the file is a symbolic link
-O *file*	true if the user running this command owns this file (Korn/Bash)
-p *file*	true if the file is a named pipe or fifo
-r *file*	true if the file is readable
-s *file*	true if the file has a size greater than zero
-S *file*	true if the file is a socket
-t *filedes*	true if file descriptor is associated with a terminal device
-u *file*	true if the file has its SUID permission bit set
-w *file*	true if the file is writable
-x *file*	true if the file is executable

String Tests

-z *string*	true if the string is empty
-n *string*	true if the string has nonzero size

s1 = *s2*	true if string s1 equals s2
s1 != *s2*	true if the strings are not equal
s1	true if string s1 is not empty
s1 < *s2*	true if s1 comes before s2 in ASCII order (Korn [[ ]])
s1 > *s2*	true if s1 comes after s2 in ASCII order (Korn [[ ]])

Integer Comparisons

Comparisons stop on first non-digit.

n1 -eq *n2*	true if *n1* is equal in value to *n2*.
n1 -ne *n2*	true if *n1* is not equal to *n2*
n1 -gt *n2*	true if *n1* is greater than *n2*
n1 -ge *n2*	true if *n1* is greater than or equal to *n2*
n1 -lt *n2*	true if *n1* is less than *n2*
n1 -le *n2*	true if *n1* is less than or equal to *n2*
! expr	true if *expr* is false (logical NOT)
-a	logical AND (Bourne)
&&	logical AND (Bash/Korn [[ ]])
-o	logical OR (Bourne)
¦¦	logical OR (Bash/Korn [[ ]])

Arithmetic Expressions (Korn/Bash Only)

Follow the general format for variable assignment:

```
let "VARIABLE=integer_expresson"
```

To embed integer calculations within a command

```
$((integer_expression))
```

Operators Allowed in Korn/Bash Integer Expressions

- Logical operators return 1 for true and 0 for false
- This list is from highest to lowest operator precedence

-	unary minus (negates the following value)
! ~	logical NOT, binary one's complement

* / %	multiply, divide, modulus (remainder operation)
+ -	add, subtract
>> <<	right, left shift, for example: `$((32 >> 2))` gives 8 (right shift 32 by 2 bits is the same as division by 4)
<= >=	less than or equal to, greater than or equal to
> <	greater than, less than
== !=	equal to, not equal to
&	bitwise AND operation, for example: `$((5 & 3))` converts 5 to binary 101 and 3 to binary 011 and ANDs the bits to give 1 as the result
^	bitwise exclusive OR operation
¦	bitwise regular OR operation
&&	logical AND
¦¦	logical OR
*= /= %=	C programming type assignment, for example, `$((a *= 2))` means multiply variable a * 2, save result in a, and substitute result
= += -=	more C programming type assignments
>>= <<=	more C programming type assignments using shift right, shift left
&= ^= ¦=	more C programming type assignments using AND, exclusive OR, regular OR

Parameters and Variables

User-Defined Variables

USERVAR=*value*	sets the contents of *USERVAR* to *value*
$*USERVAR*	substitutes the contents of *USERVAR*
${*USERVAR*}	also substitutes the contents of USERVAR. The braces are optional if there is no ambiguity.

User-defined variable names

- Must start with letter or _
- Can contain only letters, digits, or _
- Are often in capital letters to differentiate from UNIX commands

Korn/Bash 2.x Support Arrays

USERVAR[index]=value	sets a value for array element denoted by index
${USERVAR[index]}	substitutes a value into the command line
${USERVAR[*]}	substitutes all array elements
${USERVAR[@]}	substitutes all array elements as if individually double quoted

Note index must be an integer.

Korn array initialization

```
set -A USERVAR value1 value2 value3 ...
```

Bash array initialization

```
USERVAR=(value1 value2 value3 ...)
```

Built-in Shell Variables

$0	name of the command or script being executed
$n	positional parameters, that is, arguments given on the command line numbered 1 through 9
$#	number of positional parameters given on command line
$*	a list of all the command line arguments
$@	a list of all command line arguments individually double quoted
$?	The numeric exit status (that is, return code) of last command executed
$$	PID (process ID) number of current shell
$!	PID (process ID) number of last background command

Built-in Commands that Directly Affect Variables

getopts, export, read, readonly, unset

Two Types of Variables

- Environment variables are passed to any child processes.
- Local variables are not passed to any child processes.

Shell Variables

CDPATH contains colon-separated list of directories to facilitate cd command

HOME Your home directory

IFS Internal field separator characters

OPTARG The last cmd line arg processed by getopts (Korn/Bash)

OPTIND The index of the last cmd line arg processed by getopts (Korn/Bash)

PATH Contains a colon-separated list of directories to search for commands that are given without any slash

PS1 The primary shell prompt string

PS2 The secondary shell prompt string for continuation lines

PWD The current directory

RANDOM Returns a different random number (from 0 to 32,767) each time it is invoked

REPLY The last input line from read via select command (Korn/Bash)

SECONDS The numbers of seconds since shell invocation

SHLVL The number of shells currently nested

UID The numeric user ID number

A

Parameter Substitution

Parameter Substitution in Bourne/Korn/Bash

${*parameter*} substitutes the contents of the *parameter*, which can be a variable name or digit indicating a positional parameter.

${*parameter*:-*word*} substitutes the contents of the *parameter* but if it is empty or undefined, it substitutes the *word*, which might contain unquoted spaces.

${*parameter*:=*word*} substitutes the contents of the *parameter* but if it is empty or undefined, it sets *parameter* equal to the *word* and substitutes *word*.

${*parameter*:?*message*} substitutes the contents of the *parameter*, but if it is empty or undefined, aborts the script and gives the *message* as a final error. Message might contain unquoted spaces.

${*parameter*:+*word*} if *parameter* is not empty, it substitutes the *word*; otherwise it substitutes nothing.

Parameter Substitution Only in Korn/Bash

${#*parameter*} substitutes the number of characters in the contents of *parameter*.

${#*array*[*]} substitutes the number of elements in *array*.

${*parameter*#*pattern*} if the regular expression pattern given is found at start of the contents of *parameter*, it deletes the matching characters and substitutes the remainder. The smallest possible match is deleted.

${*parameter*##*pattern*} same as above but deletes the largest possible match at the start of *parameter*.

${*parameter*%*pattern*} same as above but deletes the smallest match at the end of *parameter*.

${*parameter*%%*pattern*} same as above but deletes the largest match at the end of *parameter*.

Pattern Matching

Rules for filename expansion:

- Any word on the command line containing a wildcard is expanded to a list of files which match the pattern word.
- If no filename matches are found, the pattern word is not substituted.
- Wildcards cannot match a leading period or a slash.

Pattern Wildcards Available in Bourne/Korn/Bash

*	matches 0 or more of any character
?	matches exactly 1 of any character
[*list*]	matches exactly 1 of any character in list
[!*list*]	matches exactly 1 of any character not in list

Pattern Wildcards Available Only in Korn

?(*pattern1*¦*pattern2*...) matches any of the patterns

*(*pattern1*¦*pattern2*...) matches zero or more occurrences of the patterns

+(*pattern1*¦*pattern2*...) matches one or more occurrences of the patterns

@(*pattern1*¦*pattern2*...) matches only one of the patterns

!(*pattern1*¦*pattern2*...) matches anything except one of the patterns

I/O

TABLE A.1 SUMMARY OF STANDARD UNIX I/O

Abbreviation	I/O description	File Descriptor
STDIN	Standard input	0
STDOUT	Standard output	1
STDERR	Standard error	2

A

cmd > file	save STDOUT from UNIX command in *file*
cmd 1> file	same as above
cmd >> file	append STDOUT from UNIX command to *file*
cmd 1>> file	same as above
cmd 2> file	save STDERR from UNIX command in *file*
cmd 2>> file	append STDERR from UNIX command in *file*
cmd < file	provide STDIN to UNIX command from *file* instead of keyboard
cmd 0< file	same as above

here Document

Provides STDIN to UNIX command from lines that follow until delimiter is found at start of line:

```
cmd << delimiter
one or more text lines
delimiter
```

cmd1 ¦ cmd2	pipe STDOUT of *cmd1* as STDIN to *cmd2*
cmd ¦ tee file	save STDOUT of UNIX command in *file* but also pass same text as STDOUT

`exec n> file`	redirect output of file descriptor *n* to (overwrite) file. This applies to subsequent UNIX commands.
`exec n>> file`	same as above but append to `file` instead of overwriting
`cmd 2>&1`	redirect STDERR from UNIX command to wherever STDOUT is currently going. This is useful when you want to save both output and errors in a file or pipe them together to another command, for example: `cmd > file 2>&1` This saves both STDERR and STDOUT in `file`. `2>&1` must come after `> file`.
`cmd >&2`	redirect STDOUT as STDERR. This should be done when echo displays an error message.
`cmd 1>&2`	same as above
`cmd n>&m`	redirect file descriptor *n* to wherever file descriptor *m is currently going*. This is a generalization of the above examples. Values of n and m above 2 can be used to save an I/O destination and retrieve it later.
`exec n>&-`	close file descriptor *n*

Miscellaneous Command Summaries

Here is some helpful information about several commands often used in shell programming.

echo—display arguments to standard output

\b	Backspace
\c	Suppress trailing newline
\f	Formfeed
\n	Newline
\r	Carriage return
\t	Tab
\\	Backslash
\0nn	Character whose ASCII value is octal nn

grep—display lines that contain the given pattern

-i	ignore upper versus lower case
-l	list only filenames that contain a match, not the matching lines

-n   include the file line number with each matching line displayed

-v   reverse the test, which means ignore lines that contain the pattern

printf—display formatted text output, for example:

printf "*text* %[-]m.nx" *arguments*

-            Left justify (optional)

m   Minimum field length

n   Maximum field length for string; number of characters to the right of decimal for floating point.

x   Type of argument

            s   string

            c   character value

            d   decimal integer value

            x   hexadecimal value

            o   octal value

            e   exponential floating point value

            f   fixed floating point value

            g   general floating point value

sort—display lines in sorted order

-b   ignore leading blanks

-d   ignore leading punctuation

-f   fold upper- and lowercase together

-n   sort leading numbers by magnitude

-r   sort in reverse order

+n   ignore the first n fields when sorting

Regular Expression Wildcards

grep, fgrep, egrep, sed, vi, perl, and awk allow regular expression wildcards in search patterns.

Limited Regular Expression Wildcards

All regular expression patterns can include these wildcards:

`^pattern`	only matches if *pattern* is at start of line
`pattern$`	only matches if *pattern* is at end of line
`.`	matches exactly 1 of any character
`[list]`	matches exactly 1 of any character in *list*
`[^list]`	matches exactly 1 of any character not in *list*
`*`	matches 0 or more repetitions of previous element (char or expression)
`.*`	matches 0 or more of any characters

Extended Regular Expression Wildcards

These are additional regular expression wildcards that are only supported in some commands:

`\{n\}`	matches *n* repetitions of previous element
`\{n,\}`	matches *n* or more repetitions of previous element
`\{n,m\}`	matches at least *n* but not more than *m* reps of previous element
`?`	matches 0 or 1 occurrences of previous element
`+`	matches 1 or more occurrences of previous element

Summary

This appendix provides a quick reference for shell commands and features:

- Reserved words and built-in shell commands
- Conditional expressions
- Arithmetic expressions (Korn/Bash only)
- Parameters and variables
- Parameter substitution
- Pattern matching
- I/O
- Miscellaneous command summaries
- Regular expression wildcards

As you write scripts and become familiar with the concepts, you might find this summary helps you to locate a symbol, a command name, or the correct syntax.

Questions

1. What section of this summary describes how to append output to a file?

2. What section of this summary describes how to end a case statement?

3. What section of this summary enables you to determine whether the jobs command is supported in the Bourne shell?

4. What section of this summary enables you to determine whether the + sign is a generally supported regular expression wildcard?

5. What section of this summary enables you to determine which shell variable gives the numeric result code of the last command executed?

A

APPENDIX B

Glossary

absolute path   The complete pathname to a file starting at the root directory /.

abstraction   Scripts that use abstraction retain the same basic flow by placing the conditional execution statements within functions. When a function is called, it makes a decision as to what commands execute for a given platform.

anchoring expression   Normally any part of a line will be matched by a regular expression. To match expressions that either begin or end a line, you need to anchor the regular expression. The ^ character anchors regular expressions to the beginning of a line, whereas the $ character anchors regular expressions to the end of a line.

argument   Command modifiers that change the behavior of a command. In the shell, they are specified after a command's name.

array variable   A mechanism available in bash and ksh for grouping scalar variables together. The scalar variables stored in an array are accessed using a single name in conjunction with a number. This number is referred to as an index.

awk   The awk command is a power pattern matching language that allows you to modify input lines by manipulating the fields they contain.

background   Processes usually running at a lower priority and with their input disconnected from the interactive session. Any input and output are usually directed to a file or other process.

background process   An autonomous process that runs under UNIX without requiring user interaction.

bash   Stands for GNU Bourne Again shell and is based on the Bourne shell, sh, the original command interpreter.

block special file   Provides a mechanism for communicating with device drivers via the file system. These files are called *block devices* because they transfer large blocks of data at a time. This type of file typically represents hard drives and removable media.

body   The set of commands executed by a loop is called the body of the loop.

Bourne shell   The original standard user interface to UNIX that supported limited programming capability.

BSD   Berkeley Software Distribution.

BSD UNIX   Version of UNIX developed by Berkeley Software Distribution and written at the University of California, Berkeley.

built in   A command whose code is part of the shell as opposed to a utility that exists in a separate disk file, which must be read into memory before executing the command.

C shell   A user interface for UNIX written by Bill Joy at Berkeley. It features C-programming-like syntax.

cat   The command used to view the contents of a file.

cd   The command used to change directories.

character special file   Character special files provide a mechanism for communicating with a device one character at a time.

child process   See *subprocess*.

child shell   See *subshell*.

chown   The command used to change the owner of a file or directory.

command   The name of a program and any arguments you specify to that program to cause its behavior to change. You might see the term *command* used instead of the term *utility* for simple commands, where only the program name to execute is given.

command separator   Indicates where one command ends and another begins. The most common command separator is the semicolon character, ;.

command substitution   The process by which the shell executes a command and substitutes in the output of the command.

comment   A statement that is embedded in a shell script but should not be executed by the shell.

complex command   A command that consists of a command name and a list of arguments.

compound command   A list of simple and complex commands separated by the semicolon character, ;.

compound expression   Consists of one or more expressions.

conditional execution   Alters the execution of a script, based on the system type. A script that uses conditional execution usually consists of an if statement at the beginning that sets variables to indicate the commands that should be used on a particular platform.

cp   The command used to copy files.

daemon   A system-related background process that often runs with the permissions of root and services requests from other processes.

debugging hook   A function or set of commands that executes only when a shell script executes with a special argument. Debugging hooks provide a convenient method for tracing the execution of a script in order to fix problems.

default behavior   The output that is generated when a command runs as a simple command is called the default behavior of that command.

directory   A type of file used to store other files. For users familiar with Windows or Mac OS, UNIX directories are equivalent to folders.

directory tree   UNIX uses a hierarchical structure for organizing files and directories. This structure is often referred to as a *directory tree*. The tree has a single root node, the slash character (/), and all other directories are contained below it.

environment variable   A variable that is available to any program that is started by the shell.

escape sequence   A special sequence of characters that represents another character.

escaping   Escaping a character means to put a backslash (\) just before that character. Escaping can either remove the special meaning of a character in a shell command or it can add special meaning as we saw with \n in the echo command. The character following the backslash is called an escaped character.

B

execute permission   In UNIX, only those files that have execute permission enabled can run.

exporting   A variable is placed in the environment by *exporting* it using the export command.

expression   A piece of code that are evaluated to produce a numeric result, such as 0 or 1. Some expressions that involve mathematical operations can produce other results.

field   A set of characters that are separated by one or more field separator characters. The default field separator characters are Tab and Space.

field separator   Controls the manner in which an input line is broken into fields. In the shell, the field separator is stored in the variable IFS. In awk the field separator is stored in the awk variable FS. Both the shell and awk use the default value of Space and Tab for the field separator.

file descriptor   An integer that is associated with a file. Allows you to read and write from a file using the integer instead of the filename.

filesystem   A directory structure contained within a disk drive or disk area. The total available disk space can be composed of one or more filesystems. A filesystem must be mounted before it can be accessed. To mount a filesystem, you must specify a directory to act as the mount point. Once mounted, any access to the mount point directory or its subdirectories will access the separate filesystem.

hard link   A directory entry which maps a filename to an inode number. A file may have multiple names or hard links. The link count gives the number of names by which a file is accessible. Hard links do not allow multiple names for directories and do not allow multiple names in different filesystems.

home directory   Your home directory is the directory that you start out in after you log in.

infinite loop   A loop that executes forever without terminating.

inode   A table entry within a filesystem that contains file information such as the owner, group, permissions, last modification date/time, last access date/time, and the block list of the actual file data. There is one inode for each file. The inodes are numbered sequentially. The inode does not contain the filename. A directory is a table that maps filenames to inode numbers.

input redirection   In UNIX, the process of sending input to a command from a file.

interactive mode   In interactive mode, the shell reads input from you and executes the commands that you specify. This mode is called *interactive* because the shell is interacting with a user.

invisible or hidden file   A file whose name starts with the . character. By default the ls command does not list these files. You can list them by specifying the -a option to ls.

iteration   A single execution of the body of a loop.

kernel   The heart of the UNIX system. It provides utilities with a means of accessing a machine's hardware. It also handles the scheduling and execution of commands.

Korn shell   A user interface for UNIX with extensive scripting (programming) support. Written by David G. Korn. The shell features command-line editing and will also accept scripts written for the Bourne shell.

library   A file that contains only functions. Usually libraries contain no main code.

literal character   A character with no special meaning and which causes no extra action to be taken. Quoting causes the shell to treat a wildcard as a literal character.

local variable   A variable that is present within the current instance of the shell. It is not available to programs that are started by the shell.

loop   Enables you to execute a series of commands multiple times. Two main types of loops are the while and for loops.

ls   The command used to list the files in a directory.

main code   Consists of all the commands in a shell script that are not contained within functions.

major number   UNIX uses this to associate a block special file or a character special file with a device driver.

man page   Every version of UNIX comes with an extensive collection of online help pages called man pages (short for *manual pages*). The man pages are the authoritative source about your UNIX system. They contain complete information about both the kernel and all the utilities.

metacharacter   In a regular expressions, a metacharacter is a special character that is expanded to match patterns.

minor number   UNIX uses this to associate a block special file or a character special file with a device driver.

modulus function   See *remainder function*.

B

mv The command used to rename files.

nested loop When a loop is located inside the body of another loop it is said to be nested within another loop.

newline character Literally the linefeed character whose ASCII value is 10. In general, the newline character is a special shell character that indicates a complete command line has been entered and it may now be executed.

no-op A command that does nothing and thus can be used as a dummy command or placeholder where syntax requires a command.

noninteractive mode In noninteractive mode, the shell does not interact with you, rather it reads commands stored in a file and executes them. When it reaches the end of the file, the shell exits.

numeric expression A command used to add, subtract, multiply, and divide two numbers. Numeric expressions are constructed using the numeric operators—+ (add), - (subtract), * (multiply), and / (divide).

ordinary file A file on the system that contains data, text, or program instructions.

output redirection In UNIX the process of capturing the output of a command and storing it in a file is called *output redirection*, because it redirects the output of a command into a file instead of the screen.

parent process Process that controls another often referred to as the child process or subprocess. See *process*.

parent process identifier Shown in the heading of the ps command as PPID. The process identifier of the parent process. See also *parent process*.

parent shell Shell (typically the login shell) that controls another, often referred to as the child shell or subshell. See *shell*.

piping The process used to redirect the output of one command into the input of another command. Piping is accomplished with the pipe character, ¦.

process A discrete running program under UNIX. The user's interactive session is a process. A process can invoke (run) and control another program that is then referred to as a subprocess. Ultimately, everything a user does is a subprocess of the operating system.

process identifier Shown in the heading of the ps command as pid. The unique number assigned to every process running in the system.

prompt   When you see a prompt, you can type the name of a command and press Enter. In this book, we will use the $ character to indicate the *prompt*.

PS2 variable   A shell variable whose content is usually the > character. The contents of the PS2 variable is displayed by the shell as a secondary prompt that indicates the previous command was not complete and the current command line is a continuation of that command line.

pwd   The pwd command prints the absolute path of the current directory.

quoting   Literally, to enclose selected text within some type of quotation marks. When applied to shell commands, *quoting* means to disable shell interpretation of special characters by enclosing the character within single or double quotes or by escaping the character.

read permission   The read permission of a file or directory determines which users can view the contents of that file or directory.

regular expression   A string that can describe several sequences of characters.

regular file   The most common type of files you will encounter. These files store any kind of data. This data may be stored in plain text, an application-specific format, or a special binary format that the system can execute.

relative path   Relative pathnames let you access files and directories by specifying a path to that file or directory relative to your current directory.

remainder function   The remainder of a division operation, which is the amount that is left over and thus not evenly divisible.

reserved word   A nonquoted word that is used in grouping commands or selectively executing them, such as: if, then, else, elif, fi, case, esac, for, while, until, do, or done.

rm   The command used to remove files.

scalar variable   A *scalar variable* can hold only one value at a time.

sed   The sed command is a stream editor that allows you to modify input lines using regular expressions.

set group ID (SGID)   The SGID permission causes a script to run with its group set to the group of the script, rather than the group of the user who started it.

set user ID (SUID)   The SUID permission causes a script to run as the user who is the owner of the script, rather than the user who started it.

B

shell   Provides you with an interface to the UNIX system. It gathers input from you and executes programs based on that input. After a program has finished executing, the shell displays that program's output. The shell is sometimes called a command interpreter. See also *bash*, *Bourne shell*, *C shell*, *Korn shell*, and *tcsh*.

shell initialization   After a shell is started it undergoes a phase called initialization to set up some important parameters. This is usually a two step process that involves the shell reading the files /etc/profile and .profile.

shell or command prompt   The single character or set of characters that the UNIX shell displays for which a user can enter a command or set of commands.

shell preprocessing   This describes actions taken by the shell to manipulate the command line before executing it. This is when filename, variable, command, and arithmetic substitution occur (as covered in Chapter 8, "Substitution").

shell script   A program written using a shell programming language like those supported by Bourne, Korn, or C shells. In general, a script contains a list of commands that are executed noninteractively by the shell.

shell variable   A special variable that is set by the shell and is required by the shell in order function correctly.

signal   Software interrupts sent to a program to indicate that an important event has occurred. The events can vary from user requests to illegal memory access errors. Some signals, like the interrupt signal, indicate that a user has asked the program to do something that is not in the usual flow of control.

signal handler   A function that executes when a signal is received by a shell script. Usually signal handlers clean up temporary files and then exit.

simple command   A simple command is a command that you can execute by just giving its name at the prompt.

socket file   A special file for interacting with the network via the UNIX file system.

STDERR   Standard error. A special type of output used for error messages. The file descriptor for STDERR is 2.

STDIN   Standard input. User input is read from STDIN. The file descriptor for STDIN is 0.

STDOUT   Standard output. The output of scripts is usually to STDOUT. The file descriptor for STDOUT is 1.

subdirectory   A directory that is contained within another directory.

subprocess   Process running under the control of another, often referred to as the parent process. See *process*.

subshell   Shell running under the control of another, often referred to as the parent shell (typically the login shell). See *shell*.

symbolic link or soft link   A special filetype which is a small pointer file allowing multiple names for the same file. Unlike hard links, symbolic links can be made for directories and can be made across filesystems. Commands that access the file being pointed to are said to follow the symbolic link. Commands that access the link itself do not follow the symbolic link.

system call   A C language function that is used to request services from the UNIX kernel.

tcsh   A C shell–like user interface featuring command-line editing.

uninitialized shell   When a shell is started it is uninitialized. This means that important parameters required by the shell to function correctly are not defined.

usage statement   A statement issued by a shell script when one or more of its arguments are improperly specified.

utility   Utilities are programs, such as who and date, you can run or execute.

variable substitution   The process used by the shell to substitute the value of a variable, when the variable's name is specified.

wc   The command used to count the words, lines and characters in a file.

word   An unbroken set of characters. The shell uses spaces and tabs to separate words.

write permission   Controls the users who can modify a file.

B

APPENDIX **C**

Quiz Answers

Chapter 1

1. The first is a simple command. The second is a compound command constructed from two simple commands. The last two are complex commands.

2. There is no effect. The output will be the same for both commands.

3. The two types are Bourne (sh, ksh, or bash) and C (csh, tcsh).

Chapter 2

1. The files are /etc/profile and .profile.

2. If PATH is not set, the shell cannot find the commands you want to execute. If MANPATH is not set, the shell cannot locate the online help.

3. It specifies that the shell /bin/sh should be used to execute the script.

4. The man command.

Chapter 3

1. Invisible files are files whose names start with the . character. You can list them by specifying the -a option to ls.

2. No. Each of these commands will produce the same results.

3. On Solaris and HPUX use the command

   ```
   $ wc -lm
   ```

   On Linux use the command

   ```
   $ wc -lc
   ```

4. (b) and (c) will generate error messages indicating that homework is a directory.

Chapter 4

1. (a) and (d) are absolute pathnames. (b) and (c) are relative pathnames.

2. The pwd command will output the full path to your home directory. In my case the path is

   ```
   /home/ranga
   ```

3. The following command will work:

   ```
   cp -r /usr/local /opt/pgms
   ```

4. The following commands will work:

   ```
   cp -r /usr/local /opt/pgms ; rm -r /usr/local
   ```

5. No, you cannot use the rmdir command, because the directory is not empty. You can use the following command:

   ```
   $ rm -r backup
   ```

Chapter 5

1. The file types of these files are

/dev/rdsk/c0t1d0	character special file
/etc/passwd	regular file
/usr/local	directory
/usr/sbin/ping	regular file

2. The owner and groups of these files are

`/dev/rdsk/c0t1d0`	owner `bin`	group `sys`
`/etc/passwd`	owner `root`	group `sys`
`/usr/local`	owner `bin`	group `bin`
`/usr/sbin/ping`	owner `root`	group `bin`

3. The permissions of these files are

`/dev/rdsk/c0t1d0`	owner read and `write`
	group `read`
	other `none`
`/etc/passwd`	owner `read`
	group `read`
	other `read`
`/usr/local`	owner `read, write, and execute`
	group `read, write, and execute`
	other `read, write, and execute`
`/usr/sbin/ping`	owner read and SUID `execute`
	group `read and execute`
	other read and `execute`

Chapter 6

1. By putting an ampersand at the end of the command line.
2. With the `ps` command.
3. Use the suspend key (usually Ctrl-Z) to stop the foreground process and then use the `bg` command to resume it in the background.

C

Chapter 7

1. (a) and (d) are valid variable names. (b) starts with a number thus it is invalid. (c) contains the & character, which is not a valid character for variable names.

2. These assignments are valid in `ksh` and `bash`, but not in `sh`. The shell, `sh`, only supports scalar variables.

3. To access the array item at index 5 use the following:

   `${adams[5]}`

   To access every item in the array use the following:

   `${adams[@]}`

4. An environment variable's value can be accessed by child processes of a shell. A local variable is restricted to a particular shell; it cannot be used by child processes of a shell.

Chapter 8

1. The following command will accomplish this task:

   `$ ls *hw[0-9][0-9][2-6].???`

2. If `MYPATH` is unset, it is set to the given value, which is then substituted.

3. If MYPATH is unset, the given value is substituted for it. MYPATH remains unset.

4. 10

Chapter 9

1. Double quotes accomplish this easily but not single quotes:

   `$ echo "It's <party> time!"`

2. The following command will accomplish this task:

   `$ echo "$USER owes     \$$DEBT"`

Chapter 10

1. The difference is that the first command will try to run the command without checking if it is executable. Thus if the file exists but is not executable, the command will fail. The second command takes this into account and attempts to run the command only if it is executable.

2. The output is "Your binaries are stored in your home directory."

3. Any of the following commands are valid:

```
$ test -d /usr/bin || test -h /usr/bin
$ [ -d /usr/bin ] || [ -h /usr/bin ]
$ test -d /usr/bin -o -h /usr/bin
$ [ -d /usr/bin  -o -h /usr/bin ]
```

4. The following case statement covers the given combinations and several more:

```
case "$ANS" in
    [Yy]|[Yy][Ee][Ss]) ANS="y" ;;
    *) ANS="n" ;;
esac
```

Chapter 11

1. Here is one possible implementation:

```
x=0
while [ $x -lt 10 ]
do
    x=$(($x+1))
    y=0
    while [ $y -lt $x ] ; do
  echo "$y \c"
        y=$(($y+1))
    done
    echo
done
```

2. Here is one possible implementation:

```
#!/bin/bash

select FILE in * "Exit Program"
do

    if [ -z "$FILE" ] ; then continue ; fi

    if [ "$FILE" = "Exit Program" ] ; then break ; fi

    if [ ! -f "$FILE" ] ; then
        echo "$FILE is not a regular file."
        continue
    fi

    echo $FILE
    cat $FILE
done
```

Chapter 12

1. One correct implementation is as follows:

```
#!/bin/sh

USAGE="Usage: `basename $0` [-c¦-t] [files¦directories]"

if [ $# -lt 2 ] ; then
    echo "$USAGE" ;
    exit 1 ;
fi

case "$1" in
    -t¦-x) TARGS=${1}vf ; shift
        for i in "$@" ; do
            if [ -f "$i" ] ; then
                FILES=`tar $TARGS "$i" 2>/dev/null`
                if [ $? -eq 0 ] ; then
                    echo ; echo "$i" ; echo "$FILES"
                else
                    echo "ERROR: $i not a tar file."
                fi
            else
                echo "ERROR: $i not a file."
            fi
        done
        ;;
    -c) shift ; TARGS="-cvf" ;
        tar $TARGS archive.tar "$@"
        ;;
    *) echo "$USAGE"
        exit 0
        ;;
esac
exit $?
```

2. One possible implementation is as follows:

```
#!/bin/sh

USAGE="Usage: `basename $0` [-v] [-x] [-f] [filename] [-o]
[filename]";

VERBOSE=false
EXTRACT=false

while getopts f:o:x:v OPTION ; do
    case "$OPTION" in
        f) INFILE="$OPTARG" ;;
        o) OUTFILE="$OPTARG" ;;
        v) VERBOSE=true ;;
```

```
              x)  EXTRACT=true ;;
             \?)  echo "$USAGE" ;
                  exit 1
                  ;;
         esac
done

shift `echo "$OPTIND - 1" | bc`

if [ -z "$1" -a -z "$INFILE" ] ; then
    echo "ERROR: Input file was not specified."
    exit 1
fi
if [ -z "$INFILE" ] ; then INFILE="$1" ; fi

: ${OUTFILE:=${INFILE}.uu}

if [ -f "$INFILE" ] ; then
    if [ "$EXTRACT" = "true" ] ; then
        if [ "$VERBOSE" = "true" ] ; then
            echo "uudecoding $INFILE... \c"
        fi
        uudecode "$INFILE" ; RET=$?
    else
        if [ "$VERBOSE" = "true" ] ; then
            echo "uuencoding $INFILE to $OUTFILE... \c"
        fi
        uuencode "$INFILE" "$INFILE" > "$OUTFILE" ; RET=$?
    fi

    if [ "$VERBOSE" = "true" ] ; then
        MSG="Failed" ; if [ $RET -eq 0 ] ; then MSG="Done." ; fi
        echo $MSG
    fi
else
    echo "ERROR: $INFILE is not a file."
fi
exit $RET
```

C

Chapter 13

1. The simplest possible answer is as follows:

```
#!/bin/sh

if [ $# -lt 2 ] ; then
    echo "ERROR: Insufficient arguments." ;
    exit 1 ;
fi
```

```
case "$1" in
    -o) printf "%o\n" "$2" ;;
    -x) printf "%x\n" "$2" ;;
    -e) printf "%e\n" "$2" ;;
    *) echo "ERROR: Unknown conversion, $1!" ;;
esac
```

2. The rewritten script is as follows:

```
#!/bin/sh

if [ $# -lt 2 ] ; then
    echo "ERROR: Insufficient arguments." >&2
    exit 1 ;
fi

case "$1" in
    -o) printf "%o\n" "$2" ;;
    -x) printf "%x\n" "$2" ;;
    -e) printf "%e\n" "$2" ;;
    *) echo "ERROR: Unknown conversion, $1!" >&2 ;;
esac
```

Chapter 14

1. A possible implementation is

```
mymkdir() {

    if [ $# -lt 1 ] ; then
        echo "ERROR: Insufficient arguments." >&2
        return 1
    fi

    mkdir -p "$1" > /dev/null 2>&1
    if [ $? -eq 0 ] ; then
        cd "$1" > /dev/null 2>&1
        if [ $? -eq 0 ] ; then
            pwd ;
        else
            echo "ERROR: Could not cd to $1." >&2
        fi
    else
        echo "ERROR: Could not mkdir $1." >&2
    fi
}
```

2. A possible implementation is

```
Prompt_RESPONSE() {

    if [ $# -lt 1 ] ; then
        echo "ERROR: Insufficient arguments." >&2
        return 1
    fi

    RESPONSE=
    while [ -z "$RESPONSE" ]
    do
        echo "$1 \c "
        read RESPONSE
    done

    export RESPONSE
}
```

Chapter 15

1. A sample implementation is

```
lspids() {

    USAGE="Usage: lspids [-h] process"
    HEADER=false
    PSCMD="/bin/ps -ef"

    case "$1" in
        -h) HEADER=true ; shift ;;
    esac

    if [ -z "$1" ] ; then
        echo $USAGE ;
        return 1 ;
    fi


    if [ "$HEADER" = "true" ] ; then
        $PSCMD 2> /dev/null ¦ head -n 1 ;
    fi

    $PSCMD 2> /dev/null ¦ grep "$1"¦ grep -v grep
}
```

For Linux or FreeBSD, change the variable PSCMD from

```
PSCMD="/bin/ps -ef"
```

to

```
PSCMD="/bin/ps -auwx"
```

C

2. The following is one possible implementation:

```
lspids ()
{
    USAGE="Usage: lspids [-h|-s] process";
    HEADER=false;
    SORT=false;
    PSCMD="/bin/ps -ef";
    SORTCMD="sort -rn -k 2,2";
    for OPT in $@;
    do
        case "$OPT" in
            -h)
                HEADER=true;
                shift
            ;;
            -s)
                SORT=true;
                shift
            ;;
            -*)
                echo $USAGE;
                return 1
            ;;
        esac;
    done;
    if [ -z "$1" ]; then
        echo $USAGE;
        return 1;
    fi;
    if [ "$HEADER" = "true" ]; then
        $PSCMD | head -1;
    fi;
    if [ "$SORT" = "true" ]; then
        $PSCMD 2> /dev/null | grep "$1" | grep -v grep | $SORTCMD;
    else
        $PSCMD 2> /dev/null | grep "$1" | grep -v grep;
    fi
}
```

For LINUX and FreeBSD, change the variable SORTCMD to

```
SORTCMD="sort -rn"
```

instead of

```
SORTCMD="sort -rn -k 2,2"
```

You will also need to change the variable PSCMD from

```
PSCMD="/bin/ps -ef"
```

to

```
PSCMD="/bin/ps -auwx"
```

Chapter 16

1. One possible implementation is

```
sgrep() {
    if [ $# -lt 2 ] ; then
        echo "USAGE: sgrep pattern files" >&2
        exit 1
    fi

    PAT="$1" ; shift ;

    for i in $@ ;
    do
        if [ -f "$i" ] ; then
            sed -n "/$PAT/p" $i
        else
            echo "ERROR: $i not a file." >&2
        fi
    done

    return 0
}
```

2. The following command does the job:

```
$ uptime ¦ sed 's/.* load/load/'
```

3. There are two possible solutions:

```
$ df -k ¦ sed -n '/^\//p'
$ df -k ¦ sed '/^[^\/]/d'
```

4. The following command will solve this problem:

```
/bin/ls -al ¦ sed -e '/^[^\-]/d' -e 's/ *[0-9].* / /'
```

Chapter 17

1. A possible implementation is as follows:

```
#!/bin/sh

if [ $# -lt 1 ] ; then
    echo "USAGE: `basename $0` files"
    exit 1
fi

awk '{
    for (i=NF;i>=1;i—) {
        printf("%s ",$i) ;
    }
    printf("\n") ;
}' $@
```

C

2. A possible solution is

```
#!/bin/sh
awk 'BEGIN { FS=":" ; }
    $1 == "B" {
        BAL=$NF ; next ;
    }
    $1 == "D" {
        BAL += $NF ;
    }
    ($1 == "C") || ($1 == "W") {
        BAL-=$NF ;
    }
    ($1 == "C") || ($1 == "W") || ($1 == "D") {
        printf "%10-s %8.2f\n",$2,BAL ;
    }
' account.txt ;
```

Alternatively, you can use the -F option:

```
#!/bin/sh
awk -F: '
    $1 == "B" {
        BAL=$NF ; next ;
    }
    $1 == "D" {
        BAL += $NF ;
    }
    ($1 == "C") || ($1 == "W") {
        BAL-=$NF ;
    }
    ($1 == "C") || ($1 == "W") || ($1 == "D") {
        printf "%10-s %8.2f\n",$2,BAL ;
    }
' account.txt ;
```

3. The following is a possible implementation:

```
#!/bin/sh
awk -F: '
    $1 == "B" {
        BAL=$NF ;
        next ;
    }
    $1 == "D" {
        BAL += $NF ;
    }
    ($1 == "C") || ($1 == "W") {
        BAL-=$NF ;
    }
    ($1 == "C") || ($1 == "W") || ($1 == "D") {
        printf "%10-s %8.2f\n",$2,BAL ;
    }
```

```
END {
    printf "-\n%10-s %8.2f\n","Total",BAL ;
}
' account.txt ;
```

4. A possible implementation is

```
#!/bin/sh
awk -F: '
    $1 == "B" {
        BAL=$NF ;
        next ;
    }
    $1 == "M" {
        MIN=$NF ;
        next ;
    }
    $1 == "D" {
        BAL += $NF ;
    }
    ($1 == "C") || ($1 == "W") {
        BAL-=$NF ;
    }
    ($1 == "C") || ($1 == "W") || ($1 == "D") {
        printf "%10-s %8.2f",$2,BAL ;
        if ( BAL < MIN ) { printf " * Below Min. Balance" }
        printf "\n" ;
    }
    END {
        printf "-\n%10-s %8.2f\n","Total",BAL ;
    }
' account.txt ;
```

Chapter 18

1. The following command will accomplish this task:

```
$ type process2
```

2. The following command will accomplish this task:

```
$ find /data -name '*process2*' -print
```

3. The following command will accomplish this task:

```
PRICE=`echo "scale=2; 3.5 \* $PRICE" | bc`
```

Chapter 19

1. Here is a possible implementation:

```
trap CleanUp 2 15
trap Init 1
trap "quit=true" 3
PROG="$1"
Init

while : ;
do
    wait $!
    if [ "$quit" = true ] ; then exit 0 ; fi
    $PROG &
done
```

2. Here is a possible implementation:

```
#! /bin/sh

AlarmHandler() {
    echo "Got SIGALARM, cmd took too long."
    KillSubProcs
    exit 14
}

IntHandler() {
    echo "Got SIGINT, user interrupt."
    KillSubProcs
    exit 2
}

KillSubProcs() {
    kill ${CHPROCIDS:-$!}
    if [ $? -eq 0 ] ; then echo "Sub-processes killed." ; fi
}

SetTimer() {
    DEF_TOUT=${1:-10};
    if [ $DEF_TOUT -ne 0 ] ; then
        sleep $DEF_TOUT && kill -s 14 $$ &
        CHPROCIDS="$CHPROCIDS $!"
        TIMERPROC=$!
    fi
}
```

```
UnsetTimer() {
    kill $TIMERPROC
}

# main()

trap AlarmHandler 14
trap IntHandler 2

SetTimer 15
$PROG &
CHPROCIDS="$CHPROCIDS $!"
wait $!
UnsetTimer
echo "All Done."
exit 0
```

Chapter 20

1. The three main methods are

   - Issue the script in the following fashion:

     ```
     $ /bin/sh option script arg1 arg2 arg3
     ```

   - Change the first line of the script to

     ```
     #!/bin/sh option
     ```

   - Use the set command as follows:

     ```
     set option
     ```

   Here option is the debugging option you want to enable.

2. Here is one possible implementation:

```
Debug() {
    if [ "$DEBUG" = "true" ] ; then
        if [ "$1" = "on"  -o "$1" = "ON" ] ; then
            set -x
        else
            set +x
            echo " >Press Enter To Continue< \c"
            read press_enter_to_continue
        fi
    fi
}
```

C

Chapter 21

1. One possible implementation is

```
###############################################
# Name: toLower
# Desc: changes an input string to lower case
# Args: $@ -> string to change
###############################################

toLower() {
    echo $@ | tr '[A-Z]' '[a-z]' ;
}
```

2. One possible implementation is

```
###############################################
# Name: toUpper
# Desc: changes an input string to upper case
# Args: $@ -> string to change
###############################################

toUpper() {
    echo $@ | tr '[a-z]' '[A-Z]'
}
```

3. One possible solution is

```
###############################################
# Name: isSpaceAvailable
# Desc: returns true (0) if space available
# Args: $1 -> The directory to check
#       $2 -> The amount of space to check for
###############################################

isSpaceAvailable() {

    if [ $# -lt 2 ] ; then
        printERROR "Insufficient Arguments."
        return 1
    fi

    if [ ! -d "$1" ] ; then
        printERROR "$1 is not a directory."
        return 1
    fi

    if [ `getSpaceFree "$1"` -gt "$2" ] ; then
        return 0
    fi

    return 1
}
```

4. One possible solution is

```
##################################################
# Name: isSpaceAvailable
# Desc: returns true (0) if space available
# Args: $1 -> The directory to check
#       $2 -> The amount of space to check for
#       $3 -> The units for $2 (optional)
#                  k for kilobytes
#                  m for megabytes
#                  g for gigabytes
##################################################

isSpaceAvailable() {

    if [ $# -lt 2 ] ; then
        printERROR "Insufficient Arguments."
        return 1
    fi

    if [ ! -d "$1" ] ; then
        printERROR "$1 is not a directory."
        return 1
    fi

    SPACE_MIN="$2"

    case "$3" in
        [mM]|[mM][bB])
            SPACE_MIN=`echo "$SPACE_MIN * 1024" | bc` ;;
        [gG]|[gG][bB])
            SPACE_MIN=`echo "$SPACE_MIN * 1024 * 1024" | bc` ;;
    esac

    if [ `getSpaceFree "$1"` -gt "$SPACE_MIN" ] ; then
        return 0
    fi

    return 1
}
```

5. One possible solution is

```
##################################################
# Name: isUserRoot
# Desc: returns true (0) if the users UID=0
# Args: $1 -> a user name (optional)
##################################################

isUserRoot() {
    if [ "`getUID $1`" -eq 0 ] ; then
        return 0
    fi
    return 1
}
```

C

Chapter 22

1. One possible simplification is

```
# initalize the destination directory

DESTDIR="$2";

# check if the destination exits

if [ ! -d "$DESTDIR" ] ; then

    # if the destination doesn't exist then assume the destination is
    # the new name for the directory

    DESTDIR="`/usr/bin/dirname $2`"
    NEWNAME="`/bin/basename $2`"

fi

# if dirname returns a relative dir we will be confused after cd'ing
# latter on. So reset it to the full path.

DESTDIR=`(cd $DESTDIR ; pwd ; )`

# if the parent of the destination doesn't exist,
# were in trouble. Tell the user and exit.

if [ ! -d "$DESTDIR" ] ; then
    printERROR "A parent of the destination directory $2 does not
exist"
fi
```

2. Use `grep -i` instead of `grep`.

3. They can be rewritten as functions and stored in a shell library that both scripts can access.

4. We can change the lines

```
55   grep "$1" "$TMPF1" > "$TMPF2" 2> /dev/null
56   Failed $? "No matches found."
```

to

```
55   sed -n "/^$1[^:]*:/p" "$TMPF1" > "$TMPF2" 2> /dev/null
56   test -s "$TMPF2" > /dev/null
57   Failed $? "No matches found."
```

We can also change the line

```
79          grep -v "$LINE" "$TMPF1" > "$TMPF1.new" 2> /dev/null
```

to

```
sed -e "s/^$LINE$//" "$TMPF1" > "$TMPF1.new" 2> /dev/null
```

5. Add a signal handler. A simple one might be

```
trap 'echo "Cleaning Up." ; doCleanUp ; exit 2; ' 2 3 15
```

You should add this to the script before the line:

```
cp "$MYADDRESSBOOK" "$TMPF1" 2> /dev/null
```

Chapter 23

1. A possible implementation is

```
getCharCount() {
    case `getOSName` in
        bsd|sunos|linux)
            WCOPT="-c" ;;
        *)
            WCOPT="-m" ;;
    esac

    wc $WCOPT $@
}
```

Appendix A

1. The "I/O" section; use >> to append.

2. In the section "Reserved Words and Built-in Shell Commands," find the case statement, which shows the word esac must come at the end.

3. In the section "Reserved Words and Built-in Shell Commands," find the jobs command. Note that (Korn/Bash) is indicated. This command is available in the Korn shell and Bash shell but not the Bourne shell.

4. In the section "Regular Expression Wildcards," note the + sign is not listed under "Limited Regular Expression Wildcards," which are always supported. It is in the next section, "Extended Regular Expression Wildcards," which are supported only on some commands. Check the man pages to see if a particular command supports this wildcard.

5. In the section "Parameters and Variables," subsection "Built-in Shell Variables," $? is what you are looking for.

C

INDEX

SAMS
Teach Yourself
in 24 Hours

When you only have time for the answers™

Sams Teach Yourself in 24 Hours *gets you the results you want—fast! Work through 24 proven 1-hour lessons and learn everything you need to know to get up to speed quickly. It has the answers you need at the price you can afford.*

Sams Teach Yourself UNIX in 24 Hours, 2nd Ed.

James Armstrong, Jr.
ISBN: 0-672-31480-0
$19.99 US/$28.95 CAN

Other Related Titles

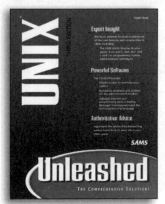

UNIX Unleashed, Third Edition
Robin Burk
ISBN: 0-672-31411-8
$49.99 US/$71.95 CAN

Sams Teach Yourself VBScript in 21 Days
Keith Brophy
1-575-21120-3
$39.99 US/$57.95 CAN

Sams Teach Yourself Microsoft Small Business Server 4.5 in 21 Days
Harry Brelsford
ISBN: 0-672-31513-0
$29.99 US/$42.95 CAN

UNIX Unleashed: Internet Edition
Robin Burk
ISBN: 0-672-31205-0
$59.99 US/$85.95 CAN

UNIX Unleashed: System Administrator's Edition
Robin Burk et al
ISBN: 0-672-30952-1
$59.99 US/$85.95 CAN

Sams Teach Yourself Java 2 Platform in 21 Days, Professional Reference Edition
Rogers Cadenhead
ISBN: 0-672-31438-X
$49.99 US/$71.95 CAN

Sams Teach Yourself Java 1.2 in 21 Days:Complete Compiler Edition
Laura Lemay
ISBN: 0-672-31534-3
$49.99 US/$71.95 CAN

Sams Teach Yourself Beginning Programming in 24 Hours
Greg Perry
ISBN: 0-672-31355-3
$19.99 US/$28.95 CAN

Sams Teach Yourself C++ in 21 Days: Complete Compiler Edition
Jesse Liberty
ISBN: 0-672-31261-1
$49.99 US/$71.95 CAN

Sams Teach Yourself Visual C++ 6 in 21 Days
Davis Chapman
ISBN: 0-672-31240-9
$34.99 US/$50.95 CAN

Sams Teach Yourself UNIX in 10 Minutes
William Ray
ISBN: 0-672-31523-8
$12.99 US/$18.95 CAN

Linux Unleashed, Third Edition
Tim Parker
ISBN: 0-672-31372-3
$39.99 US/$57.95 CAN

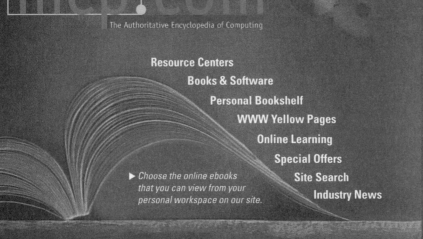